D1754780

Leading Responsibly in the Asian Century

Mario Fernando

Leading Responsibly
in the Asian Century

Springer

Mario Fernando
Faculty of Business
University of Wollongong
Wollongong, NSW, Australia

ISBN 978-3-319-21788-8   ISBN 978-3-319-21789-5 (eBook)
DOI 10.1007/978-3-319-21789-5

Library of Congress Control Number: 2015948150

Springer Cham Heidelberg New York Dordrecht London
© Springer International Publishing Switzerland 2016
This work is subject to copyright. All rights are reserved by the Publisher, whether the whole or part of the material is concerned, specifically the rights of translation, reprinting, reuse of illustrations, recitation, broadcasting, reproduction on microfilms or in any other physical way, and transmission or information storage and retrieval, electronic adaptation, computer software, or by similar or dissimilar methodology now known or hereafter developed.
The use of general descriptive names, registered names, trademarks, service marks, etc. in this publication does not imply, even in the absence of a specific statement, that such names are exempt from the relevant protective laws and regulations and therefore free for general use.
The publisher, the authors and the editors are safe to assume that the advice and information in this book are believed to be true and accurate at the date of publication. Neither the publisher nor the authors or the editors give a warranty, express or implied, with respect to the material contained herein or for any errors or omissions that may have been made.

Printed on acid-free paper

Springer International Publishing AG Switzerland is part of Springer Science+Business Media (www.springer.com)

This book is dedicated to my mother, Felicia. I will always remember you.

Foreword

The topic of this book is one that has been waiting to be explored. Mario Fernando offers us what is perhaps the first comprehensive study of what responsible leadership would look like in an Asian context. Well researched and eloquent, Fernando draws on philosophic literature, interviews with Asian leaders, and engaging practical cases and examples. He weaves together his analysis of the Asian culture, the ethics of leadership, and social responsibility into a call for innovation that will improve the well-being of people in what he calls "the Asian century."

All too often, people confuse respecting cultural differences with the idea that human beings are fundamentally different. When it comes to leadership, cultural styles, customs, priorities, and institutional arrangements may differ, but the job of a leader remains the same. Leadership is one person or a group of people who initiate, guide, direct, or collaborate with others toward various goals. These goals may relate to living together in a country, working together in any type of organization from a business, to an NGO, a community, or a social movement. How leaders work with followers – whether through force, persuasion, transactions, or dialogue – and who sets the goals vary within cultures and between cultures. While these differences can be significant, some things in the leader/follower relationship are the same. For instance, I do not know of a culture where followers do not want honest, fair, and trustworthy leaders who will treat them with respect. Moreover, I doubt that there are many people in the world who do not hope that their leaders will take responsibility for looking after their interests and well-being.

Yet, leaders disappoint their followers in far too many countries and organizations. Consider the color-coded map of the Corruption Perceptions Index that Transparency International publishes every year. The most corrupt countries tend to be the poorest, which makes us wonder if countries are corrupt because they are poor or poor because they are corrupt. The map tends to show countries where leaders in business and government fail to be ethical and effective at meeting the needs of their society or organization. In these societies leaders use their entrusted power for their own good, not the good of their constituents. Behind most poor countries and failed states, we often find leaders in business and government who either do not understand or refuse to take seriously the moral responsibilities of leadership.

Deeply embedded in the moral responsibilities of leadership lies the obligation to lead effectively, because incompetent leaders have the potential to harm their own constituents and other stakeholders. In some ways, the notion of responsibility is inherent in the job description and in the very idea of a leader. Leaders garner praise or blame for everything that goes on under their watch. This is the most ethically distinctive aspect of being a leader. We hold leaders accountable for their organizations' behavior and everything that occurs in their organizations even if they did not do it or know about it. A leader may not *be* responsible for an incident, but as a leader, he or she must *take* responsibility for it.

Fernando frames his ideas about responsible leadership in broader terms than some of the other literature on the subject, which is good because he allows us to see responsible leadership in the context of leadership ethics. The dialogue on what constitutes moral leadership has been going on for centuries and has been dominated by the most powerful nations. As Asian businesses and countries become influential players in the global economy, their leaders will occupy a key role in shaping the norms and practices of business. Fernando offers suggestions on how to research, teach, and foster responsible leadership in Asian cultures. Perhaps what is most intriguing about this book is the case that Fernando makes for the potential of Asian leaders to innovate and improve the theory and practice of responsible leadership. Since many of today's Asian business leaders have studied in the West, one hopes that in the Asian century, they will avoid the moral failures of the British and American centuries and build on the more recent focus on human rights and the environment. Ultimately, this book is not only about the Asian way; it is about finding a better way for leaders from the East and West to lead responsibly.

Jepson School of Leadership Studies Joanne B. Ciulla
University of Richmond
Richmond, VA, USA
June 9, 2015

Preface

As the twenty-first century is becoming the "Asian century," Western businesses and higher-education institutions are looking more towards Asia for market expansion and investment opportunities. At the same time, more and more Asian businesses and higher-education institutions are also expanding into Western markets. Thus, increasingly, as business professionals and students in the West are exposed to Asian perspectives, values, attributes, and practices, Asian leaders branching out into the West are challenged by different leadership styles there. These trends emphasize the need to explore an integrated view of the Western and Asian approaches to responsible leadership. Although a handful of responsible leadership scholars have written mostly from a Western perspective, there is little written about how Asian cultural factors might influence the predominantly Western-developed responsible leadership theory and practice in the Asian century. Particularly, very little is known about the influence of Asian culture on the nexus between ethical practices and leadership. Using unique Asian cultural attributes, business leaders in the Asian century have the opportunity to address a range of global social needs, promoting convergence between business and society. This will foster understanding of the distinctive interplay of ethics and leadership within Asian cultures; in turn, this understanding is likely to promote global social good.

The idea for this book came to me around 2009 when I was developing a final-year undergraduate subject titled Responsible Leadership, which I have taught to date based on a collection of readings. Three things led me to begin work on the book: the lectures for this subject, the challenges and opportunities highlighted by China's increasing economic power, which began to grow much more rapidly around 2010, and a White Paper released by the Australian government of the time, "Australia in the Asian Century". Together, they provided the impetus to examine how the Asian century might influence the theory and practice of responsible leadership. This book is aimed at addressing the gap in the micro-macro divide of studying the link between social responsibility and leadership. It focuses particularly on the Asian century opportunities and challenges as a strong contextual factor that shapes the "responsibility" of responsible leadership. The scholarly literature on the topic, the leader profiles developed through interviews and my corporate experiences in the Asia-Pacific region in leading organizations are key sources for the book's assertions. My ten-year corporate experience in a leadership position includes my work at a Sri Lankan-based Singapore Telecom start-up venture as the Human Resources Director, reporting to a Singaporean-Chinese Managing Director. The book is also a product of ideas generated, refined, and tested through my research and in my classrooms. I have been teaching business ethics and leadership to undergraduate and postgraduate students in Singapore, Hong Kong, Sri Lanka, Malaysia, New Zealand and Australia for nearly 15 years. It is rewarding to note that two of my former coursework students have been inspired to undertake responsible leadership PhD projects under my supervision.

The early chapters of the book explain the current context of leading businesses. After Chap. 1 introduces the book, the second chapter addresses the current corporate landscape and the eroding legitimacy and trust in organizations. This discussion leads to Chap. 3 which deals with the notion of responsibility and relevance of moral philosophies. The complexity of leadership is explained in Chap. 4, which includes a discussion on key leadership approaches. The theoretical context is the focus of Chap. 5 which examines and presents two key theories: Responsible Leadership for Performance (RLP) and Responsible Leadership for Relations (RLR). These two theories demand different attributes from leaders. While they explain some mechanisms of responsible leadership, more recent contributions have extended these theories and proposed novel ways of *how* responsible leadership can be enacted. These include spiritual leadership, poetic self and communicative action. The practice of responsible leadership is the focus of Chap. 6, and the discussion addresses corporate social responsibility, sustainability and environment as opportunities for enacting responsible leadership in the Asian century. Using the material presented from the preceding chapters as a foundation, in Chap. 7, this book introduces social innovation as a way to enact responsible leadership and presents a framework to understand socially innovative responsible leadership as virtuous action. After Chap. 8 addresses the future of responsible leadership theory and practice, and shares resources for developing responsible leaders, Chap. 9 presents a sample of leader interviews.

Wollongong, NSW, Australia   Mario Fernando

Acknowledgements

As they do, book projects consume much of an author's life. I must thank my wife, Shamika, and children, Mario and Andrea, for putting up with the writing of this book for the last four years, even on family holidays. Their patience and encouragement have allowed me to bring this project to a successful completion. A special thank you to all the interview participants of the project. Despite their very demanding schedules, participants have been very generous in sharing their ideas and thoughts on the topic. Baz Simmons should be mentioned for his special efforts for helping to identify suitable leaders from the region to interview. Special thanks to Laura Goodin for her editorial support and Benjamin Lee-Bates, Laura Macofsky and Breeanna Bitmead for their helpful research assistance. The four anonymous reviewers for Springer in two review rounds should be thanked for their insightful comments and critique. Their input helped me to improve the coverage of relevant topics and also the depth on key debates. To all my friends at Springer, Chris, Floor and Neil, a special thank you for being patient with me. My sincere appreciation and gratitude to Joanne Ciulla for her thought provoking Foreword. Many thanks to Ken Parry for all the support, and Laura Hartman, Geoff Moore and Brad Jackson for inspiration and advice. For the countless number of students in my first year Principles of Responsible Commerce and third year Responsible Leadership undergraduate classes, thank you for the joy and inspiration, and for reinforcing my belief in the teaching-research nexus. To my parents, Stanley and Felicia, a very special thank you for all the sacrifices made to make me who I am today.

Every effort has been made to trace all copyright holders. The publisher would like to acknowledge the copyright holders for the permission to use material from the sources identified in the book.

Contents

1	**Introduction**	1
	References	7
2	**The Context**	9
	Introduction	9
	Responsibility	10
	Social-Contract Theory	11
	A Crisis of Legitimacy and Trust	12
	Why Good People Succumb to Unethical Acts?	15
	Corporate Social Responsibility	17
	The Necessity to Consume	21
	Responsible Corporations and Capitalism	24
	Conclusion	27
	References	28
3	**The Moral Basis for Responsibility**	31
	Introduction	31
	Ethics	31
	Factors Influencing Leaders' Moral Behavior	36
	Religion	36
	Ethical Relativity	36
	Conscience and Self-Interest	37
	Power	38
	Altruism	39
	Moral Philosophies	40
	Utilitarianism	40
	Kantianism (Deontology)	41
	Virtue Ethics	43
	Application of Moral Philosophies	45
	Morality in Leadership	47
	Conclusion	50
	References	51

4 The Complexity of Leadership ... 53
Introduction ... 53
Characteristics of Leadership ... 54
Key Approaches to Leadership ... 55
    Situational-Leadership Theories ... 56
    Transactional Leadership ... 56
    Transformational Leadership ... 57
    The Full Range Leadership Model ... 57
    Transcendental Leadership ... 58
    House's Path-Goal Theory ... 58
    Spiritual Leadership ... 60
    Ethical Leadership ... 63
    Servant Leadership ... 64
    Authentic Leadership ... 65
Conclusion ... 66
References ... 66

5 Responsible Leadership in Theory ... 71
Introduction ... 71
What Is Responsible Leadership? ... 71
Antecedents of Responsible Leader Behaviour ... 75
Responsible Leadership for Performance (RLP) ... 76
Responsible Leadership for Relations (RLR) ... 80
Differences Between RLP and RLR ... 83
Responsible Leadership and Social Capital ... 84
Values and Responsible Leadership ... 87
The Poetic Self ... 90
Links with Other Leadership Approaches ... 94
    Ethical Leadership ... 95
    Shared Leadership ... 95
    Spiritual Leadership ... 96
    Servant Leadership ... 98
    Authentic Leadership ... 98
Conclusion ... 99
References ... 99

6 Responsible Leadership in Practice ... 103
Introduction ... 103
Responsible Decision-Making Options for Leaders ... 104
Corporate Social Responsibility (CSR) and Responsible Leadership ... 105
    Approaches to CSR ... 107
    Strategic CSR in the Asian Context ... 110
Responsible Leadership in Global Business ... 113
    Globalization and MNEs ... 116
    Impact of Globalization on Leading Responsibly ... 118

	Habermas and Responsible Leadership	121
	Communicative Action and Responsible Leadership Outcomes in the Asian Century	124
	Sustainability and Responsible Leadership	127
	Climate Change and Responsible Leadership	131
	Challenges to Practicing Responsible Leadership	133
	Conclusion	137
	References	137
7	**Responsible Leadership in the Asian Century**	143
	Introduction	143
	Asian Management Styles	144
	Chinese Cultural Influences on Responsible Leadership	147
	The Importance of Social-Purpose Business in the Asian Century	152
	Social Innovation	155
	Social Innovation and Responsible Leadership	158
	Social Innovation Through Performance	158
	Social Innovation Through Relationships	159
	Virtuousness Through Socially Innovative Responsible Leadership	167
	Conclusion	171
	References	172
8	**The Future for Responsible Leadership**	177
	Introduction	177
	Potential of Responsible Leadership	177
	Responsible Leadership: Another Management Fad?	179
	Developing Responsible Leaders	180
	Transformative Teaching and Learning Through Social Innovation	182
	The Subject	184
	Assessments	185
	Content of Social-Innovation Projects	186
	Conclusion	188
	References	188
9	**Appendix: Sample Asian Century Leader Interviews**	191
	Introduction	191
	Jia Li, Co-Founder, Baixing.com, China	191
	Career	191
	The Greatest Leadership Challenge	193
	Responsible Leadership	194
	Leading in Asia	194
	Recent Changes in Chinese Business Culture	195
	Summary	196
	Bernie Landy, President, BlueScope China	196
	Career	196
	Leadership	197

Advice for Leading Successfully	198
Leading in China	198
Responsible Leaders	199
Responsible Leadership and Profits	200
Impact of Leading in Asia on Responsible Leadership	200
Future of Leadership	202
Simon Linge, President, NS BlueScope Indonesia	202
Career	202
Leadership	203
Challenges of Leadership	204
Responsible Leaders	204
Responsible Leadership and Profits	204
Impact of Leading in the Asian Century on Responsible Leadership	205
Challenges and Opportunities in Different Markets and Cultures	206
Future of Leadership	207
Atul Gogna, Vice President, Strategic Marketing, NS Bluescope Coated Products, Singapore	208
Responsible Leadership in Asia	208
Challenges Facing Leadership in Asia	208
Future of Leadership in Asia	209

List of Figures

Fig. 2.1	The Economy and Nature	23
Fig. 2.2	The World Economic Pyramid	27
Fig. 3.1	Moral Leadership Styles	48
Fig. 4.1	Leadership as a process	54
Fig. 5.1	Leadership as a process embedded in responsibility	73
Fig. 5.2	Responsible leadership for performance	77
Fig. 5.3	Responsible leadership for relations theory	81
Fig. 6.1	Continuum of Responsible Decision-Making Options for Leaders	104
Fig. 7.1	Socially innovative responsible leadership	158
Fig. 7.2	Socially responsible leadership and outcomes	165
Fig. 7.3	Success-excellence relationship with goodness of purpose	168
Fig. 7.4	Virtuous responsible leadership	169

List of Tables

Table 7.1	Social-Purpose Business Attributes of RLP and RLR	155
Table 7.2	Key attributes and aims of social innovation from a sample of definitions	156
Table 8.1	Link to teaching strategies and faculty and discipline qualities	185

Chapter 1
Introduction

Alibaba is a Chinese Internet company that is best known for its large online marketplaces. It has made higher profits than those of Amazon and eBay combined (MacLeod 2014). Jack Ma, the founder of Alibaba and one of the richest men in China (CNBC 2015), is quite unique and has a past that stands out from many other Chinese corporate leaders.

Ma was born in Hangzhou in 1964 with the Chinese name Ma Yun. He grew up when the Communist Party campaigns governed daily life. During his spare time, he would collect and fight crickets, which Mao Zedong had banned (MacLeod 2014). Ma struggled with maths, but excelled in English. As he became older, Ma would be up at 5 am to practice English with tourists at the Hangzhou's main hotel, often acting as a free tour guide, which he did for 9 years. Eventually, Ma visited a family he befriended in Australia. "I realized what they told me was quite different from what I had learned in school or heard from my parents" said Ma (MacLeod 2014).

Ma attended what he considered to be the worst college in Hangzhou, after failing the national college entrance exams twice (Forbes 2014). Once he graduated in 1988, Ma married. He earned less than $15 a month by teaching English. While doing this, he attempted to find employment elsewhere, including KFC, a hotel, and the city police, but was rejected. Ma knew he wanted to enter business, which led him to start a translation company while also selling random goods on the street to stay afloat. In 1955, he assisted a Chinese company in the United States to claim funds owed by acting as a translator. During this trip, one of Ma's friends in Seattle showed him the Internet (Kaiman 2014).

Since returning to China, he developed a listing site and sold it to the Chinese government. Ma and several friends resourced $60,000 to start Alibaba, a business-to-business online platform for small Chinese exporters. Alibaba is the world's largest online retailer, and follows the name from a Arabic folk story of a poor wood cutter (Harwell 2014).

© Springer International Publishing Switzerland 2016
M. Fernando, *Leading Responsibly in the Asian Century*,
DOI 10.1007/978-3-319-21789-5_1

Ma's unique leadership style has given him the nickname "Crazy Jack Ma" (MacLeod 2014). As opposed to typical Chinese business entrepreneurs, Ma would often make jokes about himself. He is known to speak his mind, and uses a mix of Western management and Mao Zedong concepts. His eccentric performances have made Ma's leadership style quite famous. For example, he once performed an Elton John song to his 16,000 employees dressed in leather and a Mohawk (Harwell 2014). Ma enjoys various activities such as Tai Chi, so much that he brings his Tai Chi trainer when traveling, kung fu novels, which have also been made part of his company's culture, and meditation in the mountains. He follows Buddhism, Taoism and Confucianism, which Ma has also incorporated into the company culture.

Ma saw the incredible business potential of the Internet when very few other Chinese businessmen did. Alibaba has been referred to as the "Amazon of China, but has more similarities with eBay and Google" (Luckerson 2014). Although the company doesn't directly sell products itself, Alibaba rather acts as an online market where vendors of all sizes can sell their goods and services. For the exposure that sellers receive among Alibaba's 280 million users, sellers are charged a listing fee (Harwell 2014). For example, "a U.S. business that goes to Alibaba.com could set up a deal to buy yoga mats or hard drives from bulk suppliers around the world" (Harwell 2014). In addition, if everyday consumers want to buy a dress or furniture, Taobao and Tmall, Alibaba's online market places are available. These are operated mostly in Chinese. However, Alibaba just launched 11Main.com, which is an invite-only shopping website that is targeted at American buyers. Alibaba also has various stakes beyond just retail, including payment services, video streaming and cloud computing (Harwell 2014). Alibaba has priced its initial public offering at $68USD a share, making it the largest company ever to go public (Farrell 2014).

This book is about what Asian century leaders like Jack Ma bring into the leadership field. These leaders come with a unique blend of Asian cultural heritage mixed with Western management practices. However, responsible leadership discourse is yet to accommodate the influence of these types of companies and leader personalities have on the theory and practice of the concept. This book examines how the shift in economic power to Asia and the rising new global economic order can influence the theory and practice of responsible leadership. Population trends, rapid economic growth and emerging markets have shifted the attention of the world to Asia, and the twenty-first century is increasingly becoming the Asian Century. As Western businesses and higher education institutions are looking more towards Asia for market expansion and investment opportunities, Asian businesses and higher education institutions are also expanding into Western markets. These trends emphasise the value of a book on global responsible leadership offering a culturally integrated view of the topic.

Asia is home to more than half of the global population. During the past 20 years, China and India have tripled their production output (Australian Government White

Paper 2012). According to the Economist (2015), Asia now produces almost half of the world's output, and will be the largest consumer and producer. This work is aimed at researchers with a particular interest in the interplay between leadership, culture and ethics.

According to Waldman and Balven (2014), social responsibility and leadership are central to responsible leadership. It could manifest at the individual, group and organizational levels. The concept is continuing to draw increasing interest from both scholar and practitioner communities. The term 'responsible leadership' on Google Scholar generates 2,410,000 hits (September, 2015). The number of special issues in academic journals (e.g. *Academy of Management Perspectives* 2014), journal articles (e.g. in the *Journal of Business Ethics*), books (e.g. Lawrence and Beamish 2013; Doh and Stumpf 2005; Maak and Pless 2006, 2012) and conferences devoted to the topic are on the rise.

The avid appetite for embracing socially responsible initiatives is reflected in the expanding social businesses of Grameen Danone Foods and Hindustan Lever's Shakti program. These businesses are some examples of enacting responsible leadership through the triple bottom line (Elkington 1998), by giving due consideration to social, environmental and economic sustainability (i.e., people, planet and profits). Since its official launch on July 26, 2000, the UN Global Compact has grown to more than 10,000 members spread over 145 countries and constitutes over 7000 businesses (Stahl and de Luque 2014).

In his introduction to the special issue on responsible leadership in the *Academy of Management Perspectives,* Siegel (2014) argue that the concept of responsible leadership has become popular and significant due to two key reasons. First is the increasing pressure on organizations to be more socially responsible. Social responsibility constitutes of corporate actions that advance various stakeholder needs and those corporate actions that are designed to advance social objectives in the area of social and environmental performance. Unfortunately the link between social responsibility and leadership has not been examined until recently (Siegel 2014). He convincingly argues that this is despite ample evidence that social responsibility actions are embedded in business and corporate level strategies. This theoretical and empirical evidence however links social responsibility mostly at the macro level (Aguinis and Glavas 2012; Devinney 2009), establishing how social responsibility impacts on the economic performance of the organisation (Siegel 2014). In recent times however, there has been a plethora of contributions at the micro level examining the link between social responsibility practices and leadership (see Christensen et al. 2014).

Second, Siegel (2014) points out that responsible leadership has been gaining interest among scholars and practitioners due to its appeal at an interdisciplinary level. Responsible leadership is relevant to an array of disciplines such as management, marketing, business ethics, philosophy, psychology, sustainability, organizational behavior, human resource management, corporate governance, strategy, law, sociology and political science (Siegel 2014, p. 221). The many ways in which responsible leadership has been defined is probably a result of its relevance to these disciplines. For example, while 'responsibility' has been defined in terms of the fiduciary duty of a firm to maximise profits it has also been defined at a broader level, to include the demands of non-financial stakeholders (see Waldman and Siegel 2008).

To examine how the West developed responsible leadership concept is relevant to other cultural contexts, an appreciation for differences in culture is crucial in understanding how they can affect leaders' individual thinking and behavior. Despite the rapid integration of Western and Eastern views at a global level, the economic and political systems, social values and laws of the two worlds differ greatly. A large body of cross-cultural research focuses on comparing and contrasting national cultural differences (e.g., Triandis 1972; Hofstede 1998, 2010; Morris, et al. 1999; White 2002; Kao and Sinha 1997). Cross-cultural differences stem from the different backgrounds of each culture. This can lead to differences in attitudes, behaviors, functioning, communication and cultural implications (Kawar 2012). As a result, strategic decision making differs between Asian and Western cultures (Haley and Tan 1999; Hofstede 1993). Generally, research finds that Western styles of management are focused on a strongly individualistic, performance orientation with low family orientation (Gupta et al. 2009). In contrast, the Asian style of management is more focused on a collective, family-oriented and long-term approach (Hofstede 1993). There are several proposed explanations for this difference in management style. Hofstede (1994) attributes it to cultural and ethnic incongruences. Haley and Tan (1996) suggest that competitive advantage explains the differences while Haley and Stumpf (1989) name personality-type differences as the driver. Haley (1997) found that personality-type variances between different management nationalities was a significant factor, further supporting Hofstede's (1994) theory.

A common misconception is that people from the same region do not behave dramatically differently, and therefore should be treated uniformly. Therefore, in the era of a world dominated by globalization and breaking down of national boundaries, a single style of leadership behavior would not be relevant and effective concerning followers from the same locality but who are increasingly representing different ethnic origins. In terms of Triandis's (1972) criteria of a cross-cultural inquiry, a key motivator for this book is to examine the relevance of the Western-developed concept of responsible leadership in a non-Western research setting. For this purpose, a country-based definition of culture has been adopted (Lenartowicz and Roth 1999, p. 781).

The usefulness of "emic" and "etic" approaches to conducting cross-cultural studies is well documented (see Morris et al. 1999). The inside, or within, perspective of a researcher striving to understand a phenomenon from a particular culture on its own terms is often described as an emic approach. The researcher attempts to understand the phenomenon by "going native", looking at the native's understanding of the phenomenon in general, and the native behavior in particular. According to Morey and Luthans (1984), the emic approach maintains that "the subject and not the researcher is the best judge of the adequacy of the research and analysis. The subject's acceptance of the results of the research is the only necessary and sufficient validation of them" (pp. 29–30). The emic researcher attempts to understand the culture based on ground reality, giving little or no significance to prior theories. The value of the emic approach is in the rich information in the thick description (Geertz 1983).

The outside perspective of a researcher who attempts to understand a phenomenon based on a general external standard, with little input from the native and ground reality, follows the etic approach. The etic approach is based on the outsider's view of the phenomenon. Pike (1967) is credited with creating these terms. According to Morris et al. (1999), Pike's idea was based on the two main approaches used in linguistics: "phonemic analysis of the units of meaning, which reveals the unique structure of a particular language, and phonetic analysis of units of sound, which affords comparisons among languages" (p. 781).

Emic and etic approaches are complementary (Hofstede 1998). According to Hofstede, the emic approach without the help of an etic analysis is limited to native case profiles, from which the researcher cannot generalize to the external world. Similarly, the etic approach is limited in its interpretation of the native phenomenon and offers less capability to interpret the internal world of the native. Thus "the discipline is caught in a Catch 22 situation" (Fontaine and Richardson 2003, p. 76). To address this challenge, Hofstede (1998) suggests that the tactic should be to choose a method appropriate for the examined problem.

One common weakness identified in conducting a cross-cultural inquiry is the tendency to limit the study to finding similarities and differences. In contrast, this book aims to go beyond by attempting to represent and integrate the meaning of responsible leadership in a way that encompasses both emic and etic analyses. Thus this book does not only provide a list of similarities and differences that might affect the development and application of responsible leadership, focusing particularly on the Chinese context, but also examines the contextual factors that could significantly influence the development and enacting of responsible leadership in the Asian century, in which Chinese people are increasingly interacting with the rest of the world. For example, according to *The China Daily* (2013), China continues to be the top source of international students in US universities. According to the historical trends reported by the Institute of International Education (2013), since the 1980s, the number of Chinese students in the US began to grow. In the 1988/1989 school year, China displaced Taiwan as the leading supplier until it in turn was displaced by Japan in 1994/1995. In 1998/1999, China again became the top source of foreign students until displaced by India in 2001/2002, but regained the top spot in 2009/2010.

During the 2012/2013 academic year, Chinese students increased to 235,597 from 194,029 in the previous academic year, a growth of 21 % (Institute of International Education 2013). *The China Daily* (2013) reports that 28.7 % of all international students in the US were from China (39.8 % of these undergraduates, and 43.9 % graduates), and that the top three countries of origin—China, India and the Republic of Korea—now represent 49 % of the total number of international students in the US (Institute of International Education 2013). But of the top three countries, China was the only one with increasing numbers. The rising Chinese international student population is a result of the affluent Chinese middle class. In this context, the aim of the book is also to examine the corresponding potential for the influence of Chinese individual, organizational and cultural indigenous traits on responsible leadership in the increasingly Asian-dominated global economy.

In this book, my attempt is to represent both the emic and etic views of responsible leadership in the Asian century. As White (2002) points out:

> The bulk of the comparative research in Asian contexts—at all levels of analysis—also reveals a fundamental weakness related to explanation. Comparisons have been largely limited.... Nearly all of the research questions are subsumed under "What are the differences in antecedents, manifestations and/or performance among these actors?" Few studies have compared the processes given rise to or linking antecedents, manifestations or performance; i.e., "How did these differences arise?" or "How do antecedents give rise to manifestations, or manifestations to performance?" (p. 291)

Accordingly, this book has adopted a process-based approach to undertaking this inquiry. That is, it goes beyond the mere identification of the similarities and differences of responsible leadership in the Western and Asian contexts to explore in detail the factors that are likely to shape the current development of responsible leadership in both these contexts. It begins by analysing the key factors that influence the development and application of responsible leadership at the individual, organizational and cultural levels. At each level, the development and application of responsible leadership in the Asian century are explained by comparing the processes that have given rise to the current manifestation of the concept. For example, at the individual level, it explores—primarily through the emic approach—how cultural systems and processes in Asian context have influenced the development and application of responsible leadership at the internal and native levels. Most emic-based researchers' work involves qualitative data collected in the field through ethnographic observation. The academic literature, my experience in the Asia-Pacific region in enacting and teaching ethics and leadership, the leader interviews and secondary data form key sources for the book's assertions. While key interviewee observations are integrated into the main text, summaries of some of the interviews conducted for this study are included in the Appendix.

As a native of the Asian region, who was born, raised and educated in Asia, and who worked most of his corporate career with Asian colleagues and with products and services marketed in Asia, I am familiar with the business style, concepts and culture of the Asian region. I was born in Colombo, Sri Lanka, and grew up in a Roman Catholic family setting. Sri Lanka being one of the most ethnically and religiously diverse countries in the world, I was exposed at a very early age to Sinhalese, Tamil and Muslim ethnicities and four of the major religions of the world: Buddhism, Hinduism, Christianity and Islam. My entire schooling was at a Catholic school in Colombo, although Sri Lanka is predominantly Buddhist; this upbringing has been immensely helpful in understanding religious and ethnic tolerance and diversity in the Asian context.

As the book moves from analyzing at the individual level to the organizational and societal levels, the approach becomes more etic to explain the development and application of responsible leadership from an external perspective. When this book considers contemporary Western-developed concepts, and analyse their relevance in the context of Asian century organizations, it mostly uses an etic approach. From this perspective, my having lived and worked in New Zealand, the USA and Australia for over 16 years and completing my postgraduate studies there perhaps were key motivators for me to develop this book to better understand the relevance and application of Western developed responsible leadership in the Asian century.

References

Aguinis, H., & Glavas, A. (2012). What we know and don't know about corporate social responsibility: A review and research agenda. *Journal of Management, 38*, 932–968.
Australian Government White Paper. (2012). Australia in the Asian century. http://www.murdoch.edu.au/ALTC-Fellowship/_document/Resources/australia-in-the-asian-century-white-paper.pdf . Accessed 25 Oct 2014.
China Daily (USA). (2013). SAT alternative makes bid for Chinese takers [Online]. Available at http://usa.chinadaily.com.cn/us/2013-11/14/content_17103666.htm. Accessed 22 Nov 2014.
Christensen, L. J., Mackey, A., & Whetten, D. (2014). Taking responsibility for corporate responsibility: The role of leaders in creating, implementing, sustaining, or avoiding socially responsible firm behaviors. *Academy of Management Perspectives, 28*(2), 164–178.
CNBC. (2015). US dethroned as world's billionaire capital. Available at www.cnbc.com/2015/10/15/us-dethroned-as-worlds-billionaire-capital.html. Accessed 31 Oct 2015.
Devinney, T. M. (2009). Is the socially responsible corporation a myth? The good, bad, and ugly of corporate social responsibility. *Academy of Management Perspectives, 23*(2), 44–56.
Doh, J. P., & Stumpf, S. A. (2005). *Handbook on responsible leadership and governance in global business*. Cheltenham: Edward Elgar.
Elkington, J. (1998). Partnerships from cannibals with forks: The triple bottom line of 21st-century business. *Environmental Quality Management, 8*(1), 37–51.
Farrell, M. (2014). Alibaba the biggest company ever to go public. *The Australian* [Online]. Available: http://www.theaustralian.com.au/business/alibaba-the-biggest-company-ever-to-go-public/story-e6frg8zx-1227063688668?nk=1c2e9d826294bf0c8d0911261cd9deb1. Accessed 22 Sept 2014.
Fontaine, R., & Richardson, S. (2003). Cross-cultural research in Malaysia. *Cross-cultural Management: An International Journal, 10*(2), 75–89.
Forbes. (2014). What makes Alibaba's Jack Ma a great innovator? Available at http://www.forbes.com/forbes/welcome/. Accessed 30 Oct 2014.
Geertz, C. (1983). *Local knowledge: Further essays in interpretive anthropology* (Vol. 5110). New York: Basic books.
Gupta, V., Levenburg, N., Moore, L., Motwani, J., & Schwarz, T. (2009). Anglo vs. Asian Family Business: A cultural comparison and analysis. *Journal of Asia Business Studies, 3*(2), 46–55.
Haley, U. C. V. (1997). The Myers-Briggs type indicator and decision making styles: Identifying and managing cognitive trails in strategic decision making. In C. Fitzgeralf & L. Kirby (Eds.), *Developing leaders, research and applications, psychological type and leadership development* (pp. 187–223). Palo Alto: Consulting Psychologists Press.
Haley, U. C. V., & Stumpf, S. A. (1989). Cognitive trails in strategic decision-making: Linking theories of personalities and cognitions. *Journal of Management Studies, 26*(5), 477–497.
Haley, U. C. V., & Tan, C. T. (1996). The black hole of Southeast Asia: Strategic decision making in an informational void. *Management Decision, 34*(9), 37–48.
Haley, G. T., & Tan, C. (1999). East vs. West: Strategic marketing management meets the Asian networks. *Journal of Business and Industrial Marketing, 14*(2), 91–101.
Harwell, D. (2014). Web-retail titan Alibaba took over China. Could America's web be next? *The Washington Post* [Online]. Available: http://www.washingtonpost.com/business/economy/

web-retail-titan-alibaba-took-over-china-could-americas-web-be-next/2014/09/18/0176a204-3e72-11e4-b0ea-8141703bbf6f_story.html. Accessed 22 Sept 2014.

Hofstede, G. (1993). Cultural constraints in management theories. *The Executive, 7*(1), 81–94.

Hofstede, G. (1994). Cultural constraints in management theories. In D. E. Hussey (Ed.), *International review of strategic management* (Vol. 5, pp. 27–47). West Sussex: Wiley.

Hofstede, G. (1998). A case for comparing apples with oranges: International differences in values. *International Journal of Comparative Sociology, 39*(1), 16.

Hofstede, G. (2010). The GLOBE debate: Back to relevance. *Journal of International Business Studies, 41*(8), 1339–1346.

Institute of International Education. (2013). *Open doors report on international educational exchange.* http://www.iie.org/opendoors

Kaiman, J. (2014). Jack Ma profile – Alibaba's powerful but humble billionaire. *The Guardian* [Online]. Available: http://www.theguardian.com/business/2014/sep/19/jack-ma-profile-alibaba-powerful-humble-billionaire. Accessed 22 Sept 2014.

Kao, H., & Sinha, D. (Eds.). (1997). *Asian perspectives on psychology.* London: Sage.

Kawar, T. I. (2012). Cross-cultural differences in management. *International Journal of Business and Social Science, 3*(6), 105–111.

Lawrence, J. T., & Beamish, P. W. (2013). *Globally responsible leadership: Managing according to the UN global compact.* Thousand Oaks: Sage.

Lenartowicz, T., & Roth, K. (1999). A framework for culture assessment. *Journal of International Business Studies, 30*(4), 781–798.

Luckerson, V. (2014). China's Alibaba Finds Riches on Wall Street. *Time Magazine* [Online]. Available: http://time.com/3404714/alibaba-ipo-jack-ma-wall-street/. Accessed 22 Sept 2014.

Maak, T., & Pless, N. (2006). *Responsible leadership.* London: Routledge.

Maak, T., & Pless, N. (2012). *Responsible leadership.* Dordrecht: Springer.

MacLeod, C. (2014). Alibaba founder Jack Ma's road to the top. *Sydney Morning Herald* [Online]. Available: http://www.smh.com.au/business/china/alibaba-founder-jack-mas-road-to-the-top-20140919-10j3pa.html. Accessed 22 Sept 2014.

Morey, N. C., & Luthans, F. (1984). An emic perspective and ethnoscience methods for organizational research. *The Academy of Management Review, 9*(1), 27–36.

Morris, M. W., Leung, K., Ames, D., & Lickel, B. (1999). Views from inside and outside: Integrating emic and etic insights about culture and justice judgment. *The Academy of Management Review, 24*(4), 781–796.

Pike, K. L. (1967). *Language in relation to a unified theory of the structure of human behavior* (2nd ed.). The Hague: Mouton.

Siegel, D. (2014). Responsible leadership. *The Academy of Management Perspectives, 28*(3), 221–223.

Stahl, G. K., & de Luque, M. S. (2014). Antecedents of responsible leader behavior: A research synthesis, conceptual framework, and agenda for future research. *The Academy of Management Perspectives, 28*(3), 235–254.

The Economist. (2015). Made in China? http://www.economist.com/news/leaders/21646204-asias-dominance-manufacturing-will-endure-will-make-development-harder-others-made. Accessed 25 Oct 2015.

Triandis, H. C. (1972). *The analysis of subjective culture.* New York: Wiley.

Waldman, D. A., & Balven, R. M. (2014). Responsible leadership: Theoretical issues and research directions. *Academy of Management Perspectives, 28*, 224–234.

Waldman, D. A., & Siegel, D. S. (2008). Defining the socially responsible leader. *Leadership Quarterly, 19*(1), 117–131.

White, S. (2002). Rigor and relevance in Asian management research: Where are we and where can we go? *Asia Pacific Journal of Management, 19*(2), 287–352.

Chapter 2
The Context

Introduction

The term "Asian Century" originated around the time the Chinese Premier Deng Xiaoping and Indian Prime Minister Rajiv Gandhi met in 1988 (ASPC 2013). It has been widely used in the media to portray the projected dominance of the Asian economy, culture and politics in the twenty-first century. The definition of Asia varies but generally includes China, India, Japan, Taiwan, South Korea, Indonesia, Malaysia, Singapore, Thailand and 40 more others countries. China and India have shown and are expected to drive the Asian century. Both these countries have an abundance of labour and a very strong work ethic. They have 35 % of world's 6.5 billion population, and Asia is estimated to have about 60 % of the world population (Population Reference Bureau 2013).

The 18th century leading economy was China's Qing dynasty. The Qing Empire—unlike the rising Britain at roughly the same time—did not focus on trade. In 1793, King George III was informed by the emperor Qianlong that "we possess all things. I set no value on objects strange or ingenious, and I have no use for your country's manufactures" (Bloomberg 2013). Following World War II, the US emerged as the supreme trading power, leading the development of global trade and financial structures. During the same period of time, the leading trading nation of the nineteenth century, the UK, was starting to shrink its colonial power around the globe. In 1976, Chairman Mao Zedong died. Thereafter, China's economy was based on trade and foreign investment. During the period from 1978 to 2012, the average Chinese economic growth was 9.9 % per year (Hastings 2012).

China is now the largest trading partner for many leading economies and its rapid increase of power in global trade has dismantled age old trading relationships between superpowers (Bloomberg 2013). For example, by 2020, Bloomberg (2013) estimates that Germany's export volume to China would be double that of its exports to France. In this context, it is reasonable to expect the influx into the West of

Chinese leaders like Alibaba's CEO, Jack Ma, with their unique Asian management styles. How would responsible leadership be influenced?

With the rise of economic, cultural and political power of Asia, significant changes to almost every sphere of human endeavor are likely to impact how business leaders operate in the Asian century. In this context, leaders will be challenged to identify and thrive in the opportunities of the Asian century. With rising levels of energy consumption, the competition for natural resources is likely to become more intense. Leadership responsibilities in the Asian century could revolve much more around finding alternative sources to replace depleting natural resources such as water, coal, land and even air. These will soon become sources for competition between nations if supply shortages, inefficiencies of use and greater pollution are not addressed. The aging population and labour force will be another reality that Asian century business leaders will increasingly have to deal with. In addition, there are a variety of other contextual factors that could challenge business leaders such as the economic effects of corruption, impact of epidemic diseases, unemployment, poverty and social unrest. Effective policies to maximise these opportunities and to avoid pitfalls would need to be developed. Business leaders could be better placed to reap the benefits if they are more familiar with the culture, history, religions and societies in the Asian region (Ashkanasy 2002). Before focusing on these, we first explore the notion of responsibility and then the current context of business and leadership.

Responsibility

The term responsibility can be used in different forms to signify different types of responsibilities. Kermisch (2012) proposes five types; first is in the context of attributing various obligations to the holder of a role, as in role-responsibility. For instance, the CEO of the company is held responsible for the damage the company's product has caused its customers. Responsibility could also be used in the context of attributing the cause to an event, as in causal-responsibility, such as when the tsunami caused the Japanese nuclear reactors to explode. Responsibility is also used to attribute obligations to the capacity of the individual to reason and make informed decisions, as in capacity-responsibility. For instance, the pilot of an aircraft suffering a heart attack has no capacity to be held responsible for the crash. Liability-responsibility is a prospective attribution of responsibility based on law. For instance, in a car crash, if the driver was above the legal alcohol limit, the attribution of responsibility for the damages will be placed on the driver by law.

Finally, virtue-responsibility is used in the context of attributing moral obligations (Kermisch 2012). It usually is used to reflect the absence of care towards others. According to Ladd (1991), this type of responsibility seeks to attribute obligations based on a relationship. Virtue-responsibility seeks to ascertain how things are and how things should be or should have been. Thus it is applied in the descriptive and normative sense as well as in prospective and retrospective senses. Ladd (1991) makes a compelling argument as to why we should move away from the limited, legally applied blame-responsibility mindset to a notion of responsibility that is more holistic and is based on a relationship. The relationship based social-contract theory is central to understanding the responsibility of businesses to its stakeholders.

Social-Contract Theory

The social-contract theory dates back to the seventeenth and eighteenth centuries and the work of John Locke, Thomas Hobbes and Jean-Jacques Rousseau. A social contract is formed when rules and assumptions are developed on behavior patterns within sections of a society. The social contract often involves a quid pro quo (something given in return for an item or service of equivalent value). It is also often based on implicit as well as explicit agreements; for example, between a corporation and its stakeholders. Many theorists consider that corporations have a social contract with a wide variety of stakeholders. According to Donaldson (1982, 1989), based on stakeholders' consent, corporations can develop corporate legitimacy which could lead to a social contract. That is, corporations can survive only with the commitment and good will of the society. This suggests an implied agreement between the corporation and society: "If General Motors holds society responsible for providing the condition of its existence, then for what does society hold General Motors responsible? What are the terms of the social contract?" (Donaldson 1982, p. 42). He uses the social-contract theory to establish the moral foundation of the corporation: "corporations considered as productive organizations exist to enhance the welfare of society through the satisfaction of consumer and worker interests, in a way which relies on exploiting corporations' special advantages and minimizing disadvantages" (1982, p. 54).

The basis for this social contract is trust. For example, an entrepreneur wanting to launch a publicly listed company would request from the government a license to operate. This would be granted based on an implicit trust that the proposed corporation would attempt to do good, not harm, within the society. This social contract could manifest in several ways, but would usually take the form of a set of rules and assumptions about interactions with various elements in society. Effective leaders—including those in corporations—not only meet their goals efficiently but also inspire trust in their followers. Trust is very delicate and difficult to manipulate, and it takes years to develop between followers and leaders. It binds the leader's private and public morality. While leaders' private behavior may be unrelated to their public behavior, once ethical shortcomings come to the public domain, they spread doubt in society (Ciulla 2001). The trust issue is not a settled area within leadership; it is evolving. It could be based on how the followers perceive trust versus the circumstances of the particular case. The effects of power are quite obvious: it corrupts the relationship between leaders and followers if it is not carefully handled.

Due to the spate of recent corporate scandals, society now has a higher standard for corporations' social and moral obligations. The corporation is a trustee for society's resources. Therefore, corporations need to deliver goods and minimize harm when they use these resources, and to show—for example, through disclosure in annual reports—that they are engaging in these activities through a two-way, open system. Corporations need to be seen to extract and use natural, economic and social resources in a morally responsible manner, and to apply their core competencies to social involvement and community well-being.

The psychological condition plenoxia—an obsession to acquire wealth at whatever cost—works against the trust created by the social-contract theory (Ciulla 2001). Leaders who succumb to plenoxia can develop an obsession with anything that is external—money, power—and exhibit a certain amount of "gracelessness", a greed for external goods. Schwartz and Gibb (1999) hypothesise that until the Enron scandal, ethics and looking after the interests of the wider community were not considered within the purview of corporations. Thus there is often a tension between promoting individual and corporate interests.

A Crisis of Legitimacy and Trust

Business success depends on the ability of a firm to act responsibly: not just in the short term, but—and particularly—in the long term. Asian century corporations operate within a general environment of distrust and crisis of legitimacy, largely because of what has taken place in the corporate world. In the recent past, there have been several types of corporate scandals and collapses. A look at the top 100 corporate criminals of the 1990s (Anderson and Cavanagh 2000) shows that Exxon, one of the largest companies in the world, was fined $125 million for environmental damages (Mokhiber 2013). Other corporate criminals on the list include Pfizer, General Electric and IBM. The same corporations are far bigger than some of the world's largest democracies. Governments are elected by, and accountable to, the citizens they govern; corporations are owned by a limited group of rich, often influential shareholders and governed by boards of directors.

It is a common understanding that leaders' success stories are inspiring. However, according to Ciulla (2001), it's often difficult for others to replicate what they have done because their actions relate to different cultural and organizational contexts. Rather, failure in life and consequent guilt and regret are how we learn moral lessons. Ethical failures—our own and others'—also help us to think about the complexity of leadership, and provide a deeper insight about leader qualities and attributes of successful leadership. This captures the importance of looking at why leaders fail.

A number of corporate scandals notable for their magnitude and gravity have occurred in recent years. In December 2008, Bernard Madoff, a former chairman of National Association of Securities Dealers Automated Quotations (NASDAQ), turned himself in to the Federal Bureau of Investigation, and few months later pleaded guilty to eleven felony charges including money laundering. On June 29, 2009, he was found guilty and received a 150 year prison term for operating a Ponzi scheme worth several billion dollars (CNN 2014). The CNN report documents that as a hedge-fund manager Bernard Madoff laundered billions of investor dollars through an account with JPMorgan, the largest US bank, with profits topping $US20 billion a year. Media sources reported that JPMorgan agreed in 2014 to pay $US 2.6 billion to the US government and Madoff's victims to settle failure to notify the authorities of fraud suspicions regarding the Madoff hedge fund (Forbes 2014). This payment is the largest forfeiture paid by a bank to settle violations of anti-money-laundering regulations.

Concerns regarding Madoff spanned over a decade (CNN 2014). JPMorgan notified London regulators of suspicious activities, but not US regulators. According to reports, in October 2008, an analyst at the bank wrote a memo outlining the lack of transparency and suspiciously superior performance. This was reviewed by a London JPMorgan official, and a suspicious-activity report was filed with the UK Serious Organised Crime Agency (Forbes 2014). It was alleged that the account with JPMorgan received large deposits and transfers totalling around $US 150 billion from investors in Madoff Securities. The money was not used to buy securities as promised. Madoff routinely transferred money between his own account and the account of Norman Levy to overinflate the amounts, leading to higher interest payments on Levy's account (The Sydney Morning Herald 2014).

According to media reports, the main issues with the Madoff situation were the failure to report suspicious behavior and JPMorgan's withdrawing funds from Madoff-related entities to minimize their losses (Forbes 2014). JPMorgan managed to save $US200 million by withdrawing the funds just prior to Madoff's arrest. Even though the bank cut its exposure to Madoff's funds to minimize its losses, it is reported that these concerns were never communicated to US authorities. The bank was accused of lining up the dots to make profits but was not so meticulous in executing its legal obligations. Billions of dollars were laundered in what was basically a single set of accounts at JPMorgan (The Sydney Morning Herald 2014).

JPMorgan's failure to report allowed Madoff to launder billions of dollars over decades through JPMorgan (CNN 2014). No individuals at JPMorgan were held responsible. Thousands of investors lost a total of $US17.3 billion in principal (The Sydney Morning Herald 2014). Details have yet to be released on how JPMorgan will improve its anti-money-laundering efforts in the future.

In the well documented case of Enron, a US gas, electricity and commodity-trading company headquartered in Houston, perpetrated widespread accounting fraud. CEO Kenneth Lay, the son of a Baptist minister, is likely to have had the moral awareness to detect an ethical problem in his organization, and yet the violations continued for years (Achbar et al. 2004). Sherron Watkins was the whistleblower in this case (New York Times 2006). She worked directly under chief financial officer Jeffrey Skilling, and gave evidence to the House of Representatives against her employer. In sad contrast, John Clifford "Cliff" Baxter, a senior Enron executive, committed suicide after clashing with Skilling over the company's questionable practices (Achbar et al. 2004). Enron workers were left without a job and with a zero balance in their retirement accounts as the company's stock price plummeted.

In the United Kingdom, the NewsCorp phone hacking scandal compelled the media magnate Rupert Murdoch to apologize to the UK public through a one-page newspaper advertisement. Admitting that the company should have acted more quickly and aggressively to investigate any wrongdoing, the advertisement signed by Rupert Murdoch takes responsibility. Since this apology was published, Newscorp has paid compensation to those whose phones were hacked.

Australia's Heath Insurance Holdings (HIH) collapsed in 2001 due to unethical governance activities (APH 2001). Ray Williams, its CEO, had set up the company more than 30 years before and held the post until six months before its demise. According to APH (2001), by the late 1990s, HIH had become one of the largest publicly listed general insurers in Australia, specializing in volatile liability classes and paying $AUD2 billion in premiums in 1999. It had a reputation in the market for aggressive pricing to win business. Posts in an online forum on the collapse of HIH reflected what goes wrong when senior executives act without responsibility (see Four Corners 2001).

The case of Australian building-products manufacturing firm James Hardie Industries represents a new breed of ethical misconduct. James Hardie Industries was alleged to be responsible for over half of the reported Australian cases of mesothelioma, an asbestos related form of lung cancer (Fernando and Sim 2011).

These incidents of high-profile corporate misconduct give rise to the question, "Why do executives engage in unethical actions?" The above examples of corporate unethical action have a common theme. That is, just as many good German citizens followed Nazi authority and orders at the time, many ordinary working people in organizations follow their orders because they perceive that their role is to help the organisation achieve its goals. They do not question the legitimacy of the order.

However, there have also been good examples of leading responsibly. Anita Roddick, founder of The Body Shop, is often cited as an example of a capitalist with a conscience (Pless 2011). According to the Independent (2011), Dame Anita Roddick was born in 1942 to an Italian migrant couple in Littlehampton. She trained as a teacher but then began to tour around the world representing the United Nation's Environment Programme. In 1976 Dame Anita created The Body Shop, opening its first store in Brighton (Independent 2011). Three decades after The Body Shop was created, it was revealed that Dame Anita was carrying Hepatitis C, believed to have been contracted from infected blood given to her during the birth of her youngest daughter in 1972. Independent (2011) reported that two years after Anita found out, she revealed her diagnosis on her internet blog: "I have Hepatitis C. It's a bit of a bummer but you groan and move on."

Anita Roddick campaigned strongly on human-rights causes varying from opposition to the death penalty to stopping domestic violence, but it was as the founder of The Body Shop that she was best known (Pless 2011). The Body Shop focuses on social responsibility, respect for human rights, concern for the environment and animal protection.

In 2006, The Body Shop was sold to French company L'Oreal for £652 m (Independent 2011). Dame Anita was confident that the values and purpose of The Body Shop would survive the transition, and was excited to work with such a large company and enter into new ways of doing business, specifically sourcing ingredients from developing countries. She passed away at age 64 in 2007 from a major brain hemorrhage, with her husband and daughters by her bedside (Independent 2011). She had been advocating for human-rights causes weeks before her death.

As a response to increasing instances of corporate scandals and executives' unethical and corrupt conduct, there are now widespread societal expectations that corporations need not only to achieve traditional economic profits, but to deliver on the "triple bottom line": profits, planet and people. Parties or stakeholders interested in a corporation's profits, its economic impact and its effects on and interaction with the community often have conflicting demands. A corporation is thus challenged to create value for all stakeholders, including its shareholders, consumers, suppliers, employees, the community and other interested parties. A responsible approach to leadership in corporations is vital for generating win-win outcomes for all stakeholders, who generally have different agendas in a corporation. Responsible leadership is about leading with integrity and making profits without compromising principles. But why do "good" people succumb to pressures to act unethically?

Why Good People Succumb to Unethical Acts?

A key contributing factor is obedience to authority (Hartman et al. 2008). For example, in the case of Lynndie England, a soldier accused in the Abu Ghraib prisoner abuse case, and also in Nazi Germany, these officers' defense of their engagement in inhumane acts was the need to obey authority (NBC News 2013). As we have seen in several court cases, such as in England's case and at Nuremberg, this justification does not hold up at the legal level, let alone at the (higher) ethical level.

The second factor that contributes to why good people tend to succumb to pressure to engage in unethical acts is peer pressure and consensus (Hartman et al. 2008). This exerts a force not just because people want to fit in and succeed in an organization, but because in the face of groupthink, people's thinking can actually change. An example can be drawn from the collapse of the largest insurer in Australia, HIH. The company invested in the Taiwanese military without conducting due diligence (APH 2013). The entire board of directors would have had to approve such an investment. A single holdout board member might have felt quite a bit of self-doubt and pressure to conform. The greater the degree to which people can identify this effect and look at it consciously, the less power it has (Hartman et al. 2008). It is also possible to "turn the tables" through making a strong and persuasive argument to build one's own group of supporters for ethical action. The consequences can be very painful. The most common is expulsion from the group and denial of rights—although if enough people diverge from the norm, they can create a new majority, and societal norms can change.

Third, self-serving bias can contribute to good people committing unethical acts (Hartman et al. 2008). It allows individuals to selectively remember and retain only those views that confirm their pre-existing views. No-one wants to be wrong, as that feels like a threat to the ego. Whistleblowers can overcome this by finding alternative interpretations of the same data: choosing new sources, identifying persuasive arguments; and moving toward a less self-serving interpretation.

A fourth reason for good people to succumb to external pressures to engage in unethical acts could be the effect of the "slippery slope" (Hartman et al. 2008). An initial small lapse in ethical behavior can lead incrementally to larger lapses. After the first, the person feels guilty, but because there is no punishment or because the person finds they can tolerate the guilt, they become more competent in negating the inner, nagging voice of conscience, and the offenses grow, incrementally. However, this tendency can be turned to good: if even small lapses are detected and rectified, this can have a significant impact on generating ethical action.

Lastly, good people can succumb to external pressures to engage in unethical acts due to the desire to avoid losing the sunk cost—the investment that has already gone into a situation, including the resources of time, effort and money—and avoid the risk of additional cost (Hartman et al. 2008). Sometimes when wrongdoing is detected, there is very little chance of recovering these investments. Risk-aversion becomes a factor when something or someone important to the person can be threatened by a potential course of action. This can be overcome by considering what has already been gained or learned by the sunk investment, not just in monetary terms. Whistleblowers in particular are able to say, "I'm not concerned with the financial aspects; I need to have a clear conscience. I need to be able to live with myself", and accordingly blow the whistle. As an example, I offer this story.

In a postgraduate management subject I was teaching, the last scheduled lecture was on "Ethics and Strategic Human Resources Management". We were discussing Lowry's (2006) ethical-awareness model and whether an employee is ethically mute or ethically active, with these two states being the poles on a continuum. After the lecture, two students came up to me. They had a situation in their workplace where they suspected a superior was engaging in unethical and illegal behavior, fabricating reasons to dismiss people to achieve cost savings. They asked, "If we keep silent, which category would we fall into on that continuum?" I told them they would be ethically mute, the least ethical category. The discussion went on for some time, and they didn't agree with me. Sometime later, when I was overseas, I received an email from one of the students saying that she now agreed with me, and had decided to blow the whistle. She didn't want to wait for me to return to the country to discuss it further; she had decided to act and wanted to get it over with. I felt sad that I had led her to make this decision and she might be out of a job, particularly as I knew she was a single parent.

When I got back, she came to see me with the other student and a third person, who had been one of the improperly retrenched employees. My student was in good spirits because the organization had accepted the allegations. The third person had been offered her job again and she wanted to thank me. This is a very rare story of whistleblowers for whom things turned out well. As a whistleblower, my student described the turmoil she went through. Her experiences illustrate the concepts of the sunk cost and cost-aversion. This person had invested 4 years in this job (the sunk cost), which was the motivation for cost-aversion. The hardest aspect of whistleblowing is to enact what is ethical. Even if we know that we need to blow the whistle, we may not because of the consequences. There is a great deal of literature that supports the view that merely teaching someone what is ethical, and the various theories of ethical behavior, does not necessarily lead to them becoming ethically active or more ethical. Knowing what to do is a different issue from doing it. Options where the individual decision-maker's ethical awareness and moral courage are developed may be more effective than rule- and governance-based approaches. While Milton Friedman, the Nobel laureate in economics, would say that the only responsibility of an organization is to make profits, the modern view asserts that social responsibility extends the level of responsibility beyond profits to safeguarding society's welfare. Organizations are expected to engage in corporate responsibility.

Corporate Social Responsibility

While philosophers have been theorising using moral philosophies to develop the discipline of business ethics, in practice, leaders have focused on corporate social responsibility (CSR) as an integral part of corporate strategy making (Fisher 2004). Thus ethics and CSR are used interchangeably although the two concepts convey different meanings. I concur with Fisher's (2004) distinction "social responsibility focuses on the impact that business activity has on society while ethics is concerned with the conduct of people within organisations" (p. 393). The role of business and society has been debated for some time (e.g., Porter and Kramer 2011; 2006; Basu and Palazzo 2008; Godfrey and Hatch 2007; Jamali 2007; McWilliams et al. 2006; Maitland 2002). There has been growing support for a strategic view that incorporates CSR. Most CSR definitions focus on the extent of engagement with economic, social and environmental domains. Very early in the conceptualisation process of CSR, Carroll (1979) defined CSR as addressing economic, legal, ethical and philanthropic aspects of the corporation's activities. Economic responsibilities involve, as articulated by Milton Friedman, a commitment to protecting the interests of shareholders, specifically in terms of maximizing and protecting profits. If a company has the means to engage in philanthropy, the company may do so as long as this will not abrogate its responsibilities to its shareholders.

Legal responsibilities involve meeting the minimum legal standards that apply to the company's activities. Ethical responsibilities involve the company's decision-makers consciously trying to determine the right thing to do. Philanthropic responsibilities involve a company putting itself in a position of performing a good action based on the concept of human kinship, without any expectation of a return.

Because the broader society has grown to expect CSR, some corporations engage in it in an instrumental sense: to be popular with stakeholders, to jump on the bandwagon so that their reputation is not harmed (see Fernando 2001). If a commercial bank is launching a program for the homeless, other banks might follow, as they need to compete with this image. Unfortunately, there is no easy way to determine how sincere and authentic corporations are when they engage in CSR activities. The stockholder and stakeholder approaches give a basis for this dichotomy between the classical and the socioeconomic view (see Waldman and Siegel 2008). While the financial benefit to the stockholders is the primary focus of the stockholder approach, in contrast, all stakeholders that interact with the organization are the focus of the stakeholder approach.

In his now-famous quote in the *Wealth of Nations*, Adam Smith outlined the role of self-interest in business: "It is not from the benevolence of the butcher, the brewer, or the baker, that we expect our dinner, but from their regard to their own interest. We address ourselves, not to their humanity but to their self-love, and never talk to them of our necessities but of their advantages" (Smith 1776, Book 1, Chapter 2). From this perspective, if all agents in a market economy follow self-interest (consumers seeking the lowest prices and producers the highest), all the market forces will combine to produce a market guided by an "invisible hand" into doing good for the society. Smith argued that when all parties have perfect information, the invisible hand will guide the best interest of the buyer and seller in a market. For example, under perfect market conditions, a potential buyer in the stock market can obtain information about all the shares, the economic outlook and the business, political and social contexts. If perfect information is not available, those acting in the market will make substandard decisions, thus hindering the invisible hand in looking after the community's needs. Smith believed that governments should stay at arm's length from the market, and should not interfere in determining market prices. If the government intervenes, the invisible hand does not work. If a corporation doesn't want to engage in CSR, a government can enact legislation to force it to do so. But the free-market argument asserts that the government must not interfere.

The stakeholder theory has been proposed as an approach firms can use in allocating resources to internal and external stakeholders (Donaldson and Preston 1995). In stakeholder theory, an organization's primary stakeholders include its shareholders (in other words, the owners), the customers, the suppliers and the employees; its secondary stakeholders include, for example, governments, activists and others, depending on the industry and the company. According to stakeholder theory, all these parties should be treated fairly by corporations; it could lead to better market performance.

Business organizations' primary purpose is to make profits. Without this profit objective, there's no rationale for a company's existence. However, companies can also engage in doing good as they make profits. The stockholder approach focuses solely on financial and economic relationships with stockholders or owners as the key beneficiaries of company initiatives.

Adam Smith justified the effectiveness of the narrow or stockholder view of corporate responsibility using several arguments. First, he was of the view that companies should not be held morally responsible for matters outside the economic operations of the company. He argued that this would tantamount to disturbing the company objectives (the economic mission of business)—and even threaten the very foundations of the free-enterprise system. Second, Smith argued that it is not proper to encourage corporations to address non-business issues. They lack the necessary expertise, and corporations are likely to impose their materialistic values on society. Yet some corporations have demonstrated that they accept responsibility for the well-being of their immediate and wider communities. In 1982, the Johnson & Johnson manufactured Tylenol capsules caused the death of seven people from cyanide poisoning. These had been sold in five Chicago stores. At that time, the market share of Tylenol was 35 % of the $1.2 billion worth analgesic market. After the deaths, Johnson & Johnson's market share dropped to 7 % (Knowledge@Wharton 2012).

Jim Burke, the company's then-CEO, immediately expressed commitment to and concern for customers. He chose to pull the products from the market and lose sales in the short term to protect public safety. Honesty and commitment elevated consumer trust in the company, and the damage to the Tylenol brand in the longer term was minimal. Johnson & Johnson's recall of 31 million bottles costed $100 million. Two moths later, using tamper proof packaging, Burke relaunched the product. His actions have now become the template to follow in corporate crisis management (Knowledge@Wharton 2012). Jim Burke's handling of the Tylenol incident redefined the way that firms should act on public safety issues, to go beyond talking and taking action.

Third, Smith argued that if corporations stray from purely economic matters, they will impose their values on society. Rather than moralising corporate activity, they will materialise society. Yet corporations already exert considerable discretionary power over society.

While the stockholder view has several positives, it has also been criticized by scholars on several grounds. Modern corporations bear little resemblance to the self-sufficient farmers and craftspersons on whom Adam Smith based his theory. A company as large as ExxonMobil is in the position to dictate the terms of consumers' buying behavior for oil products. Toyota Motor Company can influence car-buying behavior by the sheer size of its resources and its inescapable advertising campaigns. Thus the stockholder approach needs to be expanded with a broader look at more systemic issues of running a corporation.

Milton Friedman's approach simply implies that as long as a company can generate a dollar out of doing good, that course should be followed. However, this involves the notion of instrumentality: exploiting doing good to others as a tool, as an instrument to advance companies' profit-maximizing objectives. Many companies can be perceived to be engaging in this type of behavior, intentionally or not. Unilever Sri Lanka, for example, allocated a quarter of the SLR100 million funded by its parent company to the Sri Lankan government to help the victims of the Boxing Day Asian tsunami in 2004, and developed major plans to help the victims through projects such as building and donating houses. The company's intentions in the first 12 months after the disaster reflected a spontaneous response to an horrific natural disaster (Fernando 2007, 2010). However, 3 years later the company was yet to fulfill some of its objectives for various reasons. The company's initial promises could have been perceived by stakeholders as an instrumental approach to further the company's own financial goals through the benefits of positive public relations and tax reductions. So are firms' intentions in these types of philanthropy efforts ever really genuine? What did the company or the board of directors intend when they developed the tsunami-relief plan? Does intent matter if the action provides ultimate good to some people? This is an important question that requires the application of moral philosophies, and which I will consider later. The question to be dealt with in this introductory chapter is this: is the goodness of a corporation's philanthropic action diluted if the corporation stands to benefit from that good deed?

Two cases highlight this point: James Hardie Industries Limited (Australia) and the Toyota Prius. In Fernando and Sim (2011), we outline the James Hardie case in detail. Briefly, the James Hardie case is about a company that continued to manufacture and distribute a harmful product knowingly. The company has been manufacturing asbestos related products in Australia for over 70 years. It has been documented that the company knew for over 30 years that asbestos was linked to mesothelioma, a type of lung cancer. According to Prince et al. (2004), asbestos related claims were estimated at around $6 billion. Since 1945, Murray (2005) estimates that about 7000 Australians would have died from mesothelioma and by 2020, this is expected to increase to 18,000. This type of cancer develops only after about 40 years and this has been a major obstacle in attributing responsibility to the company. Due to the prolonged delay of mesothelioma symptoms showing up, compensation planning for victims has been a challenging task. According to Hills (2001), the first James Hardie worker died in 1960. After more than 4000 complaints were filed against James Hardie and other associated asbestos manufacturing companies, James Hardie ceased asbestos manufacturing in 1986 (see Fernando and Sim 2011).

The company set up a compensation fund of $293 million (James Hardie Industries Limited 2001) but James Hardie, not long after, announced a shortfall in the fund (Hills 2001, 2005). In 2007, the Australian Securities and Investments Commission (ASIC) initiated civil cases against 10 former directors and managers.

The main activist for Hardie victims, Bernie Banton, died in 2007. With his mini-oxygen tank, he became a symbol for the asbestos victims' struggle for compensation. On April 23rd, 2009, 10 directors were held guilty of misleading the public with a media release (Fernando and Sim 2011). The company was also found to have been transferring funds to the Netherlands; the Australian media called this one of the most morally and legally repugnant acts in Australian corporate history (7.30 Report 2004). All directors were held liable for failing to act with duty of care. In 2010, the appeals lodged by the directors (except for the CEO) in the New South Wales Court of Appeal (The West Australian 2010) were upheld (see The Australian 2010). James Hardie Industries Limited's appeal however failed and the company was required to pay 90 % of ASIC's legal costs. The CEO was prohibited from managing companies over a 15 year-period and was fined AUS$ 350,000 (The Australian 2010).

The case of the development of the Toyota Prius offers an interesting contrast. The company has been applauded for producing a socially responsible hybrid car that generates lower levels of emissions compared to other comparable models. This option in the market would excite a section of the consumer market to pay a higher price; assuming that reducing the harm to the environment is of value to these consumers (McWilliams et al. 2006). Such product differentiation that creates a societal good could strengthen the firm's reputation.

These two contrasting cases can simultaneously fulfill Friedman's narrow view of corporate responsibility (of making profits and only profits) and the more Asian century view of a broader corporate responsibility, in which corporations are expected to engage in promoting the triple bottom line. Is "doing well by doing good" responsible and ethical? That is, is doing good for society with the expectation of a benefit still an ethical action? We will address this question later.

As a key driver of capitalism, consumption levels in the highly globalised Asian century can increase the rising instances of unethical misconduct in organizations. Consumption trends are linked to elements of an economic system. Abnormal levels of consumption in a society have the potential to spawn many vices. Why is consumption necessary?

The Necessity to Consume

A key facet of the post-industrial revolution is the necessity to consume. In capitalism, consumption is a driver for job creation, and from the job income, employees will continue to purchase which is essential for the economy to function smoothly. Continuous consumption is the key imperative of capitalism. The role of consumption in capitalist societies is highlighted when climate change initiatives are introduced that affect trends in consumption. Climate change initiatives are usually challenged on the basis of their potential to reduce jobs and slow down consumption. Therefore, consumption is the vital cog in the wheel of capitalism, allowing individuals and communities to promote self-interest to feel good about owning branded and high-end products that the upper class own (that is, promoting status).

Of the world's 100 largest economic entities, 51 were corporations (Anderson and Cavanagh 2000). General Motors, at number 23, was the highest-ranked corporation, with an economy bigger than Denmark's. IBM's annual turnover was bigger than Singapore's gross domestic product. In the case of these enormous companies, one can ask: who is wielding the power to exploit resources, dispose of waste, set prices, enter communities and compete with small, independent businesses? What obligation do these corporations have toward external stakeholders, particularly the community? This includes not only their adherence to laws, rights and values and respect for cultures, but also to be a good global citizen by promoting all facets of human development. Moreover, how do these corporations protect, respect, improve and sustain the environment, and follow practices of sustainable growth? The role of consumption needs to be examined in relation to environmental sustainability. "The individual serves the industrial system not by supplying savings and the resulting capital, but by consuming its products" (Galbraith 1967, p. 38). Thus consumption in an economic context plays an integral role in capitalism, the dominant economic system in most societies. Hence during the Global Financial Crisis, stimulus packages were a critical element in boosting consumption and keeping national economies from falling into recession. All nations and economies are now compelled to address climate change, and the role of nature in human activities has come to focus of late.

Working from left to right through the simple economy model depicted in Fig. 2.1, firms and households treat nature as a source of inputs. For example, beverage manufacturers locate their factories near waterways to maximize the use of free access to water in their bottling operations. Households process nature as inputs as well, and pay rates to the government for the use of land and water. Households also provide labor to firms in return for wages, and firms provide commodities in return for consumer spending. What happens to the waste during the production of this economic activity? The cost of waste, and of dealing with waste, until recently at least, was not incorporated into firms' price structure. Firms used to externalise these cost factors to a third party, namely the government. Cost shifting is at the core of what economists refer to as externality. This process of shifting a cost item to another party is called negative externality. Nature was regarded not only as a reservoir to draw resources, but as a sink and a dump for waste. Although most from the West do not tend to regard nature as sacred, believers of Confucian philosophy feel that nature is not to be conquered or controlled. Rather, one is to be in harmony with nature.

Veblen's classic book *The Theory of the Leisure Class* (1899), highlights this concept extremely well. He argues that firms were able to dump their waste products in a nearby river or lake and saved money that might otherwise have spent on managing that waste. The externalising of costs, which is shifting costs to another party, is not deemed ethical. The responsible course of action would be to acknowledge all relevant costs in a product or service pricing structure, and market the product or service accordingly. Of late some far-thinking countries such as Switzerland (and, for several years, Australia, although it has since been repealed) have even gone to the extent of mandating a carbon tax on the level of emissions attributable to economic activity. China is to follow soon.

THE ECONOMY AND NATURE: A SIMPLE MODEL

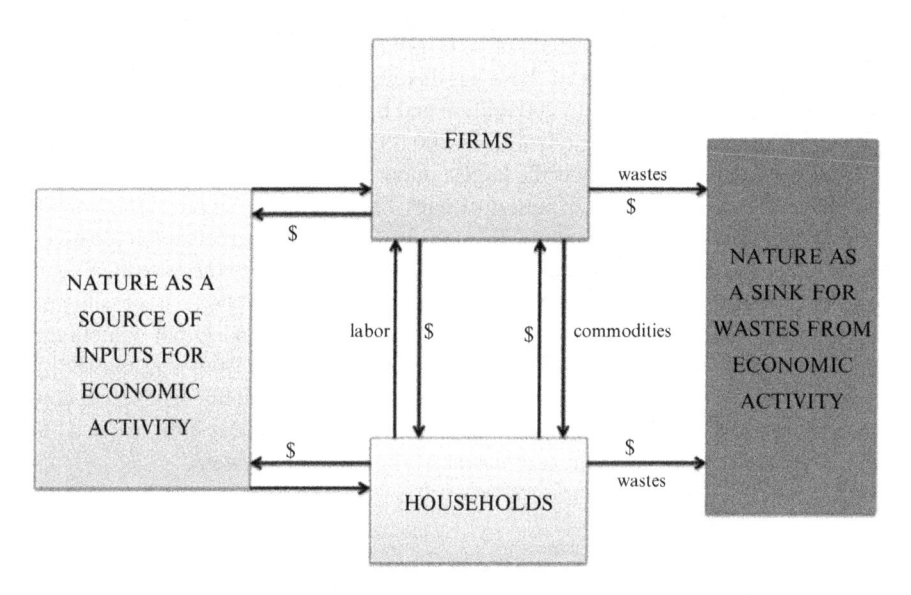

Fig. 2.1 The Economy and Nature (with kind permission from Daniel Bromley 2011)

Veblen (1899) blames the capitalist system for certain flaws, one of which is the division of society into three classes. The upper class is characterised by its obsession for conspicuous consumption; the middle class aiming to replicate this level of consumption. The middle class assumes that by imitating the consumption behaviors of the upper class, they will be considered and accepted as being part of that class. However, the third class, the lower class, is brutalised because the two other classes have but one goal: to consume at the lowest possible cost to themselves. The voice of the lower class is so thoroughly overwhelmed that they have become, in effect, voiceless.

Thus in the Asian century, there are several leadership challenges in the midst of a limitless demand for goods and services. The rapid development of the Chinese and Indian economies is posing leadership challenges particularly in the areas of urbanisation, pollution and economic infrastructure. In addition, the growing Asian consumer market is placing an unprecedented demand on various markets in the global economy. The need for a global outlook in responsible leadership with an understanding of hitherto voiceless stakeholders is felt more than ever. For example, the sustainability of continuing to produce the goods and services in ever increasing quantities and speeds will no doubt place a heavy strain on natural resources and the way we live in the future. Leading responsibly in the Asian century would demand that leaders explore new and sustainable ways of producing goods and services. Hard questions need to be asked.

Let us consider for instance the egg industry. According to the International Egg Commission (2014), there are about 4.93 billion egg-laying hens in the world. China has 800–1,000 million of these egg-laying hens. USA has 276 million, followed by European Union with 290 million and India with 133 million. China is the largest producer of eggs in the world. In 2002, the global production of eggs was 53.4 million tonnes. Germany is the largest importer of eggs. The issues involved in the mere production and distribution of eggs has significant implications for all stakeholders of the global economy. Responsible leaders concerned about the treatment of caged hens and the use of antibiotics and other tactics to increase the rate of egg production could explore ways of sustainable production. Is it possible to develop a product naturally that satisfies all the goodness of an egg but without the hen? Imagine the power of this idea and the effect it can have from a sustainability perspective. So in an increasingly shifting and unfamiliar economic landscape, how can corporations operate responsibly? In order to answer this question, we need to first explore the systemic context of business: the economic system.

Responsible Corporations and Capitalism

Corporations do not operate in a vacuum; there is a larger systemic environment. The most dominant system in this environment is the economic system. Some argue that the capitalism that is practised now is vastly different to what was proposed originally. The classical view of capitalism assumes a variety of small businesses existing in a situation of vigorous competition and random market forces. However, this view no longer necessarily applies to the corporate world. For example, in the oil industry, a few large companies dominate an oligopolistic market. The worldwide resource power of companies such as ExxonMobil can overwhelm even the influencing power of a government. According to the classical notion of capitalism, businesses must be allowed to fail—not through scandal, but through bankruptcy—allowing new company ventures, operations and services to emerge and inject a fresh impetus into the market. In contrast, modern capitalism has seen the development of large businesses that are "too large to fail", as their failure would have too many economic follow-on effects. Thus governments intervene to save these large companies (such as the US company AIG) from bankruptcy. However, while capitalism is no longer implemented in its classical form, its current form may not be the only alternative to the existing capitalist system.

Some countries have adopted Marxist and socialist models, but China and Russia have moved toward free-market economies (traditionally a cornerstone of capitalism). In the Asian century, according Bill Gates, what is needed now is "creative capitalism" (Kiviat and Gates 2008). He argues that so far, corporations have been catering to the affluent, but that they should also be engaging with poorer communities, thus uplifting the well-being of society as a whole. Not many contemporary capitalists see that contemporary capitalism is perfect. For example, Bill Gates formulated the concept of "creative capitalism", contending that the disparity between the poorest and the rest of the world prompts a consideration of how to apply the "caring and innovation power" and resources of corporations to the needs of the poorest (for example, developing and disseminating breakthroughs in medicine and nutrition or new forms of banking). Indeed, meeting the needs of poorer consumers can sometimes fit in with traditional ideas of successful business—for example, they may constitute a new and larger market for a firm's products or services. Young people are now wanting the company they work for to have some sort of social engagement, and not be solely for the benefit of the richest. Caliber Collection, a jewelry line from the US firm Jewelry for a Cause, is an example. Jessica Mindich, the CEO and founder of Jewelry for a Cause, has been quoted by Reuters (2013) as saying, "The Caliber Collection is a line of jewelry made in part from illegal guns and brass shell casings taken off the streets of Newark, New Jersey and a portion of the proceeds go back to Newark Police Department to benefit their gun buy-back/amnesty program". Newark Police Director Samuel Demaio confirmed that the crime rate has dropped as more guns have been removed from the streets. The first series of bracelets went on sale in late November of 2012, but Mindich says sales have soared since the shooting incident at an elementary school in Newtown, Connecticut (Reuters 2013).

A corporation is an entity that can exist beyond the life years of organizational members, and can sue and be sued—it is a legal person in the eyes of the law. It can own property and borrow funds from ventures of limited liability. It has a clear purpose: to make profits. Milton Friedman said, "There is one and only one social responsibility of business—to use its resources and engage in activities designed to increase its profits so long as it…engages in open and free competition, without deception or fraud" (Friedman 1962, p. 133). Corporations are also concerned with brand names, and with trust, which generally takes the form of collaboration between stockholders and stakeholders. Stockholders own the business. Stakeholders, more broadly, include any party that can either benefit from or be harmed by the organization's activities. Stockholders and stakeholders constantly compete for a company's limited resources. For example, if the company makes a quarterly profit, the board of directors needs to decide whether to use it to benefit the employees (in other words, a salary increase) or the stockholders (a dividend increase). Will the corporation invest in the environment, or in its shareholders' interests? Will it look after customers with, perhaps, an advanced product or service, or pass that profit on to its shareholders? This inherent tension places corporations in the position of having to consider their own moral agency. The size and the almost robotic structure of the corporation can give rise to an absence of responsibility. It is difficult to assign responsibility to specific individuals because the corporate structure envelops members. Who should be responsible for corporate actions?

Corporations cannot be sent to jail for their irresponsible actions. Obviously they have neither "a soul to lose nor a body to kick". Yet the question remains: how can corporations be held responsible for their decisions in the Asian century? They are legal agents, but are they moral agents? Executives as individuals are moral agents. Executives can think, rationalize, have a values framework—an ethical framework—that can be used to make decisions. Executives can always say, "I made this decision that hurts you, or this other person, for these particular reasons. And I'm sorry if you don't see my point of view, but this is the best I could do under the circumstances." But can a corporation say that to its competing stakeholders? It can act as a person, but should it then be held morally responsible? The issue is not normative; it is pragmatic: *how* can it be held responsible? The common view is that only those individuals who run the corporations have the ability to make decisions. Therefore, when irresponsible decisions have been made, those individuals who are responsible for running the organization should be held accountable.

According to Nik Frances, in his influential book *The End of Charity: Time for Social Enterprise* (2008), handing out money and resources inhibits the entrepreneurial spirit of the receiver. Frances asserts that the time has come for social entrepreneurship, which he says should actually be called entrepreneurship for social innovation, and that the ingredients for entrepreneurship, such as creativity, courage and perseverance, must be applied to bring about social change. Frances asserts that there is no fundamental conflict between the market and good social outcomes: "Milton Friedman famously said the business of business is business, but I think a company's concern for the welfare of its community is sustainable business" (Frances 2008, p. 111).

C. K. Prahalad highlighted the importance of linking a social purpose to corporate profit-making in his seminal book *The Fortune at the Bottom of the Pyramid* (2009). He argued that when world economic wealth is depicted in terms of a pyramid, corporations have been serving those in the top three tiers, who earn more than $US1,500 annually (Fig. 2.2).

The "bottom of the pyramid" in Prahalad's title denotes (a) individuals who live primarily in developing countries and whose annual per-capita incomes fall below US$1,500; and (b) an emerging field of business strategy that focuses on products, services and enterprises to serve these individuals.

Prahalad claimed that while it includes highly diverse populations, a fast-growing consumer market is present at the bottom of the pyramid with a production sector which has vast amounts of under-utilized entrepreneurial energy. According to Prahalad, this market includes 60 % of the population of India and China— 68 % in the rural sectors—representing about 3.7 billion people (2009). These people are largely excluded from formal markets because they earn less than US$8 a day. However, with annual growth levels of 8 % per annum, this market projects a substantial growth opportunity for corporations. Prahalad challenged corporations to have a social-purpose-driven business, in which the company's profit motive is linked to achieving a social purpose as well.

Prahalad (2009) related how the Unilever Hindustan product Sunsilk shampoo was marketed in a standard-sized bottle in India. As a strategy consultant to the company, he developed the idea of a single wash sachet for the company. At a fraction of the cost of a normal sized shampoo bottle, anyone who could not afford the standard bottle could participate in the sense of luxury offered by the product.

THE WORLD ECONOMIC PYRAMID

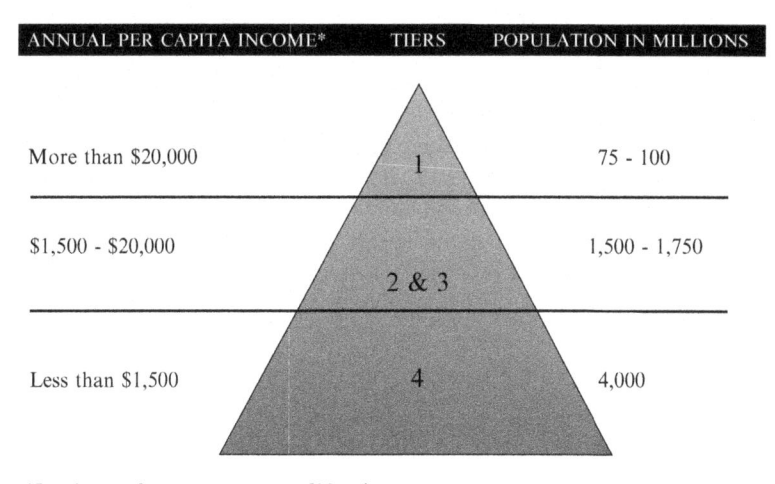

ANNUAL PER CAPITA INCOME*	TIERS	POPULATION IN MILLIONS
More than $20,000	1	75 - 100
$1,500 - $20,000	2 & 3	1,500 - 1,750
Less than $1,500	4	4,000

*Based on purchasing power parity in U.S. $
Source: U.N. World Development Reports

Fig. 2.2 The World Economic Pyramid (Reprinted with permission from "The Fortune at the Bottom of the Pyramid" by C. K. Prahalad and Stuart L. Hart from the First Quarter 2002 issue of *strategy + business* magazine, published by PwC Strategy& LLC. © 2002 PwC. All rights reserved. PwC refers to the PwC network and/or one or more of its member firms, each of which is a separate legal entity. Please see www.pwc.com/structure for further details. www.strategy-business.com)

Those consumers could now use a product that had once been beyond their economic reach, and no longer felt deprived and marginalized. Prahalad claimed that Unilever not only increased profits, but enhanced the well-being and resilience of people who had not previously been their customers.

In the Asian century, with the increasing demand for consumption of goods and services, and the corresponding competition for resources, business leaders would need to think outside the box to develop novel and inclusive ways to operate responsibly. The question arises as to how leaders can balance the tension created by the stockholders and the larger stakeholder interests fairly, with—hopefully—win-win outcomes for all. In other words, on what basis can leaders carry out the responsibility of allocating resources to generating profits, protecting the environment and safeguarding communities? The answer to this question can be explored by considering the individual level moral responsibility of business leaders.

Conclusion

The aim of this chapter was to lay the context for the rest of the book. It outlined that business leaders need to recognise the shifting economic and power balance and recognise the need to identify challenges and opportunities in the new era. The chapter noted that the rate of corporate scandals continues without any signs of slowing, and explained several cases of unethical corporate conduct. In light of this context, it was presented that it would be reasonable to accept a crisis of legitimacy and trust in corporations. Despite policy and regulatory measures taken in various jurisdictions, such as the Sarbanes Oxley Act of 2001 in the US, and increases in compliance requirements of board directors in UK, Australia and elsewhere, the continued rise of corporate scandals due to unethical executive conduct questions the effectiveness of imposing more and more regulatory mechanisms. Instead, it can be argued that the improvement of ethical action at the individual level can be more effective in curbing increases in unethical executive misconduct. Chapter 3 will examine the moral basis for responsibility at the individual level.

References

7.30 Report. (2004). James Hardie executives accused of fraud. ABC Corporation. Available at http://www.abc.net.au/7.30/content/2004/s1164158.htm. Accessed 23 Sept 2015.
Achbar, M., Abbott, J., & Bakan, J. (2004). *The corporation* [video recording], Madman Cinema.
Anderson, S., & Cavanagh, J. (2000). The rise of corporate global power. Available at http://www.corpwatch.org/article.php?id377. Accessed 23 Sep 2015.
APH. (2001). *HIH insurance group collapse*. Available at http://www.aph.gov.au/About_Parliament/Parliamentary_Departments/Parliamentary_Library/Publications_Archive/archive/hihinsurance. Accessed 12 Oct 2015.
Ashkanasy, N. M. (2002). Leadership in the Asian century: Lessons from GLOBE. *International Journal of Organisational Behaviour, 5*(3), 150–163.
ASPC. (2013). *Human capital matters 2013/4: The Asian century*. http://www.apsc.gov.au/publications-and-media/current-publications/human-capital-matters/2013/hcm4. Accessed 23 Aug 2015.
Basu, K., & Palazzo, P. (2008). Corporate social responsibility: A process model of sensemaking. *Academy of Management Review, 22*, 122–136.
Bloomberg. (2013). *China Eclipses U.S. as biggest trading nation*. Available at http://www.bloomberg.com/news/2013-02-09/china-passes-u-s-to-become-the-world-s-biggest-trading-nation.html. Accessed 23 Nov 2014.
Bromley, D. (2011). *Simple economic model*. Available at http://www.aae.wisc.edu/aae344/7-pollution.ppt. Accessed 23 Jan 2011.
Carroll, A. B. (1979). A three-dimensional conceptual model of corporate social performance. *Academy of Management Review, 4*(4), 497–505.
Ciulla, J. (2001). Carving leaders from the warped wood of humanity. *Canadian Journal of Administrative Sciences, 18*(4), 313–319.
CNN. (2014). *Bernard Madoff Fast facts*. Available at http://edition.cnn.com/2013/03/11/us/bernard-madoff-fast-facts/. Accessed 23 Nov 2104.
Donaldson, T. (1982). *Corporations and morality*. Englewood Cliffs: Prentice-Hall.
Donaldson, T. (1989). *The ethics of international business*. New York: Oxford University Press.
Donaldson, T., & Preston, L. E. (1995). The stakeholder theory of the corporation: Concepts, evidence and implications. *Academy of Management Review, 20*(1), 65–91.
Fernando, M. (2001). Are popular management techniques a waste of time? *Academy of Management Perspectives, 15*(3), 138–140.

Fernando, M. (2007). Corporate social responsibility in the wake of the Asian tsunami: A comparative case study of two Sri Lankan companies. *European Management Journal, 25*(1), 1–10.
Fernando, M. (2010). Corporate social responsibility in the wake of the Asian tsunami: Effect of time on the genuineness of CSR initiatives. *European Management Journal, 28*(1), 68–79.
Fernando, M., & Sim, A. B. (2011). Strategic ambiguity and leaders' responsibility beyond maximizing profits. *European Management Journal, 29*(6), 504–513.
Fisher, J. (2004). Social responsibility and ethics: Clarifying the concepts. *Journal of Business Ethics, 52*(4), 391–400.
Forbes. (2014). *JPMorgan chase to pay $1.7 billion in largest bank forfeiture in history, settles criminal Madoff charges.* Available at http://www.forbes.com/sites/nathanvardi/2014/01/07/jpmorgan-chase-to-pay-1-7-billion-in-largest-bank-forfeiture-in-history-settles-criminal-madoff-charges/. Accessed 2 Jan 2015.
Four Corners (2001). *HIH online forum.* Available at http://www2b.abc.net.au/4corners/sforum58/default.htm. Accessed 23 Nov 2014.
Frances, N. (2008). *The end of charity: Time for social enterprise.* Crows Nest: Allen & Unwin.
Friedman, M. (1962). *Capitalism and freedom.* Chicago: University of Chicago Press.
Galbraith, J. K. (1967). *The new industrial state.* Boston: Houghton Mifflin.
Godfrey, P. C., & Hatch, N. W. (2007). Researching corporate social responsibility: An agenda for the 21st century. *Journal of Business Ethics, 70*(1), 87–98.
Hartman, L. P., DesJardins, J. R., & MacDonald, C. (2008). *Business ethics: Decision-making for personal integrity and social responsibility.* New York: McGraw-Hill/Irwin.
Hastings, P. (2012). *Wages and benefits in China.* Available at http://www.americanbenefitscouncil.org/pub/e6142160-026e-80d1-3557-51776b149a3f. Accessed 12 April 2015.
Hills, B. (2001). James Hardie_s forgotten victims. *The Sydney Morning Herald* (p. 11). Available at http://www.benhills.com/articles/articles/ASB02a.html. Accessed 10 Nov 2009.
Hills, B. (2005). The James Hardie story: Asbestos victims_ claimsevaded by manufacturer. *International Journal of Occupational and Environmental Health, 11*(2), 212–214.
Independent. (2011). *Anita Roddick, capitalist with a conscience, dies at 64.* Available at http://www.independent.co.uk/news/uk/this-britain/anita-roddick-capitalist-with-a-conscience-dies-at-64-402014.html. Accessed 12 May 2014.
International Egg Commission. (2014). *The world egg industry.* Available at https://www.internationalegg.com/corporate/eggindustry/details.asp?id=18&cid=24. Accessed 24 Nov 2014.
Jamali, D. (2007). The case for strategic corporate social responsibility in developing countries. *Business and Society Review, 112*, 1–27.
James Hardie Industries Limited. (2001, February). *Media release: James Hardie resolves its asbestos liability favourably for claimants and shareholders.* Available at http://www.asx.com.au/asx/statistics/displayAnnouncement.do?display=text&issuerId=602&announcementId=645410. Accessed 23 Sep 2015.
Kermisch, C. (2012). Risk and responsibility: A complex and evolving relationship. *Science and Engineering Ethics, 18*(1), 91–102.
Kiviat, B., & Gates, B. (2008). *Making capitalism more creative.* Available at http://content.time.com/time/magazine/article/0,9171,1828417,00.html. Accessed 24 Nov 2014.
Knowledge@Wharton. (2012). *Tylenol and the legacy of J&J's James Burke.* Available at http://knowledge.wharton.upenn.edu/article/tylenol-and-the-legacy-of-jjs-james-burke/, Accessed 23 Nov 2014.
Ladd, J. (1991). Bhopal: An essay on moral responsibility and civic virtue. *Journal of Social Philosophy, 22*(1), 73–91.
Lowry, D. (2006). HR managers as ethical decision-makers: Mapping the terrain. *Asia Pacific Journal of Human Resources, 44*(2), 171–183.
Maitland, I. (2002). The human face of self-interest. *Journal of Business Ethics, 38*, 3–17.
McWilliams, A., Siegel, D. S., & Wright, P. M. (2006). Corporate social responsibility: Strategic implications. *Journal of Management Studies, 43*, 1–18.

Mokhiber, R. (2013). *Top 100 corporate criminals of the decade*. Available at http://www.corporatecrimereporter.com/top100.html. Accessed 23 Nov 2014.

Murray, A. (2005). *Asbestos-related claims (management of commonwealth liabilities) Bill 2005*. Australian Democrat Speeches, Senator Andrew Murray Portfolio: Workplace Relations.

NBC News. (2013). *Iraq war 10 years later: Where are they now? Lynndie England (Abu Ghraib)*. Available at http://worldnews.nbcnews.com/_news/2013/03/19/17373769-iraq-war-10-years-later-where-are-they-now-lynndie-england-abu-ghraib. Accessed 12 June 2014.

New York Times. (2006). *Enron founder dies before sentencing*. Available at http://www.nytimes.com/2006/07/05/business/05cnd-lay.html?_r=0. Accessed 2 Aug 2014.

Pless, N. M. (2011). Women leading a responsible global business: A study of dame Anita Roddick, founder of the Body Shop. In P. Werhane & M. Painter-Morland (Eds.), *Leadership, gender and organisation* (pp. 245–258). Dordrecht: Springer.

Population Reference Bureau. (2013). *World population data sheet 2013*. Available at http://www.prb.org/Publications/Datasheets/2013/2013-world-population-data-sheet/data-sheet.aspx. Accessed 25 Oct 2014.

Porter, M., & Kramer, M. (2006). Strategy and society: The link between competitive advantage and corporate social responsibility. *Harvard Business Review, 84*, 78–92.

Porter, M., & Kramer, M. (2011). Creating shared value. *Harvard Business Review, 89*(January–February), 62–77.

Prahalad, C. K. (2009). *The fortune at the bottom of the pyramid: Eradicating poverty through profits*. Prentice Hall: Pearson.

Prahalad, C. K., & Hart, S. L. (2002). The fortune at the bottom of the pyramid. *Strategy + Business, 26*(first quarter), 4.

Prince, P., Davidson, J., & Dudley, S. (2004). *In the shadow of the corporate veil: James Hardie and asbestos compensation* (Research Note No. 12 2004–05, Law and Bills Digest Section). Canberra: Commonwealth of Australia.

Reuters. (2013). *Connecticut woman turns guns into jewelry*. Available at http://www.reuters.com/video/2013/01/23/connecticut-woman-turns-guns-into-jewelr?videoId=240666416. Accessed 24 Nov 2014.

Schwartz, P., & Gibb, B. (1999). *When good companies do bad things*. New York: Wiley.

Smith, A. (1776). *An inquiry into the nature and causes of the wealth of nations*. Book 1, Chapter 2, Available at http://geolib.com/smith.adam/woncont.html, Accessed 23 Nov 2014.

The Australian. (2010). *Former James Hardie directors win appeal*. Available on http://www.theaustralian.com.au/business/industry-sectors/former-james-hardie-directors-win-appeal/story-e6frg96x-1225972622207. Accessed 26 Mar 2011.

The Sydney Morning Herald. (2014). *Tough penalty for JP Morgan over Madoff scandal*. Available at http://www.smh.com.au/business/world-business/tough-penalty-for-jpmorgan-over-madoff-scandal-20140108-30gw1.html. Accessed 2 Oct 2015.

The West Australian. (2010). Appeal hearing for James Hardie directors begins. Available at http://www.au.news.yahoo.com/thewest/business/a/-/national/7080635/appeal-hearing-for-james-hardie-directors-begins/. Accessed 31 May 2010.

Veblen, T. (1899). *The theory of the leisure class*. New York: The New American Library.

Waldman, D. A., & Siegel, D. S. (2008). Defining the socially responsible leader. *Leadership Quarterly, 19*(1), 117–131.

Chapter 3
The Moral Basis for Responsibility

Introduction

This chapter begins an examination of the individual factors that influence ethical conduct. Specifically, it identifies the factors that influence the ethical conduct of leaders in relation to the notion of responsibility. With intensifying Asian century global issues in economic (e.g. fiscal crises), environmental (e.g. failure to address climate change effects), geopolitical (e.g. national conflicts), societal (e.g. rising income disparity) and technological (e.g. piracy) domains, the World Economic Forum (2014) identified the risk of global governance failure as one of the risks that is at the heart of most of these global issues. The Asian century business leader would be required to make ever more ethically challenging responsible decisions. It would be difficult to explain the concept of responsibility without reference to moral philosophies and ethical conduct. Ethical conduct and responsibility are inextricably linked. Responsibility is a quality or state of being answerable, and is associated with moral, legal or mental accountability. A responsible leader is reliable and trustworthy. This chapter explains the moral basis for responsibility through key moral philosophies, starting with an examination of ethics.

Ethics

Ethics is commonly thought of as being about right and wrong, of duties and obligations, character and responsibility. In the context of business ethics, it seeks to discover how a corporation can ensure how not to harm others in the operation of its business.

Corporations need to ensure compliance with their duty not only to their stockholders but to every other stakeholder. A good example is the tobacco industry. There is enough medical evidence for a layperson to arrive at a decision that smoking results in lung cancer. Based on that level of evidence, in 2012, the Australian government was one of the first in the world to take initiatives to ban brand advertisements such as logos and attractive artwork on cigarette packages. The tobacco companies in Australia were worried about the negative branding due to warning messages and graphic photographs of damage to the body caused by cigarette smoking. Tobacco companies' (including Philip Morris) attempts to overturn the law were defeated in the Australian High Court (The Sydney Morning Herald 2013). Philip Morris sued the Australian government on its ground- breaking tobacco plain-packaging legislation. The company is alleged to have restructured its assets to become a Hong Kong investor so that it could use a 1993 treaty to mount its case that the tobacco advertising ban was an infringement of its right to conduct business freely in Australia (The Sydney Morning Herald 2013). This context raises an important ethical question: how can tobacco companies incorporate a consideration of social profit into their practices? There is opportunity for these corporations to embrace a new form of product that targets the same markets and may even lead to the same level of consumer satisfaction, without causing the societal and environmental harm of cigarettes in their current form. Isn't it morally justifiable and ethical to do so, and a responsible way to make profits?

For a sound understanding of ethics, one needs to be aware of some fundamental debates within the field. The first is morality versus legality. One aspect of business ethics involves examining how moral norms apply to the activities and goals of business. Ethics is not a dogmatic set of principles. It is flexible and dynamic; it evolves with society over time. Legal regulations always tend to lag behind the evolving societal understanding of what is ethical. Therefore, there is in reality, a gap between the enacted law and the moral standards of a society. A legally allowable action is not necessarily ethical or moral. The issue of euthanasia provides an example. Imagine a couple—a man 90 years old and a woman 85 years old—who have been married for more than 60 years. The man is suffering badly from ill health and pain, and requires complete, 24-hour care. He asks his wife, "Can you kill me? Can you do anything to save me from this pain? I don't want to live this life anymore." It may be that from the wife's perspective, it is morally right, although illegal in most jurisdictions, to perform euthanasia in this case. On the other hand, an action can be legal but morally wrong. Take the case of abortion. If the local legal system allows the abortion of a fetus, then the act of aborting is legal. But is it morally right? Many in our society believe that a fetus has the same rights as a human being, and harming it is immoral. What, then, is the higher norm, the legal standard or the moral standard? Ethics as a discipline holds that law is the minimum, in terms of ethical expectations. In other words, just abiding by the law does not necessarily make someone ethical. For example, consider the case of the fast-food industry. At least some businesses in the industry have, without legal compulsion, regulated themselves to respond to the society in which they operate, becoming more health-conscious.

A second issue of ethics in business is the relationship between ethics and professional codes. These aim to regulate the behaviour of members in a profession such as in accounting, law and medicine. These can also operate at a higher level than mere legality. However, the prevalence of these codes in various professions does not ensure that the members of those professions will act ethically. Corporations also have ethics codes governing their business. For example, before it collapsed, Enron had a 64-page ethics code (Novak 1996). Unless the individual professionals themselves feel—and appreciate—that in violating these codes they are actually breaking a moral norm, change is unlikely. Individuals have the responsibility to critically assess the rules of the organizations and professions they belong to; however these rules are not by any means a comprehensive guide to achieving ethical behaviour. Going beyond the professional and organizational codes, scholars have been learning, debating, discussing and perhaps even agreeing, to a certain extent, that a uniform, universal code of ethics can be helpful to ensure that everyone behaves ethically in an organizational, social or even global environment. What international initiatives like the Kyoto Protocol have attempted to achieve has been to identify and define some very basic, common human values. More recently, it has been shown that universal acceptance of moral norms is essential for global initiatives like the United Nations Global Compact, Principles of Responsible Management Education (PRME) and other climate-change initiatives to work effectively.

In my ethics classes, I use a collaborative classroom exercise to explore the potential for developing universal moral codes. I ask my students to quickly sketch a house. Across several educational levels, taught in Australia, Singapore, Hong Kong and Malaysia, all the houses students draw look essentially the same: squarish houses, with square windows, a chimney, and a door in the center. I then ask, how many live in these types of houses? It is always the minority. Where do we acquire the habit of drawing similar-looking houses that we do not actually live in? The most common response from students is that at preschool, when we are learning our alphabet, "H" is for house—this typical squarish house with square windows used to illustrate "H" is perhaps conditioning us to draw houses in this shape. I use this exercise to suggest that people at a very fundamental level may be able to universally agree on key values like honesty and integrity if learned at a very young age.

My corporate career and subsequent study of ethics in organizations have convinced me that mere rules to guide behavior during ethically challenging situations will not always produce ethical outcomes. I believe in the central role played by the characteristics of the individual decision maker in the ethical or unethical outcomes of an action. This brings up a third issue in the field of ethics: how do individuals know what is right and what is wrong? Where does our sense of morality originate? There is some emphasis on valuing each individual's personal ethics, rather than trying to impose a collective, uniform point of view. But at the same time there is no guarantee that teaching or learning personal ethics will necessarily lead to heightened ethical behavior or sensitivity. Each individual's personal ethics develops within a context, which includes contingent factors that can promote or hamper the development of a consistent ethical system. Ethically challenging decisions are linked to several factors: individual factors related to the decision-maker, the context and the decision-making process.

The presence of ethics and morality are central to acknowledging one's responsibilities. Both are sometimes used interchangeably. Morality can be defined as a foundational, first-order set of beliefs and practices on how to live a good life. The origin of morality is linked to "mos", meaning custom. Morality gives the meaning of a code of conduct as well as behaviour. The source of morality is recognised as internal to the individual. Ethics, which sits within morality, is second-order conscious reflection: there is some action required to "know" what is ethical. The origin of the word ethics is linked to "ethos", meaning character. Some refer to ethics as a general guide to behaviour that an individual accepts. The source of ethics could be external to the individual, such as societal expectations. One needs to consciously reflect on, think about and critique the efficacy of moral beliefs. Thus morality can be viewed as the subject of ethical enquiry. The ultimate goal for an individual is moral health. When we consciously reflect, we feel good about ourselves. When we come to the conclusion, "I am satisfied with those standards in terms of meeting this ethical dilemma", our conscience allows us to have a good night's sleep. That is good moral health. Corporations are also now acknowledging the notion of moral responsibility. At a strategic level, values are important, and a set of key values is now integrated into most organizational missions and goals.

There is a big difference between the "right to act" and "rightful action". A whistleblower, such as Joseph Darby in the Abu Ghraib prisoner-abuse case (NBC News 2013), may think, "I can't live like this as if nothing's happening, I have to act. I have the right to act because I see that other human beings are unjustifiably harmed, whether or not there is anything specifically illegal going on." Do these people, whistleblowers in particular, have the right to act, regardless of the consequences that flow on from their acts to others? What if someone is harmed by whistleblowers' rightful action? When Anders Behring Breivik went on a rampage and killed 77 people in Norway, he thought he needed to act in a symbolic manner to deliver a message to the rest of the world about his idea of what Europe should look like. As an individual, he obviously had the right to act. This is the right inherent in a civilized society. However, one cannot justify a massacre of people as a righteous act. Many of us might feel in a given situation, "We must act, we don't feel right in this situation." But sometimes societal norms, expectations and precedents challenge us with the uneasiness of suspecting that the rest of society would not agree with us. That is, the action that seems right to us would likely to violate a societal norm.

That is, someone might feel, individually speaking, that they have a right to act, but when we transfer that right to the societal level, this right to act becomes diffused if it is not accepted by most members of the society. Thus there is a communal element to what is considered ethical. What seems "right" to us at an individual level becomes not so "right" at the communal level. This perennial "I" versus "them" tension emerges in many daily decision-making situations. The notion of responsibility comes into play when finding an amicable way to do the right thing that is acceptable to society and the individual. As members of the human race, we crave to belong through connections with others.

The concept of groupthink in organizational behavior tells us that we tend to align our decisions with the majority view in decision-making situations. Because we are largely driven by a clan-based mentality, we try to please the group in our actions to win recognition, status and security. Our actions thus have a social-desirability aspect, especially when we are in the presence of strangers. At times, an individual needs to ask, "What should I do, and how should I act?" The idea of groupthink says that if someone has an idea that is different from the rest of the group, when there is an overwhelming majority acting differently, that individual will feel a compulsion to follow the group norm. The social dimension to the question "How should I act?" has a bearing on how business institutions ought to be structured, and on how—and whether—an organization adheres to ideals of corporate social responsibility, or to its obligations to all stakeholders, not just shareholders. The traditional view of corporate social responsibility is that the decision-makers in an organization must take into account the many interests represented by suppliers, customers, shareholders, the government, the general public and others that can be affected by the company's decisions and actions.

In sum, at its most basic level, ethics is about how people act and how people live. Thus ethics from this perspective is more practical. It has more to do with how people act, decide and behave. Ethics is also normative; that is, ethics is concerned about how we *should* be acting in a given situation. An example can be useful in looking at these ideas. Lynndie England, a US soldier who participated in the alleged abuse of Abu Ghraib prisoners during interrogation, and 10 of her fellow soldiers were dishonorably discharged from the army after the 2004 release of explosive photographs that showed physical, sexual and psychological abuse of Iraqi detainees (NBC News 2013). In 2005, Lynndie England served 521 days in a military prison for a range of offences including maltreatment of detainees. Sergeant Joseph Darby was the whistleblower who first contacted his commanding officers and exposed these interrogation techniques. The two military personnel were from the same organization with the same organizational goals in terms of winning the war against terror; what made them different? Why would Joseph Darby take the initiative to blow the whistle, and Lynndie England follow the orders of her superiors to go through with the interrogation techniques?

One could summarize how the academic literature examines this question in terms of prerequisites for ethical action:

1. Awareness of an ethical problem. Joseph Darby's high-school football coach said he wasn't surprised to find that Darby had blown the whistle, because he had always demonstrated he had a sense of right and wrong. Darby's family members, too, said in interviews that they felt he'd been destined to do this (Vargas 2004). The type of person who has a very strong awareness of right and wrong tends to be the kind who can, in particular situations, become a whistleblower.
2. Ability to reason. For someone to act ethically, they should not only be aware of something that isn't right, but be able to weigh the various aspects of an ethical dilemma. Joseph Darby was hailed as the epitome of a soldier of conscience (Vargas 2004). He was able to assess the nature of the abuse, and report it according to his strong conscience.

3. Motivation to act. An ethical act must be prompted by a compelling desire to do the right thing. Whistleblowers know they face enormous consequences because of their actions: loss of livelihood, even being displaced from their homes. And yet they are still motivated to act, based on their sense of right and wrong. Having the motivation to act ethically differentiates whistleblowers from the general population. While most people are aware of what is right and wrong, and have the ability to reason, facing the consequences of whistleblowing is perhaps something too challenging. Whistleblowers have the persistence to implement an ethical action in the face of inevitable obstacles and consequences.
4. Fortitude. An ethical act is not just an impulse; it requires the determination to consistently maintain the necessity of the action, and to see the process through to its end.

This four-step process can be understood more deeply using normative ethical theories or moral philosophies. "Normative" implies an expectation of a norm, a standard within a societal perspective. For example, there is a societal understanding that one cannot kill people. The normative aspect of an action is the ideal, the "oughtness" of an action, the "should" aspect. The aim of ethics is to provide guidance to meet the challenges posed in ethically challenging situations. These ethically challenging situations could be between actions that promote self-interest and society's interest. Business ethics is about how corporations ought to be making decisions on their structure and corporate social responsibility involving a range of stakeholders. But the moral behaviour of business leaders is known to be influenced by several factors.

Factors Influencing Leaders' Moral Behavior

Religion

Religion has often been identified as a source of morality, helping determine what is right and what is wrong and providing incentives to be moral. People feel good, and do not feel guilt, if they don't succumb to doing wrong. Religion provides moral guidance; for example, from the Five Precepts of Buddhism, the Ten Commandments in Christianity and Judaism and the Quran in Islam. In a religious view of morality, moral norms are, in essence, divine commands, given to humanity by some superhuman being or entity. But many individuals are not affiliated to any religion. What guides them?

Ethical Relativity

Each person can be guided by their own values framework, which has been inculcated by parents, teachers and society. This leads to a problem: what is ethical in one cultural context may not apply in other societies. Cultures can differ in terms of their expectations of what is and is not an ethical action. This is the problem of ethical relativity: the view that moral norms are not universal; instead, that moral norms derive justification from the habits and traditions of the society.

In contrast to the idea that there are universal moral norms, moral relativism has a number of serious implications for personal and corporate behavior. First, it means there is a reliable norm by which to assess the behaviour of other societies. Second, the idea of ethical and moral development loses is critical importance; some cultures value certain practices that look to be, and are understood as, immoral by other cultures, and the moral relativist is not permitted to judge one culture as higher or better than another. And third, it is senseless to act against the moral code of one's culture. For example, why did Anders Behring Breivik in 2011 killed 77 people in Norway? He did not agree with the values of his society: he thought that the European continent was not progressing according to something he would like to be part of. He decided to become a symbol to initiate change by giving his actions some prominence. Essentially, the society determines whether Breivik is right or wrong. Not religion, not the individual. Why, then, is it important to look at moral principles? Many feel the need to develop a set of moral principles that are always able to guide anyone, anywhere, anytime when confronted with ethically challenging situations. Having principles that extend beyond intellectual recognition; it demands individual commitment to a values framework.

Conscience and Self-Interest

Conscience plays a major part in developing this profound sense of commitment to a set of values. As children we might remember one of our early dishonest activities, perhaps stealing a coin or two from our parents' wallets, something we knew was wrong when we did it. We felt guilty, but perhaps over a period of time, we tended to forget these feelings, and eventually we did it again, and when no harm came, it escalated to greater dishonest acts. This is the "slippery slope"—we minimize the incremental effect our conscience has on us (Hartman et al. 2008). If our actions constitute a major issue, concerning ourselves or someone we love, our conscience might not let us sleep. But this disquiet can be negated, even cancelled. It can also be conflicted, and, in some cases, erroneous, so it can't always be trusted.

Throughout history, acting in self-interest has been one of the most powerful sources for immoral behavior. When self-interest prevails, we are tempted to engage in unethical actions. Additional—and even greater—tensions are introduced with the concept of priority ranking: are we assigning our highest priority to ourselves, and in what instances would we actually accommodate others even if it involves our own suffering? Would we have acted any differently from the directors of James Hardie (see Chap. 2)? Would we have siphoned off profits overseas that might have otherwise been allocated to asbestos victims? Would we allocate $293 million and say that it is enough to compensate all asbestos victims, but only two years later say that the compensation fund is grossly underfunded by about a billion dollars?

The business leaders who have faltered along the way have succumbed to this pressure between self-interest and a life led according to principles. Enron CEO Kenneth Lay was the son of a Baptist minister, so it can't be argued that he wasn't exposed to values (Achbar et al. 2004). He had a Ph.D. in economics, which suggests that he was aware of how to run a business as well. But to do what he did to Enron and its stakeholders was to succumb to this pressure: putting oneself first over everything else. A well-developed moral framework demands that co-existence is more important than self-interest. Breivik's self-interest caused him to decide that he did not like the way his society was evolving, and that he could put his wishes above everyone else's, as opposed to maintaining social coexistence by, for example, launching a political party and attempting to promote his ideas. In times of conflict between moral principles and self-interest, shared principles might offer the best justification to adopt a course of action. For example, by pursuing this action, how would everyone benefit? If executives in financial, environmental and ethical disasters had asked this question at key points in their careers, there might have been very different outcomes. Power is one critical element that clouds executive judgment in ethically challenging situations.

Power

Most societies place higher expectations on people who are in power. According to Ciulla (2001), the difference between the personal morality of leaders and the morality of their actions at work becomes more intense when power is a factor. Power poses a distinctive ethical challenge to leadership. Ciulla (2001) claims that in most unethical leader actions leading to corporate scandals, the attempts to cover-up the action is more repugnant than the unethical act itself. These cover-ups usually involves the abuse of a leader's power in an excessive manner.

At a recent conference I attended, researchers reported on a study conducted on the British Members of Parliament and the cover-up of their abuse of the official housing allowance. This allowance was to be used to furnish and maintain one designated residence. The accounts of various members of Parliament were found to have been altered so that they bought furniture for a second or third house, or a girlfriend's house, while still claiming it was for the one designated house. Researchers identified a process. First, when the media approached the alleged offenders, they rejected the accusations as "absolute nonsense". When the allegations started to come in more quickly, information began to trickle out. Alleged offenders admitted: "Maybe there's been an error; I have to check with my accountant." Although in this case the information eventually emerged, their position of power let them cover their actions up for a significant length of time (see also Fernando and Gross 2006; Brunsson 2004). This suggests that, indeed, leaders must be held to a higher standard of behavior than others, because the ramifications of their actions are so much more widespread.

Private and public morality could be two different things for someone in power. A person who is ethical, quiet and well-mannered in private life could be very different in public life, and vice versa. Even if public and private morality are unrelated, when ethical shortcomings enter the public domain, they create doubt in the society. Due to the power that people in leadership positions hold, we demand that they must not do wrong, because the implications could be drastic.

Altruism

Ciulla (2001), in her widely cited article "Carving leaders from the warped wood of humanity" in the *Canadian Journal of Administrative Sciences* (pp. 313–319), poses a critical question: is leadership more ethical when leaders are guided by altruism? That is, if a leader engages in altruistic activities, does that necessarily make them more ethical? Ciulla argues that altruism is not just a moral standard, but rather the central part of a leader's job description (p. 315). Through altruism, an effective leader should be empathic, should be transforming, should be freely giving resources and expertise to followers—not in a sense where they are actually doling out company resources or their personal resources, but more in the sense of taking care of their followers and other constituents.

According to Ciulla (2001), leaders who fail to consider the interests of their followers are unethical and ineffective. That has been the argument against the transactional leadership style: that it is inhumane, unethical and ineffective, as (in the transactional sense) leaders demoralize and exploit their followers. The practice of leadership is to guide people, and look after their interests and well-being; to put the benefits of one's constituents first. The notion of altruism (as expressed in concepts like corporate social responsibility) at the organizational level should be distinguished from the altruism of leaders. Leaders' altruism would be more focused on putting their constituents first. But this does not mean that when leaders prioritise their constituents' needs first, their actions are ethical. How the leader does it—the way, the process, the means through which the leader actually demonstrates caring—must also be ethical. For example, a leader could be extremely altruistic purely for the purpose of promoting the corporation's products and services or to reduce taxes. This type of instrumentalism and how a leader actually executes altruism can take the gloss off its genuineness or authenticity.

In sum, when leaders are confronted with ethical decisions, more often than not, what they are facing is a tension between what is best for them and the organization, and what is best for others. The application of ethics or moral philosophies attempts to explain how this tension can be balanced.

Moral Philosophies

There are two groups of ethical theories: consequentialist and non-consequentialist. Consequential analysis bases ethical judgments on the outcomes, the consequences, of an action. While utilitarianism is classified as a consequential moral philosophy, Kantianism and virtue ethics are known as non-consequential moral philosophies.

Utilitarianism

The utilitarianism theory is credited to Jeremy Bentham and John Stuart Mill. It is based on the principle of utility as governed by "two sovereign masters, pain and pleasure" (Bentham, 2009). He claims that pain and pleasure direct us what we ought to do. Utilitarianism was developed around in the 18th and 19th centuries. It came about as part of the birth of modern democratic capitalism. It asserts that actions are right to the extent they appear to generate happiness, and wrong to the extent they appear to promote unhappiness. In fact, Bentham went onto introduce a way to calculate the value of pleasures and pains from an action (Bentham 2009). The calculation is based on intensity, duration, certainty/uncertainty and propinquity/remoteness of the value of pleasure or pain. If an action produced two units of happiness and three units of unhappiness, the utilitarian would argue that the action is unethical. If it produced three units of happiness and two of unhappiness, that action would be ethical. Utilitarianism demands that actions should produce the greatest balance of good over bad for all affected by such action: the greatest good for the greatest number. In contrast, if the only option for an action's outcome is two units of unhappiness, no matter how that action is performed, one cannot ethically proceed. There can be certain types of utilitarianism as well (see Lyons 1965). In "act utilitarianism", the judgment about whether happiness for everyone is maximized is applied to the performance of an action. In "rule utilitarianism", the focus is on the procedure, rather than the action itself. The distinction between the two depends on whether the principle of utility is applied to an action or rule.

For example, the Principles of Responsible Management Education (PRME) is a UN protocol that aims to make business and management students aware of their responsibilities toward society. In the same way, the UN Global Compact attempts to emphasize some universal moral principles, such as the prevention of exploitation of labor and of environmental degradation. These assertions are based on the assumption that it is possible to have a universal moral code. At a very basic level, it assumes at least some hope that people can all agree on some essential, fundamental, humane principles that can govern the progress of humanity. Utilitarianism is commonly so embedded in an organization (for example, in the form of "majority rule"), it's hardly noticeable even as it guides decisions and actions of most processes.

However, there are drawbacks to utilitarianism too. It raises the question: is it humane to ignore the minority, on the assumption that the majority's needs take precedence? It would be a very courageous leader who could ensure that minorities' views are looked after. Another drawback is whether some actions are wrong even if they produce good. For example, many ethicists have asserted the possibility of a just war: one that prevents a mass-scale wrongdoing. For others, even a "just" war continues to harm individuals, which they consider wrong. Kantianism helps us to address some of these issues.

Kantianism (Deontology)

Kantian ethics was proposed by the German philosopher Immanuel Kant (Kant 1797/1991). The theory is based solely on goodwill toward, and respecting the dignity of, one's fellow human beings. If one aims to produce any type of harm to a fellow human being, one's actions cannot be deemed ethical. The outcomes are not the focus in deciding the ethicality of an action, but the intention. A fundamental concept in Kantian ethics is the categorical imperative: a moral rule to which there can be no exceptions. An example is "You should never steal." This is quite a harsh rule. What if someone is hungry? What if the government is restricting someone's ability to earn a living, and is taking the food rations given by other foreign governments? Can one make an exception: "Never steal except when you are hungry"? That sort of exception is not allowed in Kantian ethics. Each rule must be universally applied. But one of the critiques of Kantian ethics is that there can be situations where categorical imperatives need to be qualified.

Kantian ethics considers humanity as an end, never as the means. One cannot use another person or exploit their goodwill to advance one's own good. Respecting the dignity of each individual human being is central to Kantian ethics. Lynndie England's defense was, in effect, "I am just a foot soldier. I am in the military environment, which is hierarchical. If I didn't follow orders, I wouldn't have my job." This introduces the problematic notion of duty. Duty-based ethics is a key element in Kantian ethics. There is external duty to a superior, but more crucial is the duty one owes to oneself, according to Kant. As Stahl and de Luque point out, his distinction between "duties of perfect and of imperfect obligation" (duties to refrain from harm and duties to advance the aims of others) (Kant 1797/1991) is central to this issue. Whistleblowers are prime examples of followers of Kantian deontological ethics. Joseph Darby did exactly this in the Abu Ghraib prisoner abuse case by blowing the whistle. In another example, Dr. Jayant Patel was at the center of a 2005 scandal at the Bundaberg Hospital in Queensland, Australia: he'd been accused of killing patients because of his incompetence, even as his commitment to achieving good financial results for the hospital earned him performance bonuses (The Age 2005). Head Nurse Toni Hoffman blew the whistle. Whistleblowers believe they must disobey authority figures and obey their internal duty to themselves.

The Milgram experiment (1974) is a classic example that highlights the human tendency to obey authority figures. Stanely Milgram, an American social psychologist, developed an experiment in 1961 at Yale University to examine human responses to authority. In the experiment, a professor and his associates—wearing white coats and giving instructions—were perceived as authority figures. They ordered unsuspecting participants to administer electric shocks to a learner, whom they could not see, and who was supposedly taking part in a test, each time the learner got an answer wrong. Each mistake led to 15-V intensity increments of electric shock, ranging from 15 to 450 V. Some of the participants—the people administering the shocks—continued to give up to 430 or 450 V. Obviously these shocks were not actually given to the person answering the question, but the participants did not know this, and obeyed the authority figures. The experiment shows that it is entirely plausible that in the face of pressure from authority figures, ordinary people can ignore the respect Kantian ethics asserts they owe their fellow human beings. Authority figures seem to create a strong sense of external duty to them at the expense of their followers' internal duty to themselves. Whistleblowers are able to overcome this tension by placing more importance on their internal duty.

The categorical imperative gives an organization a firm rule to follow in moral decision-making: that it cannot harm even one individual human being in the pursuit of profit-making. This introduces an important humanist dimension into business decision-making. For example, Nike's use of child labor in its South Asian operations in the 1980s cannot be held ethical under Kantian ethics. Kant stresses the importance of motivation and acting in principle: of intent as an input into action, rather than the outcomes of actions.

Another example can be drawn from the findings of a study I conducted in 2007 on the corporate relief efforts associated with the Boxing Day Asian tsunami in 2004 (Fernando 2007). The Boxing Day tsunami killed about 60,000 people in Indonesia and about 40,000 in Sri Lanka. The study examined companies such as Unilever, a large multinational corporation with operations in Sri Lanka that was pioneering the relief effort. I asked the interviewees who were board directors about the experience of mounting a pioneering relief effort. The responses reflected that in the face of overwhelming damage to life and property, the company simply wanted to do the "right thing"; in other words, they placed more emphasis on the intention to do good than on the outcomes of their actions (Fernando 2007, 2010).

This example from Fernando (2007, 2010) provides a classic situation of the application of Kantian ethics in terms of the focus being on the intention, wanting to do the right thing. However, it is not as easy to apply Kantian ethics to most organizational situations.

From the standpoint of Kantian ethics, it would be very hard to justify any type of profit-maximization in a capitalist environment. As part of my research into business ethics, I sent out a survey to examine the application of Kantian ethics in business, and a senior manager from a prominent shampoo-manufacturing company said, "I can't respond just using your scale of 1 to 5 because I have a lot to say about it." She sent me a lengthy email saying that she knows that some of the ingredients in the shampoo have the potential to cause cancer. But she needs the job, and hence continues to work for the company. In these types of situations, Kantian ethics is not pragmatic. When any type of product is manufactured, there is at least some level of harm to one or more stakeholders of that production entity. It could be in terms of emission levels, or it could be that an increase in shareholders' profits means the company cannot provide the salary increase it promised the trade union it would give. In a business setting, decision-makers have to balance these tensions among the stakeholders in a sensitive manner. For these reasons, it's extremely difficult to apply Kantian ethics in organizational contexts. Kant stresses the importance of motivation, of acting on principles. Whistleblowers who are likely to view situations with a clear and strong conscience will find working in organizations difficult if the organizations are not balancing stakeholders' needs pragmatically.

The critiques of Kantian ethics include the concept of moral worth. In utilitarianism, outcomes are expressed in units of happiness. Differentiating the moral worth of various stakeholders' interests is not so clear from the perspective of Kantian ethics. For example, if dividends are higher, shareholders are happy but employees are unhappy. If employees receive a pay increase, shareholders will start to ask questions such as "Why couldn't that money have been paid as dividends?" A business only has limited resources to satisfy these increasing tensions between different stakeholders. Is the categorical imperative an adequate test of what it is to be right? Is religion? Values? Whose religion? Whose values? One person's "right" and another's are different and subjective. Balancing what different stakeholders consider "right" is not as simple and direct as applying utilitarianism in an organizational context.

Virtue Ethics

Another approach to ethics is through virtue ethics. This approach, which has its origins in Aristotelian ethics, is based on a person's character (Moore 2012). First and foremost, it postulates that character is at the centre of human action: projecting good emotional balance (temperance), thinking before one acts (prudence), the courage to carry on with an ethical action (fortitude) and virtues of justice (Fernando and Chowdhury 2016). Such character based attributes are instilled in individuals and they are therefore conditioned by them. Character can be formed by interacting with others and one's environment. Human beings have a unique ability to reflect, to talk to themselves, to develop themselves step by step.

The process of developing a values framework does not necessarily require interaction with another individual, but can be practiced—and formed—by action. Virtue ethics therefore aims to understand the way in which character traits are formed, which traits are developed, and which compromise a truly satisfying and meaningful life. Virtue ethics provides a comprehensive description of life rather than labeling the individual good or bad.

Virtue ethics has drawn a considerable amount of interest from the business ethics scholar community. While a majority of scholars (see Koehn 1998; McCloskey

2006; Sison 2011; Sison and Fontrodona 2012; Solomon 2004; Tsoukas and Cummings 1997) have contributed to Aristotelian or neo-Aristotelian virtue ethics, several others such as Mele (2009), Slote (1996, 2001) and Swanton (2003) have developed alternative models (see also Fernando and Moore 2014).

Joanna Ciulla, a proponent of "virtue ethics", views virtues—for example, honesty or integrity—as things people only have if they practice them. The morally virtuous leader is also a competent leader: "in virtue ethics there is no split between the morality of a leader and the morality of his or her leadership" (Ciulla 2001, p. 317). Virtue—the application and practice of values—requires the ability to morally reason. When one faces a moral dilemma, what are the logical reasoning processes involved when choosing one ethical option over another? If an individual is lucky, there will be two options that ultimately produce a benefit (for example, two worthy NGOs need a contribution, but there are resources for a donation to only one). There are, however, cases where the choice is between two bad options, as with the "just war" problem. Either choice will lead to negative results, making it very hard to discern the correct one by reason.

According to virtue ethics, the person faced with an ethical dilemma should ask, "What would a person with integrity do?" The person might look to a role model, and think, "How would this person I admire and respect resolve this issue?" These individuals are operating within the boundaries of virtue ethics, because they are looking at someone else's character, using what they know of the role model's previous actions, to solve a problem. One fundamental benefit of virtue ethics over every other ethical theory is that it does not separate the action from the characteristics of the actor or decision-maker. For example, in utilitarian ethics, the outcomes are separate from the actor: anyone can perform an action; the focus is on what comes out of it. In virtue ethics, the actor, the action and the outcomes are all considered in one theory. This is a fundamental distinction between virtues ethics, utilitarianism and Kantian ethics.

Analysing the two key moral frameworks of utilitarianism and Kantianism (deontology), Ciulla asserts that virtue ethics comes to a median position between the two moral frameworks. Virtue ethics is not about outputs or inputs, but about which characteristics of the individual contributed to their choice and implementation of an action. In this approach, there is also an intimate relationship between the virtuous character of a society and the virtuous character of the people in it: as societal members decide on actions, they individually develop their personality and character within the context of their society (Ciulla 2001). One can assign an imaginary personality to anything (for example, Wilson, the volleyball in the film *Castaway* (2000), starring Tom Hanks), thus creating a microcosm of society, and form a reflexive relationship with this artificial construct, thus developing one's personality.

The philosopher Alasdair MacIntyre (2007) claims that virtues are related to practices, and that this relationship determines our job performance and effectiveness (Moore 2012; Fernando and Moore 2014). He proposes that various organizations require different virtues in employees. When leaders practice virtuousness, MacIntyre claims that it will lead to effectiveness and excellence. A business must cultivate virtues that, as with an individual, develop its character. These virtues should be compatible with the mission of the company and its stakeholder obligations. Virtues are generated through daily practices. The extent of virtue as opposed to vice present in individuals' actions can explain individual character. In Aristotelian ethics, virtuous behaviour is also assumed to be excellent and effective behaviour (Fernando and Chowdhury 2016).

In virtue ethics, the structure of organizations can also contribute to an understanding of why good corporations engage in unethical activities. An organization's structure can promote or hamper the practice of two types of virtues: moral and technical. If a physician or a professor must engage in an uphill task to secure what is morally right, Ciulla (2001, p. 317) claims that there is something wrong with the leadership of the organization. For example, whistleblowers, who are clearly aggrieved by the organization, clearly cannot operate within the structure, and rebel.

In an organizational context, virtue ethics is being increasingly applied through the notion of virtuousness (Bright et al. 2006; Cameron et al. 2004). Acting virtuously require organizations to operate at a level above the "do no harm" maxim. It is defined as the "the pursuit of the highest aspirations in the human condition. It is characterized by human impact, moral goodness, and unconditional societal betterment" (Bright et al. 2006, p. 249). The concept can be presented in two forms; virtue *in* organizations and virtue *through* organizations (Bright et al. 2006). The former refers to the conduct in firms that promote individuals to blossom. These actions generate virtues such as hope, gratitude, wisdom, forgiveness and courage (Seligman 2002; Emmons and Crumpler 2000; Snyder 2000). The latter refers to firm initiatives such as CSR programs that promote virtuousness. Compared to individual actions, groups have more potential to generate virtuousness through their collective conduct (Bright et al. 2006). Virtues can also be tonic or phasic (Park and Peterson 2003). The first is always present in organizations (e.g. hope, kindness). The latter form of virtuousness generates through events such as when crafting organizational responses to natural disasters or retrenchment (Bright et al. 2006).

Application of Moral Philosophies

For the German philosopher Immanuel Kant, an action's utility, how many units of happiness or joy it brings, is irrelevant; what matters is what intention the agent had in the first place. From the utilitarian, outcome-based perspective, the question is: what ultimate value would the action have? Whistleblowers' actions can be explained more from a Kantian perspective. They are commonly identified as "black-and-white" people as they seem to know exactly what is right and what is wrong. Whistleblowers want to react in situations that harm other people. Kant would say whistleblowers are highly ethical, if their intentions concerning the act of whistleblowing are to prevent harm to others.

When Sherron Watkins, the former Vice President at Enron, informed of the irregularities of Enron's financial affairs to Ken Lay, with the ensuing bankruptcy, many people lost their jobs and their livelihoods overnight (New York Times 2006). They could actually find fault with Sherron Watkins for not keeping quiet. But from the standpoint of deontological theory, what thoughts went into her action—the intention with which she approached it—is what is important in determining whether the action was ethical.

In terms of attributing responsibility, the application of Kantian and utilitarian theories has a number of shortcomings. One major criticism of Kantian ethics is the absence of emotions in the application of the philosophy. Reliance on pure practical reason overlooks the role of emotions in one's responsibility towards the other. Thus in developing and maintaining relationships, our ability to rely on emotions for decision making has no place in Kantian ethics. This shortcoming has a major impact on virtue-responsibility (Ladd 1991), which relies on relationships. From the utilitarian perspective, one of the shortcomings of the application of the philosophy is in collective action situations. For instance, in combatting climate change, my decision to stop driving my car to work daily to help reduce carbon emissions and thereby reduce the impact on climate change will have little impact if everyone else contributes to ignoring climate change and living the way they used to.

The above discussion on the application of moral philosophies brings us to the notion of "spheres of responsibility". The spheres of responsibility ultimately pose four questions to business leaders: "(1) which course of action will do the most good and the least harm?; (2) which alternative best serves others' rights, including shareholders' rights?; (3) what plan can I live with, which is consistent with the basic values and commitments of my company?; and (4) which course of action is feasible in the world as it is?" (Badaracco 1992, p. 75). These spheres of responsibility are proposed to help business leaders resolve conflicting moral dilemmas.

Furthermore, while the Kantian and utilitarian theories differ significantly, they both separate the person from his or her actions. The person of Sherron Watkins, who she is, why she blew the whistle, is separated from whether the action was ethical or not. Ciulla (2001) says that ancient Greek theories of morality do not have the problem of separating the person from their actions. For example, it was necessary that the person Sherron Watkins was aware that there was an ethical problem that she had to report. And again, at Bundaberg Hospital in Queensland Australia, the Head Nurse, Toni Hoffman (who was studying medical ethics for her master's degree), blew the whistle on a surgeon who was alleged to have been harming patients because he was incompetent.

From the perspective of virtue ethics, virtues exist only insofar as they are practiced, and virtues are different from values, which need not be practiced (Ciulla 2001). One can say, "I uphold the value of honesty." That is one's normative sense, a belief in the notion that honesty is a good thing to have. But one cannot talk about a virtue in the same sense. It has to be practiced, demonstrated consistently, if one wants to claim to be a virtuous person (Moore, 2012). Citing Aristotle, Ciulla (2001) states that the function of humans is to reason. Reasoning helps to be morally virtuous, because reason guides us on how and when to practice the virtues (Ciulla 2001, p. 317). If a whistleblower claims, "I am an ethical person, I know what is right and what is wrong," that knowledge only becomes virtuous when it is put into practice.

Reason is key, because it provides motivation and understanding of one's actions and consequences. The virtuous leader has to reason, find justification for what to do, debate within him- or herself and examine the pros and cons. Hence, a morally virtuous leader is likely to be a competent leader, a leader who has used reason. In virtue ethics there is no split between the personal morality of a leader and that of his or her leadership, or between the leader and the action; they are part of a whole (Ciulla 2001, p. 317).

She claims that in a similar manner, the virtues of a society and the virtues of the people of that society are based on a relationship. This introduces the debate on nature versus nurture: where do an individual's values come from? Are people universally born with a template of values? Imagine a baby, one month old, floating over the ocean, who lands on an island: there are no animals, but only trees. Somehow, the baby survives and grows to adulthood. What would this person be like when they come back to interact with others? What sort of values would such a person have? What is crucial to understand in this context is that we are *encultured*, changed, affected and influenced by what is going on around us. We interact, and gain from the benefit of our experiences. Ciulla (2001) says, "On a practical level, Aristotle observed that the way a society was organised, its laws, practices and so on, contributed to shaping the morality of the people in it. Different practices such as sculpting and sailing require different technical virtues and excellence. Similarly, different kinds of organizations require different virtues in their employees" (p. 317).

Aristotle argues that if personal reasoning is used, what comes out is necessarily excellence. If one reasons to the best of one's ability, not in an incompetent manner, and practices what one reasons to the best of one's ability, the result will be excellence. Virtue ethics does away with the distinction between effective versus ethical leaders: a leader who is applying reason correctly will, by definition, be both. Virtue ethics is perhaps one of the best answers available for dealing with the effective-versus-ethical debate in leadership. Some would say that being ethical requires compromising the stockholders' expectations, and being effective requires compromising one's ethics. Thus, virtue ethics offers a significant improvement in bridging the gap between effectiveness and ethical behavior.

Morality in Leadership

Certain types of leadership behavior support the promotion of values in the workplace. On a continuum from less ethical to more ethical (Fig. 3.1), Weiss (2014) suggests that the least ethical is the leader displaying manipulative behavior: at every opportunity, this leader will use Machiavellian techniques to pressure or trick people into complying, while justifying what he or she is doing. This type of leader might choose not to motivate others, but to confuse them, communicate ambiguously, ensure there is enough leeway to manipulate and exploit followers. The end goal dictates what means the leader will adopt to achieve the goal. A business leader

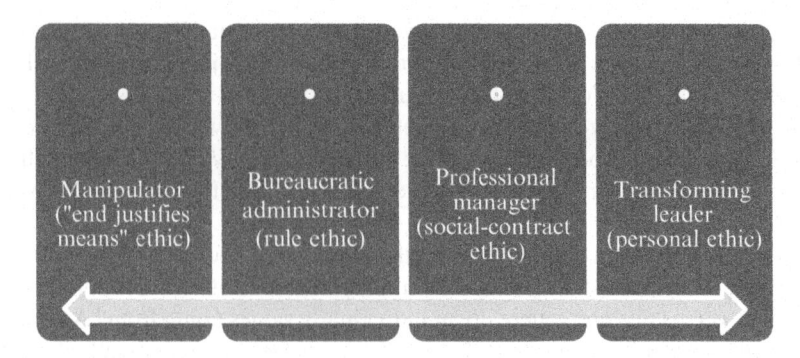

Fig. 3.1 Moral Leadership Styles (Reprinted with permission of the publisher. From Business Ethics: A Stakeholder and Issues Management Approach, copyright© (2014) by Joseph Weiss, Berrett-Koehler Publishers, Inc., San Francisco, CA. All rights reserved. www.bkconnection.com)

with this style does not worry about values, standards or the means used in getting what they want. Power is a very significant component. Kantian ethics—which is concerned with intent in determining what is ethical—is irrelevant for the person with a manipulative leadership style; in contrast, in utilitarian ethics a manipulative approach would be feasible under certain circumstances. A Machiavellian leader seeks to operate amorally, outside the application of moral perceptions and moral judgments.

The next ethical level is that of leaders who are obsessed with "doing things right": here one finds the leader similar to a bureaucratic administrator, using rules-based ethics. This bureaucratic style has been described based on Max Weber's (1947) principles of bureaucracy. The actor is bound by a web of rules and principles, and is more concerned with doing things right (that is, as set out by the rules) than doing them effectively. Although leaders may be confronted by a *situation* outside the rules, they feel they cannot choose an *action* outside the rules. For example, such a leader might insist that employees with personal problems that conflict with work schedules comply with all administrative requirements to the letter before being given time off, however deserving they may be. In not granting leave, this type of leader might typically comment, "My hands are tied. But you can appeal my decision."

Next is the level of leadership morality concerned with "doing the right things". The leader is expected to understand the situation, not blindly apply, or be a slave to, the rules. The danger in relying on this style is that, as noted in earlier chapters, it is subject to a phenomenon referred to in the organizational behavior literature as *groupthink*. In this case, being continually surrounded by the same circle of people would orient one to a particular view, a particular way of thinking about issues. Once individuals in a group situation see the group arguing and voting against their individual position or suggestion, even if they don't agree with the majority view, they may still go along with it. The discomfort of not conforming to the group affects people's views of which actions are right and which are wrong. For leaders using the professional-manager style, the emphasis is on effectiveness. Managers are taught to take stock of contingencies and circumstances in decision-making, and to honor the social contract with their stakeholders. However, in this context, a manager has to be cautious.

Organizations such as Enron, HIH and Worldcom, all of which have been criticized for lack of moral leadership, have employed the best professional managers. But while there might be an individual who can identify unethical actions, because that individual is part of a group such as a board of directors, they might feel a compulsion to go along with the group in decisions producing unethical outcomes. For example, a manager might disagree to comply with striking action recommended by the union, as it harms the customers. But when it comes to the cultural context, which in this case is mateship with work colleagues, in a groupthink-affected thinking process, the manager might think, "I might have to succumb to this particular action because I don't want to be an outcast," and join the strike action: doing what the group is engaged in although it might be against the manager's own better judgment.

According to Weiss (2014), transforming leaders are the most ethical type. Transforming leaders are driven by a personal ethic, not a social-contract, rules-based or end-justifies-means ethic. They are very strong in their conscience; they know what is right and wrong. Their task is to transform their followers, to help them develop and improve themselves, without looking at the rulebook. Transformational leadership is primarily an individual-level phenomenon, narrower than responsible leadership. It entails a process of building commitment and empowerment among followers (but not necessarily among all stakeholders—again, a limiting factor) to accomplish organizational goals. There is nothing of social change here, little of inspiring others and little shared sense of meaning, as in responsible leadership. This type of style is also associated with transcendental or authentic: "transcendental" in that leaders aim to bring their followers to rise above the status quo to a higher level of motivation, commitment or being. These leaders transform not only the business and their projects, but individual followers as well. They are so passionate, so committed to their cause, through role-modeling they transcend the environment and their individual followers, and bring the entire leadership context to a higher plane. The question, then, is how authentic are modern-day transformational leaders?

A particular CEO who participated in one of my research projects on workplace spirituality (see Fernando and Jackson 2006) provides an example of applying the moral leadership style continuum. He is a Muslim, but not in a fundamentalist sense. I interviewed this CEO, who manages 12 subsidiaries in the Sri Lankan tourism sector. He was educated in Britain, in an Anglican school. Therefore his notion of religion and spirituality is quite broad. I asked him, "What is your best example of enacting your spirituality at work?" He told me, "In the tourism industry, after the events of 24 July, 2001, when the international airport in Colombo was bombed by terrorists, and just two months later the World Trade Center was brought down, my company had to reduce staff by two-thirds. This was not a publicly listed company, it was family-owned. At first, various decisions were made by outside consultants and HR people, but I said no, we had to be entirely transparent. We communicated to the staff right from the beginning to the very end. We had a voluntary retirement scheme, but leading up to that, people were given a complete scenario of the company and its options. Coupled with the voluntary retirement scheme, we also provided courses with outside consultants as to how employees could learn to do their CVs and job applications, and present themselves at interviews. Those who accepted the voluntary retirement scheme would be given as much help as possible through business contacts to find another job. If they didn't find another job, we would take them back. There was a safety net, because these employees were right at the bottom. Many of them agreed to resign for the sake of the company. We didn't have a single problem with the unions or the workers' forum. Communication was excellent, strengthening the affected workers so as to make this an opportunity."

His argument was that he was acting in the best possible manner as a leader, taking care of his followers. In Sri Lanka, at that time, that sort of management was very rare. Given this context, where would this leader be on this continuum? Transforming? Somewhere between professional and transforming?

The leader in this particular example may not be at the transforming level yet, because while he did the best he could in being transparent, a higher justification is required to consider someone to be a transforming leader; that higher justification is not necessarily present in this case. Is he a responsible leader? What are the attributes of a responsible leader? How are these attributes different from general leadership and other forms of leadership styles? The next two chapters attempt to address these questions.

Conclusion

This chapter examined the notion of responsibility and the factors that influence responsible behavior of leaders from an ethical standpoint. In the Asian century, with intensifying global problems in economic, environmental, geopolitical, societal and technological fronts, business leaders' moral action could be influenced by various factors. These could be explained by the application of moral philosophies. The next task is to examine the notion of leadership. Leadership in the organizational behavior discipline has a very complex and broad literature spanning several decades. The next chapter attempts to capture the essence of the complexity of leadership with a view to understanding how this complex concept informs the notion of responsible leadership.

References

Achbar, M., Abbott, J., & Bakan, J. (2004). *The corporation* [video recording], Madman Cinema.
Badaracco, J. L., Jr. (1992). Business ethics: Four spheres of executive responsibility. *California Management Review, 34*(3), 64–79.
Bentham, J. (2009). *An introduction to the principles of morals and legislation* (Dover philosophical classics). New York: Dover Publications.
Bright, D. S., Cameron, K. S., & Caza, A. (2006). The amplifying and buffering effects of virtuousness in downsized organizations. *Journal of Business Ethics, 64*(3), 249–269.
Brunsson, N. (2004). *The organization of hypocrisy: Talk, decisions and actions*. Herndon: Copenhagen Business School Press.
Cameron, K. S., Bright, D., & Caza, A. (2004). Exploring the relationships between organizational virtuousness and performance. *American Behavioral Scientist, 47*(6), 766–790.
Ciulla, J. (2001). Carving leaders from the warped wood of humanity. *Canadian Journal of Administrative Sciences, 18*(4), 313–319.
Emmons, R. A., & Crumpler, C. A. (2000). Gratitude as a human strength: Appraising the evidence. *Journal of Social and Clinical Psychology, 19*(1), 56–69.
Fernando, M. (2007). Corporate social responsibility in the wake of the Asian Tsunami: A comparative case study of two Sri Lankan companies. *European Management Journal, 25*(1), 1–10.
Fernando, M. (2010). Corporate social responsibility in the wake of the Asian tsunami: Effect of time on the genuineness of CSR initiatives. *European Management Journal, 28*(1), 68–79.
Fernando, M., & Gross, M. (2006). Workplace spirituality and organizational hypocrisy: The Holy Water-Gate Case. Australia New Zealand Academy of Management (ANZAM) Proceedings, Queensland.
Fernando, M., & Jackson, B. (2006). The influence of religion-based workplace spirituality on business leaders' decision making: An inner-faith study. *Journal of Management and Organisation, 12*(1), 23–39.
Fernando, M., & Moore, G. (2014). MacIntyrean virtue ethics in business: A cross-cultural comparison. *Journal of Business Ethics,* Online First, 1–18.
Fernando, M., & Almeida, S. J. (2012). The organizational virtuousness of strategic corporate social responsibility: A case study of the Sri Lankan family-owned enterprise MAS holdings. *European Management Journal, 30*(6), 564–576.
Fernando, M., & Chowdhury, R. (2016). Cultivation of virtuousness and self-actualization in the workplace. In A. J. Sison (Ed.), *The handbook of virtue ethics in business and management*. New York: Springer.
Hanks, T., Rapke, J., Starkey, S., Zemeckis, R (Producer)., & Zemeckis, R (Director). (2000). Cast Away: 20th Century Fox.
Hartman, L. P., DesJardins, J. R., & MacDonald, C. (2008). *Business ethics: Decision-making for personal integrity and social responsibility*. New York: McGraw-Hill/Irwin.
Kant, I. (1797/1991). *The metaphysics of morals*. In M. Gregor (Trans.). Cambridge: Cambridge University Press. (Original work published 1797)
Koehn, D. (1998). Virtue ethics, the firm and moral psychology. *Business Ethics Quarterly, 8*(3), 497–513.
Ladd, J. (1991). Bhopal: An essay on moral responsibility and civic virtue. *Journal of Social Philosophy, 22*(1), 73–91.
Lyons, D. (1965). *Forms and limits of utilitarianism*. Oxford: Clarendon.
MacIntyre, A. (2007). *After virtue* (3rd ed.). London: Duckworth.
McCloskey, D. (2006). Hobbes, Nussbaum, and all seven of the virtues. *Development and Change, 37*(6), 1309–1312.
Mele, D. (2009). Integrating personalism into virtue-based business ethics: The personalist and the common good principles. *Journal of Business Ethics, 88*(1), 227–244.
Milgram, S. (1974). *Obedience to authority*. New York: Harper & Row.

Moore, G. (2012). Virtue in business: Alliance Boots and an empirical exploration of MacIntyre's conceptual framework. *Organization Studies, 33*(3), 363–387.

NBC News. (2013). *Iraq war 10 years later: Where are they now? Lynndie England (Abu Ghraib)*. Available at http://worldnews.nbcnews.com/_news/2013/03/19/17373769-iraq-war-10-years-later-where-are-they-now-lynndie-england-abu-ghraib. Accessed 12 June 2014.

New York Times. (2006). *Enron founder dies before sentencing*. Available at http://www.nytimes.com/2006/07/05/business/05cnd-lay.html?_r=0. Accessed 2 Aug 2014.

Novak, M. (1996). *Business as a calling: Work and the examined life*. New York: The Free Press.

Park, N., & Peterson, C. (2003). Virtues and organizations. In K. S. Cameron, J. E. Dutton, & R. E. Quinn (Eds.), *Positive organizational scholarship: Foundations of a new discipline*. San Francisco: Berrett Koehler.

Seligman, M. E. P. (2002). *Authentic happiness: Using the new positive psychology to realize your potential for lasting fufillment*. New York: Free Press/Simon and Schuste.

Sison, A. (2011). Aristotelian citizenship and corporate citizenship: Who is a citizen of the corporate polis? *Journal of Business Ethics, 100*(1), 3–9.

Sison, A. J. G., & Fontrodona, J. (2012). The common good of the firm in the Aristotelian-Thomistic tradition. *Business Ethics Quarterly, 22*(2), 211–246.

Slote, M. (1996). *From morality to virtue*. Oxford: Oxford University Press.

Slote, M. (2001). *Morals from motives*. Oxford: Oxford University Press.

Snyder, C. R. (2000). The past and possible futures of hope. *Journal of Social and Clinical Psychology, 19*, 11–28.

Solomon, R. (2004). Aristotle, ethics and business organizations. *Organization Studies, 25*(6), 1021–1043.

Swanton, C. (2003). *Virtue ethics, a pluralistic view*. Oxford: Oxford University Press.

The Age. (2005). *The scandal of 'Dr death'*. Available at http://www.theage.com.au/news/General/The-scandal-of-Dr-Death/2005/05/27/1117129900672.html. Accessed 12 April 2013.

The Sydney Morning Herald. (2013). *Australia 'fails' anti-tobacco bid*. Available at http://www.smh.com.au/federal-politics/political-news/australia-fails-antitobacco-bid-20131212-2zaml.html. Accessed 15 Oct 2015.

Tsoukas, H., & Cummings, S. (1997). Marginalization and recovery: The emergence of Aristotelian themes in organization studies. *Organization Studies, 18*(4), 655–683.

Vargas, E. (2004). *People of the year: Joseph Darby*. Available on http://abcnews.go.com/WNT/PersonOfWeek/story?id=365920. Accessed 25 Nov 2014.

World Economic Forum. (2014). *Top 10 risks for the decade ahead*. Available at http://forumblog.org/2014/01/top-10-risks-decade-ahead/. Accessed 25 Nov 2014.

Weber, M. (1947). *The theory of social and economic organization*. New York: Free Press.

Weiss, J. (2014). *Business ethics: A stakeholder and issues management approach*. San Francisco: Berrett-Koehler Publishers.

Chapter 4
The Complexity of Leadership

Introduction

Examinations of leadership in the academic literature have found it to be an elusive concept. The debate continues about what constitutes effective leadership, and indeed whether leadership is actually necessary. Scholars such as Alvesson and Sveningsson (2003) have examined the possibility of non-relevance of the notion of leadership. They claim that "leadership in any straightforward and clear sense is perhaps a rare bird indeed" (p. 378). However, leadership seems entirely necessary in human activities that require cooperation: families, sports teams and group work. Is this always true?

For example, an elderly lady I met in New Zealand had been in the same workplace as a supermarket counter cashier for over 10 years. Management had offered her a senior position, but she did not want it. She told me she loves what she's doing. She explained, "Well, I'm a loner. I don't have any family. I have one cat at home. The only human interaction I have is when I come to work. And I take real joy serving behind this counter and serving these people, seeing these familiar faces and saying good morning." If the work—at whatever level, from a janitor to a CEO—is so satisfying that the person is self-motivated toward achieving the work goals, a leader's input actually could be detrimental or disruptive to the worker's productivity and well-being. Even in professional work contexts, such as a firm of accountants, medical practitioners or lawyers, where everyone has a speciality, the nominated head of the firm will rarely dictate the specifics of what these specialists do. Thus in some instances where employees are highly engaged in satisfying work, or where there is a professional work context or even a context of a large percentage of experienced employees, leadership may not add anything useful to the overall individual and organizational performance. However, in many other instances, leadership has been found necessary to achieve individual and organizational outcomes effectively and efficiently.

Certainly in the Asian century, not only will the need for effective leadership be felt more than ever, but its complexity is expected to grow. The increasing intensity of competition for natural resources will lead to unprecedented demand for leaders with a vision for developing renewable energy sources and sustainable alternatives for almost every aspect of human endeavour. In this chapter, we will explore the leadership process generally, and examine key leadership approaches to develop a more focused understanding of responsibility in leading in the Asian century.

Characteristics of Leadership

A multitude of scholars at various times have attempted to define and understand the concept of leadership (e.g. Bass 1985; Bass and Avolio 1997; Avolio and Bass 2002). Bolman and Deal (2003) define leadership as "a subtle process of mutual influence fusing thought, feeling, and action to produce cooperative effort in the service of purpose and values embraced by both the leader and the led" (p. 339). According to Wang and Chee (2011), the Chinese translation of leadership is "leading ability", referring to a series of strategies and personal skills for mangers to develop. Bass (1985) notes that the relationship between leader and follower requires the leader to show appreciation for followers who are expected to invest their energies and efforts to achieving set goals. It is widely agreed that there is a clear difference between leadership and management (Bolman and Deal 2003): leaders have a vision, produce changes and inspire followers to high levels of effort, while managers create order and consistency.

A simple leadership process in organizations has several characteristics (Fig. 4.1). The first is that leadership does not operate in a vacuum: every leadership process

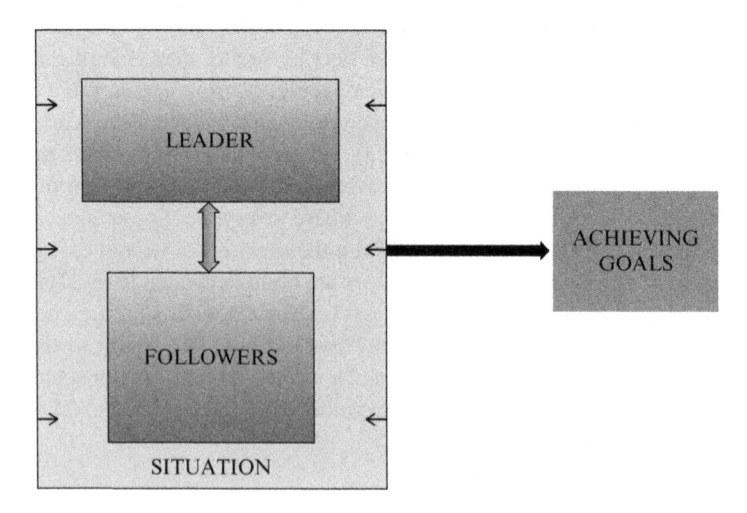

Fig. 4.1 Leadership as a process

has a context that exerts various pressures on the leadership process, and in particular on the relationship between the leader and the followers. Second, leaders can influence, as well as direct, their followers and subordinates toward achieving individual and organizational goals. For example, if a leader is someone who has followers, and a great leader is someone who has many followers, both Ghandi and Hitler qualify as great leaders. Hitler was able to influence other people to engage in mass killings, perhaps one of the most difficult tasks to influence people to perform. But for anyone with a moral compass and respect for human dignity, this would be almost an idiotic assertion (Klau 2010). Third, the distribution of power is unequal between leaders and followers. The notion of power in the leadership process generates varying levels of leadership outcomes.

Thus our simple leadership process requires a leader and followers, and interactions between these two. This leadership relationship exists within a context: a dynamic, fluid situation that exerts certain amounts of pressure on the relationship. These pressures will sometimes influence how a leader behaves toward followers, and how followers respond to their leader. Leadership assumes that the group desires to achieve a set complement of goals that they agree on in common. Based on the relative importance placed on each of the characteristics of the leadership process, several major leadership theories, styles and approaches have been proposed over time. To understand responsible leadership and the need for it in Asian century business organizations requires some knowledge of the key leadership approaches.

Key Approaches to Leadership[1]

In essence, leadership is about managing relationships and performance objectives when exercising the influence by a person or group of people over others. The quality of leadership is a critical determinant of how well an organization achieves its goals. Leadership is described as "any type of process or act of influence which in any way gets people to do something" (Ciulla 1995, p. 12). It constitutes a dynamic interpersonal relation of influence. The followers' behavior has to be voluntary—it cannot be required or demanded (Guillén and González 2001).

Some of the early theories in leadership assumed that the key driver of leadership effectiveness was leaders' personal traits—their physical and personality characteristics (Jago 1982). For example, it was thought that taller, well-spoken, charismatic, well-educated people would be effective leaders. However, over time, researchers began to think that they should look not just at leaders' traits, but at how they behave. In that context, how would a leader behave in an ethically challenging situation, where the followers are challenging the leader's decisions? Would the leader be calm? Authoritative? Or consultative and democratic in decision-making?

In reaction to the more stable perspective of early studies, others focused on the dynamic aspects of leader behavior, explaining leaders' influence in terms of how they act—what they actually do when dealing with subordinates, and how the subor-

---

[1] This section includes an updated version of ideas first presented in Fernando et al. (2009).

dinates react, both emotionally and behaviorally (Blake and McCanse 1991; Lewin and Lippitt 1938; Tannenbaum and Schmidt 1973). However, these theories had limited applicability and were unable to explain the leadership process in different contexts. The context of leadership studies thus broadened as researchers realized that leaders' behaviors couldn't be looked at in isolation from the situation or environment in which the leaders acted. Situations were seen as being able to shift between positive and negative, between people-oriented and task-oriented.

Situational-Leadership Theories

Situational-leadership theories look at how a leader would behave in various situations. Various contributions have attempted to develop universal theories of leadership to understand leadership across every situation (Kerns 2015; Hersey and Blanchard 1988; House 1996; House and Howell 1992; House and Mitchell 1974). These theories studied leadership styles in different environments. Without ignoring previous attempts, newer contributions focused more on the nature and drivers of the leader-follower relationship. Thus, these contributions examined not only the leader attributes, but also the follower attributes in attempting to understand the leader-follower relationship in various situational contexts. These contributions gave birth to two of the most researched leadership approaches; transactional leadership and transformational leadership. While the former explains leadership as an economic transaction between leaders and followers, the latter considers leadership as a more holistic process, involving the development of the whole being of the followers (Bass 1985; Burns 1978; Greenleaf 1977; Guillén and González 2001; Yammarino 1993). Encompassing these two leadership theories, the Full Range Leadership model was developed by Bass (1995). To develop the thesis in the book, transactional and transformational leadership and the Full Range Leadership model require a closer look.

Transactional Leadership

Transactional leadership is based on an economically based exchange relationship (House and Antonakis 2014). This leadership style assumes that the leadership process is a transaction between the leader and followers, a "carrot-and-stick" situation (Kuvaas et al. 2012). According to Cardona (2000, p. 203), the leader attempts to generate uniformity by providing extrinsic (positive or negative) rewards to the collaborators. Geroy et al. (2005) claim that transactional-leadership behaviors such as coaching activities promote capacity development, resulting in better organisational performance. This approach was thought by many to be quite inhumane. Followers were treated as merely another resource, without taking into consideration their specific needs and challenges in the transaction process.

Transformational Leadership

Transformational leadership is perhaps the most researched and empirically studied leadership style (Avolio and Yammarino 2013). The leader's task is not to engage in a transaction or be driven by economic pursuits; instead, the leader is motivated by a more moral, more social purpose: to transform followers as total beings (To et al. 2015). Mahatma Gandhi would be an example of someone who transformed his followers; another might be Anita Roddick, founder of the Body Shop. Several studies have shown that transformational leaders who are both charismatic and visionary energise others to transcend their needs for the overall success of the organization (Parry and Kempster 2014).

One of the better-known models explaining the process of leadership is the Full Range Leadership (FRL) model; the next section will examine this model.

The Full Range Leadership Model

The Full Range Leadership (FRL) model (Avolio 2010; Bass 1995; Bass and Avolio 1997) conceptualises transactional and transformational forms of leadership. My colleagues and I have elaborated on this model in Fernando et al. (2009, p. 524), and note that studies have found links between transformational leadership and several positive outcomes (Bass and Stogdill 1990; Barbuto et al. 2007). The FRL model explains leadership behaviour from laissez-faire to transformational styles (Fukushige and Spicer 2007). While three types of transactional leaders (contingent-reward leaders, active management-by-exception leaders and passive management-by-exception leaders) are identified by the model, transformational leaders are identified by four components: idealized influence, inspirational motivation, individualized consideration and intellectual stimulation. The shortcomings of transformational leadership include its one-directional influence from the leader to the follower and overdependence on the leader (see Yukl 1999). This leadership style is also criticized for the absence of morals and ethics (see Fernando et al. 2009).

The FRL model fails to integrate all leadership styles (Avolio 1999). Rather, the model's intent was to examine the particular leadership styles included in the model, to the fullest (Bass and Avolio 1997). Therefore there are other leadership styles that need to be further explored; this approach provides a context for examining the attributes of transcendental leaders.

Transcendental Leadership

Transcendental leaders are expected to develop the spiritual needs of both leaders and their followers (Madison and Kellermanns 2013; Cardona 2000; Fry 2003; Sanders et al. 2003). As opposed to transformational leaders, transcendental leaders are motivated by altruistic love and feeling of worthiness, well-being and harmony (Fernando et al. 2009). Thus as opposed to the leader focus in transformational leadership, transcendental leadership is both leader and follower focused. Transcendental leaders are expected to move to a higher plain of influence, going beyond their egos to understand the meaning spiritualty in their lives (Sanders et al. 2003, p. 23).

Transcendental leaders "have the capacity to address organizational expectations and needs, but also influence all facets of an individual's life" (Geroy et al. 2005, p. 28). According to Cardona (2000), transcendental leaders are "concerned with the people themselves and tries to contribute to their personal development" (p. 205), and the key competence of these leaders is "their integrity and capacity to sacrifice themselves in the service of their collaborators, even at the expense of their own interests" (Cardona 2000, p. 205).

In summary, the discussion so far on the development of various leadership approaches shows a pattern where theories have been developed to overcome the emphasis placed on one aspect of the leadership process. For example, the trait theory placed more emphasis on the leader, neglecting the follower, context and goal dimensions. The situational theories, on the other hand, placed more emphasis on the context, somewhat ignoring the leader, follower and goal aspects of the process. However, House's Path-Goal Theory (1971) is perhaps the leadership approach that can be related to all four variables in the leadership process (leader, follower, situation and goals).

House's Path-Goal Theory

House's (1971) theory focuses on the impact of leaders on follower satisfaction, motivation and performance. It concerns relationships between supervisors and subordinates; i.e. how supervisors can influence their subordinates' motivation and satisfaction (House 1996).

Path-Goal Theory advocates that the leaders' function is to increase "personal pay-offs to subordinates for work-goal attainment and make the path to these pay-offs easier to travel by clarifying it, reducing road blocks and pitfalls, and increasing the opportunities for personal satisfaction en route" (House 1971, p. 324). Additionally, an effective leader helps subordinates through various paths that lead to outcomes that are valued by employees and the organization (Schriesheim and Neider 1996).

The need for this type of leadership is a function of the characteristics of both the environment and the subordinates (House and Mitchell 1974). Bass (1990) explains this need as complimenting what is missing in a situation to increase the motivation, performance and satisfaction of subordinates. This theory has stimulated much research and has been included in numerous major organizational behavior textbooks; its impact and contribution cannot be denied (Wofford and Liska 1993).

Research into path goal theory has provided mixed and sometimes contradictory findings (Wofford and Liska 1993; House 1996). This may be attributed to the measures used to test the theory being confounded and the variation in constructs (Schriesheim and Neider 1996; Bass 1990; Wofford and Liska 1993). According to Schriesheim and Neider (1996), development of the Path-Goal Theory has come to a standstill. Difficulty in developing meaningful modifications and the fact that the most clear relationships have already been tested have resulted in scholars and researchers generally being uncomfortable with attempting to refine or extend House's (1971) theory (Schriesheim and Neider 1996). There have been several suggestions for moving the theory away from its stagnated state: recognizing those main functions that drive follower motivation, satisfaction and performance; being aware of the extent to which those main functions are facilitated by other factors than the leader (e.g. task, training); and predicting the effect of varied leadership behaviors using previous assessments (Schriesheim and Neider 1996).

House (1996) offers a reformulated view of the original path goal theory (House 1971). This revised theory, the Path-Goal Theory of Work Unit Leadership, identifies leader behaviors that focus on the work unit, and the development of subordinate satisfaction, effectiveness, and their empowerment. It also evaluates leaders' impact on the motivation and abilities of subordinates and work units (House 1996). House (1996) outlines eight classes of leadership behaviors that are motivational for subordinates: path-goal clarifying behaviors (e.g. clarifying performance goals and performance measures), achievement-oriented leader behavior (e.g. an emphasis on performance and work pride), work facilitation (e.g. planning, scheduling and organizing), supportive leader behavior (e.g. psychological support for subordinates), interaction facilitation (e.g. facilitating communication, resolving disputes), group-oriented decision process (e.g. the quality of the decisions and the extent to which these decisions impact on decision outcomes), representation and networking (e.g. work unit representation, relative power and legitimacy in organizations) and value-based leader behavior (e.g. special focus on follower commitment and recognizing core values of subordinates).

House (1996) suggests that value-based leadership is contingent on the situation. Situations that require highly involved, active leadership and emotional commitment, present meaningful values, involve highly stressful or competitive environments and do not favor transactional leadership, all increase the effectiveness of value-based leadership (House 1996). The reformulated theory, working from modifications suggested by Schriesheim and Neider (1996), addresses empowerment of subordinates, and identifies the leader behaviors that influence satisfaction, motivation and performance, the effect of these behaviors and under what situations they will be most effective (House 1996).

Path-Goal Theory (House 1971) and the Path-Goal Theory of Work Unit Leadership (House 1996) posit that leader behavior is effective and meaningful only if it is satisfying and useful to subordinate performance. House's (1971) original theory has had a significant impact on organizational behavior research, although some findings are contradictory. These incongruences could be addressed through standardization of measurements (Wofford and Liska 1993; House 1996). House (1996) suggests that further improvements and reformulations of the Work Unit theory should be the result of empirical testing.

Spiritual Leadership[2]

While a range of leadership theories have sought to explain the leadership phenomenon by applying various facets of the physical, mental and emotional dimensions of organizational member interactions, these theories neglected the spiritual component (Fry 2003; Malone and Fry 2003). The spiritual-leadership theory is a relatively novel approach to recognizing this spiritual element in leading.

The embryonic stage of spiritual leadership is apparent when the literature on other leadership areas is considered, some of which dates back to 500 B.C. However, the popularity of the concept in the management discipline shows an increasing trend in journal articles (e.g., Phipps 2012; Aydin and Ceylan 2009; Baglione and Zimmerer 2007; Benefiel 2005; Dent et al. 2005; Fernando et al. 2009; Fry and Cohen 2009; Karadag 2009; Kriger and Seng 2005; Reave 2005) and books (e.g., Benefiel 2005; Fernando 2007; Hicks 2003). The essence of spiritual leadership can be captured by Peter Vaill's idea that as a leader, one is responsible for leading

> a system of spiritually conscious and spiritually concerned people. This is not a choice; it probably isn't even just another way to frame the situation…because you have knowing, self-referencing subjects as your organizational members, no matter what your frame, and these knowing, self-referencing subjects are agreeing to start thinking about What It All Means. They are going to be seeking meaning, expressing their meaning needs (Vaill 1998, p. 178).

Leaders of spirituality-based organizations such as parish churches generally score higher on leadership effectiveness than leaders from other contexts (Druskat 1994). Although workplace spirituality scholars have acknowledged for some time the importance of leadership to the development of their field, until recently they have not acknowledged such a relationship between leadership and workplace spirituality. For example, I note in Fernando (2007) that Zwart's (2000) study of 266 American business leaders failed to find any linkages between the transformational leadership described by Bass and Avolio (1989) and the dimensions of spirituality identified by Beazley (1998). However, after reviewing over 150 studies, Reave (2005) notes that there is a clear alignment between spiritual values and practices and effective leadership:

> [V]alues that have long been considered spiritual ideals, such as integrity, honesty, and humility, have been demonstrated to have an effect on leadership success. Similarly, practices traditionally associated with spirituality as demonstrated in daily life have also been shown to be connected to leadership effectiveness. All of the following practices have been

---

[2] This section includes an updated version of ideas first presented in Fernando (2007) and in Fernando and Nilakant (2008).

emphasized in many spiritual teachings, and they have also been found to be crucial leadership skills: showing respect for others, demonstrating fair treatment, expressing caring and concern, listening responsively, recognizing the contributions of others, and engaging in reflective practice (p. 655).

Since Reave's views were published, several studies have promoted the link between leadership and spirituality (e.g. Phipps 2012; Fernando 2011; Fernando et al. 2009; Fry and Cohen 2009; Smith and Rayment 2007). Louis Fry's (2003) spiritual leadership theory introduces leader and follower higher-order needs—something higher than basic needs—and cultural and organizational effectiveness into a causal framework (2003, p. 696). This causality aspect in Fry's model, which is highly relevant to examinations of responsible leadership, was the first in the spiritual leadership literature.

A key quality of spiritual leadership that can promote responsible leadership is connection with self, others and reality. These connections can coexist, but even one would suffice to experience spirituality. Establishing and maintaining a connection with self, for example, would require leaders to be self-reflective concerning their actions. Conscious reflection on one's actions can bring about good deeds and rectify less-good deeds. Fernando and Nilakant's (2008) study based on self-growth-based spirituality is especially relevant here. The study set out to examine Sri Lankan business leaders' self-actualization in relation to their experience of workplace spirituality. During a spiritual experience, leaders commonly showed a need to grow, become and evolve towards an ideal self. A motivation to connect with one's self was key to developing this need. The study found that self-actualizing job designs could potentially lead to developing workplace spirituality. It was argued that self-actualized spirituality overcomes the zealotry challenges that have been known to plague the practice of religion-based workplace spirituality. In terms of connection with others, spiritual leadership offers new approaches to practicing responsible leadership. For example, a key element of spiritual leadership is a constant desire to direct one's self and others to shape a culture founded on a strong sense of community (Fernando 2011).

Spiritual leadership qualities embody the notion that has been variously expressed as benevolent social inclusion, community engagement, becoming a global citizen or corporate social responsibility. Fry (2003) defines spiritual leadership as the "values, attitudes, and behaviors that are necessary to intrinsically motivate one's self and others so that they have a sense of spiritual survival through calling and membership" (pp. 694–695). According to Fry (2003), developing an alignment with mission and values at strategic and operational structures of the organization is a key purpose of spiritual leadership. This is expected to influence teams and individuals to produce higher-level organizational commitment and productivity. It embodies concepts like organizational virtue based on Aristotelian principles. Spirituality in the workplace might also include concepts like altruistic love, which could include trust and loyalty, and hope (or faith), which could include endurance.

My research (see Fernando 2007) shows that regardless of whether leaders feel an internal or an external connection, or both, as part of their spirituality, business leaders practicing spirituality practice similar values. They try to lead honest lives, and to consider others in their pursuit of their business goals. I found that the older leaders become, the more they shift from an internal to an external connection. Leaders report that they gain an inner well-being when they incorporate spirituality into their business practices. In my contributions to the topic of workplace spirituality, I define spirituality as a quality that generates an awareness of a need to connect with an ultimate: something, someone, some object that is more powerful, dignified and humane than oneself, to which one can look for guidance, and which drives one to engage in behaviors that lead towards experiencing and becoming that ultimate (Fernando 2007). I found that the leaders I studied (Fernando 2007) tended to practice one of three types of spiritualities, regardless of whether they were Christian, Hindu, Buddhist or Muslim, that affected how they made their decisions.

Type 1 leaders enacted religious practices at work. For example, once a year Dilmah Tea company conducts a Roman Catholic mass at their Sri Lankan head office, in which all the workers participate, even though the majority of the workforce is Buddhist. Attendance is voluntary. In another example, a particular Hindu business leader would perform a religious practice before making a major decision. In an interview with the author, this leader said, "Sometimes you take a certain amount of risk and you wonder what your chances are." In these instances, he elaborated, "It might be a weakness in me. I sit and think—pray to God [asking] whether I am doing the right thing. Am I going the right way?" He emphasized, "I have to make the right decisions," and described to follow a path as determined by his faith in God. He sought help to do the right thing, in the right manner. He said, "Perhaps it is psychotic but I have done this for the last 30–35 years. I feel it [praying] makes me a better man, and it helps me to take the right decisions." In this manner, Type 1 leaders seek the assistance and guidance of a higher power to navigate difficult decision-making situations.

Type 2 leaders engage in value-based practices at work that express their belief in a code of ethics. For example, a particular Muslim leader I interviewed felt that religious dignitaries had "bastardized" his religion, and he had no faith in the people who control Islam, so he had developed his own form of religion. He said, "I don't believe in the form of a god. I believe in religion in its intrinsic form. I certainly believe that there is somebody, something or some force that guides destiny and lot of it is there in your own value system. It is within yourself. If you subscribe to it—those values within you—then that is religion. So therefore, I think everybody has his or her own religion." This Muslim leader developed a set of values that he thought was important for someone to lead a successful life. When he launched his own group of companies, this leader adopted these as core values for his organization. Every employee had to conduct official business according to these values, which included honesty, integrity and respect.

The last type is based on self-growth-based spirituality. These leaders, as opposed to religious or values-based leaders who explicitly practice spirituality, use realizing the potential of the self as a form of experiencing spirtualty at work. For example, for one Buddhist leader of a business conglomerate with 3,000 employees, this type of spirituality was the basis for starting a cross-functional self-growth committee. This leader actively promoted self-growth. Developing a work culture where each of his employees can achieve full potential was an important business goal. He did not want employees to follow a regimental pattern. He claimed that such patterns permanently stifle one's creativity. He wanted to give his employees an opportunity to break free from these predetermined arrangements and "blossom". In this manner, Type 3 leaders seek to create a work environment that provides opportunities for employees to achieve to their highest capabilities.

Ethical Leadership

Ethical leadership is the "demonstration of normatively appropriate conduct through personal actions and interpersonal relationships, and the promotion of such conduct to followers through two-way communication, reinforcement, and decision-making" (Brown et al. 2005, p. 120). This type of leadership is strongly focused on the leader's ethical awareness and behaviour (Mayer et al. 2012; Ciulla 2013; Brown and Treviño 2006).

Ethical leadership is concerned with doing what is morally right, just and good, and creating awareness in followers to do the same (Ciulla 2013). The three key challenges of ethical leadership are the leader's power, the types of ethical justification and the leader's authenticity. Because it creates inequalities, power can corrupt the relationship between the leader and followers if not handled correctly. Power creates temptations for leaders, potentially making them act in ways they would not normally act, and corrupting their values and their behavior towards others.

We have seen that there can be several types of ethical justifications for specific behaviors. A challenge for ethical leadership is which type of ethical theory to use to justify an action. Possibilities include ethics of divine command (such as those expressed in the Ten Commandments in Christianity and Judaism), virtue ethics, a teleological perspective of ethics, in which the outcome determines whether the action was ethical (utilitarianism) and the deontological perspective of ethics, which centers on Kantianism or duty-based ethics that asserts that it is our obligation to respect and avoid harming others.

The application of these types of ethical justifications create enormous moral challenges. An example is the discussion of Nike in the early 1990s and its use of Asian sweat shops and child labor to manufacture its goods (DeTienne and Lewis 2005). In addition to the issues surrounding inhumane conditions of work, many Americans frowned on this practice, particularly as towns such as Flint, in Michigan, USA, at the time had high levels of unemployment. From this perspective Nike could have been seen as unethical, as it was taking jobs away from local Americans.

However, most of the Americans who objected did not know that Nike's use of cheap labor in Asian countries aided in the survival of many more people than the numbers of Americans it could have employed. In many developing nations, including those in which Nike had its manufacturing operations, child workers were often the only means of income for entire families. If they were denied work because Nike closed its operations and went back to the US, these children and the developing economy in their countries would suffer. This example is an extreme situation, but is a challenge faced by many leaders trying to act ethically. One can ask what the role of the government and other multinational enterprises is. Nike is seen to be unethical by the Flint community, but shouldn't the US government and multinational enterprises (MNEs) other than Nike be held accountable as well? Nike, as one corporation, may not be responsible for comprehensively solving a complex issue involving many stakeholder groups by itself.

Attacking an action or situation through a different ethical lens, as in the Nike example, shows just how challenging ethical leadership can be, as it often needs to respond to ethical dilemmas in which no alternative is appropriate because someone always suffers harm.

Finally, the challenge of authenticity and ethical leadership must be examined. Authenticity is about being true and loyal to oneself. A significant facet of authenticity is being genuine or virtuous, and not portraying oneself as having qualities one does not possess. The challenge with ethical leadership is that if leaders are not seen to be applying what they assert to be ethical, the trust in the relationship between the leader and followers may be affected. Authenticity requires leaders to behave consistently with the values and morals they assert to be theirs. Authentic leaders who behave ethically, promote ethical values and norms and practice them establish credibility among their followers, and those who do not may not be effective if their followers see them as inauthentic. This is the challenge to ethical leadership: being perceived as authentic to gain trust and commitment from one's followers.

Both power and authenticity affect followers' trust in the leadership process, regardless of the leader's actual behavior. Moreover, this behavior can be differently interpreted as ethical or unethical, and the leader-follower relationship differently affected, depending on the perspective of the observer.

Servant Leadership

Offshoots of transformational leadership such as servant leadership and authentic transformational leadership are proposed due to the conceptual weaknesses of transformational leadership. According to Barbuto and Wheeler (2006), servant leaders' service orientation is geared to promote "wise organizations". On the other hand, transcendental leaders inspire followers to connect with the ultimate power, the extraordinary. The contrast between servant and transcendental leaders can be seen in the extent of concern and care of the servant towards others; that other people's needs are first served.

Greenleaf (1977) first conceptualized the concept of servant leadership, describing it as a process beginning with the "natural feeling that one wants to serve first", followed by a conscious choice to "aspire to lead" (p. 12). Four key themes of servant leadership are prominence of service to others over self, affirmation through listening, developing trust and developing followers to become wholesome individuals (Daft 1999).

Overlap between the transcendental and servant leadership styles have been observed. Fernando et al. (2009) argue that the transcendental leader is not just a servant, but also a transactional and charismatic leader. As servant leaders must care for the interests of their collaborators as a priority, servant leader qualities make it impossible for transcendental leaders to exploit others.

Authentic Leadership

It is easy for leaders to hide in a cloak of goodness and ethicality and project an image of perfect morality. In terms of leadership, and especially in terms of ethical and moral leadership, there is then the question of instrumentality: is the leader using pseudo-ethics to further their own goals? These goals could be motivating others, or influencing followers and stakeholders, just as I was influenced as a junior executive (as I will relate below). Yet leadership should be authentic, genuine. A major proponent of this leadership style is Bruce Avolio, who characterizes authentic leadership as "a process that draws from both psychological capacities and a highly developed organizational context" (see Luthans and Avolio 2003, p. 243). He points out that psychological tools—in other words, instruments or processes—come in to play when one talks about an authentic style of leadership.

Authentic leadership fosters "the modal values of honesty, loyalty, and fairness, as well as the end values of justice, equality, and human rights" (Bass and Steidlmeier 1999, p. 192). Fernando et al. (2009) note that even though Bass and Steidlmeier explains how values are embedded in cultures, good and bad transformational leaders are not easy to identify. The close unison in the leader and follower relationship in follower development is a unique feature of transcendental leadership (Avolio and Gardner 2005; Walumbwa et al. 2008).

The following story illustrates the idea of authentic leadership. I used to work for a large Sri Lankan business conglomerate. Absenteeism was a problem in that particular office, and I thought it would be good for me to show up at 8 a.m. sharp to have eye contact with the employees who came in late. I was quite regularly there at the main entrance to the building at 8, when the senior directors were also coming in. Because of this, I observed every morning that these senior directors would come in from their limousines to enter the building, and after they entered, they would turn so that they would face the main door, and back themselves into the lift. I didn't understand why they were doing this. After some time, I realized the reason: on top of the main door was a series of pictures of various religious deities, and this was a way of respecting and venerating these gods while they were first stepping into the office for the day. They also participated in a religious ceremony each morning. As a junior executive, also religious at the time, I found that this practice of the senior leaders had a profound effect on me (the follower). I believed that these senior directors' behavior meant that they were so holy, they would not engage in anything wrong. I respected them for this reason and tried to follow their instructions. Religion was a major part of the culture of that organization, and the senior directors even asserted that some of the successes of the organization were due to their religious affiliations. After some time, and after I became a director myself, I thought it would be interesting to examine how authentic these senior directors' projected behaviors were. The higher I got up the corporate ladder, the more I realized that these executives engaged in the same level of competitive, and sometimes unethical, behavior as anyone else in that environment to achieve a competitive edge. This is a problem that authentic leadership attempts to address.

Conclusion

The different leadership styles explored in this chapter provides a foundation for us to examine the notion of responsible leadership. What is clear is that leadership requires a bringing together of many variables; the situation, follower, leader and achievement of goal aspects. In the next chapter, we will use this foundation to examine the substantial difference between general leadership and responsible leadership. The extent of the difference is effectively juxtaposed through a consideration of, for instance, the leadership of Mahatma Ghandi and Adolf Hitler. It is without doubt that both individuals were successful, aspirational and inspirational leaders. However, one was responsible and the other was not. This analogy also extends into the organizational setting. In the wake of corporate disasters and managerial corruption such as that displayed within Volkswagen, JP Morgan, Enron, James Hardie and HIH, particularly in comparison with other organizations that have thrived both socially and commercially, it would be evident not only that responsible leadership is substantially different from general leadership, but that responsible leaders are very clearly visible to the public as being responsible. In the next chapter, we will examine how the word "responsible" connotes reliability, trustworthiness, amenability and integrity. It is argued that in the Asian century society of modern capitalism and globalization, leaders need to demonstrate responsibility through their understanding and implementation of corporate social responsibility. By the same token, it must be recognized that not all leaders who appear to be "responsible" are so.

References

Alvesson, M., & Sveningsson, S. (2003). The great disappearance act: Difficulties in doing 'leadership'. *Leadership Quarterly., 14*, 359–81.
Avolio, B. J. (1999). *Full leadership development: Building the vital forces in organizations*. Thousand Oaks: Sage.
Avolio, B. J. (2010). *Full range leadership development*. Thousand Oaks: Sage.

References

Avolio, B. J., & Bass, B. (2002). *Manual for the multifactor leadership questionnaire (Form 5X)*. Redwood City: Mindgarden.

Avolio, B. J., & Gardner, W. L. (2005). Authentic leadership development: Getting to the root of positive forms of leadership. *The Leadership Quarterly, 16*(3), 315–338.

Avolio, B. J., & Yammarino, F. J. (Eds.). (2013). *Transformational and charismatic leadership: The road ahead*. Bingley: Emerald Group Publishing.

Aydin, B., & Ceylan, A. (2009). The effect of spiritual leadership on organizational learning capacity. *African Journal of Business Management, 3*(5), 184–190.

Baglione, S. L., & Zimmerer, T. W. (2007). Spirituality, values, and leadership beliefs and practices: An empirical study of US and Chinese business leaders. *Journal of International Business Strategy, 7*(1).

Barbuto, J., & Wheeler, D. (2006). Scale development and construct clarification of servant leadership. *Group & Organization Management, 31*(3), 300–326.

Barbuto, J., Fritz, S., Matkin, G., & Marx, D. (2007). Effects of gender, education, and age upon leaders' use of influence tactics and full range leadership behaviors. *Sex Roles, 56*(1), 71–83.

Bass, B. M. (1985). *Leadership and performance*. New York: Free Press.

Bass, B. M. (1990). From transactional to transformational leadership: Learning to share the vision. *Organizational Dynamics, 18*(3), 19–31.

Bass, B. M. (1995). Theory of transformational leadership redux. *The Leadership Quarterly, 6*(4), 463–478.

Bass, B. M., & Avolio, B. J. (1989). Potential biases in leadership measures: How prototypes, leniency, and general satisfaction relate to ratings and rankings of transformational and transactional leadership constructs. *Educational and Psychological Measurement, 49*(3), 509–527.

Bass, B. M., & Avolio, B. J. (1997). *Full range leadership development: Manual for the multifactor leadership questionnaire*. Palo Alto: Mind Garden.

Bass, B. M., & Steidlmeier, P. (1999). Ethics, character, and authentic transformational leadership behavior. *The Leadership Quarterly, 10*(2), 181–217.

Bass, B. M., & Stogdill, R. M. (1990). *Handbook of leadership: Theory, research & managerial applications*. New York: Free Press.

Beazley, H. (1998). *Meaning and measurement of spirituality in organizational settings: Development of a spirituality assessment scale*. ProQuest: UMI Dissertations Publishing.

Benefiel, M. (2005). The second half of the journey: Spiritual leadership for organizational transformation. *The Leadership Quarterly, 16*(5), 723–747.

Blake, R. R., & McCanse, A. A. (1991). *Leadership dilemmas: Grid solutions*. Houston: Gulf Publishing Company.

Bolman, L. G., & Deal, T. E. (2003). *Reframing organizations: Artistry, choice, and leadership* (3rd ed.). San Francisco: Jossey-Bass.

Brown, M. E., & Treviño, L. K. (2006). Ethical leadership: A review and future directions. *The Leadership Quarterly, 17*(6), 595–616.

Brown, M. E., Treviño, L. K., & Harrison, D. A. (2005). Ethical leadership: A social learning perspective for construct development and testing. *Organizational Behavior and Human Decision Processes, 97*(2), 117–134.

Brunsson, N. (2004). *The organization of hypocrisy: Talk, decisions and actions*. Herndon: Copenhagen Business School Press.

Burns, J. M. (1978). *Leadership*. New York: Harper & Row.

Cardona, P. (2000). Transcendental leadership. *Leadership & Organization Development Journal, 21*(4), 201–207.

Ciulla, J. B. (1995). Leadership ethics: Mapping the territory. *Business Ethics Quarterly, 5*(1), 5–28.

Ciulla, J. B. (2013). *Leadership ethics*. Thousand Oaks: Sage.

Daft, R. L. (1999). *Leadership: Theory and practice*. Fort Worth: Dryden Press.

Dent, E. B., Higgins, M. E., & Wharff, D. M. (2005). Spirituality and leadership: An empirical review of definitions, distinctions, and embedded assumptions. *The Leadership Quarterly, 16*(5), 625–653.

DeTienne, K. B., & Lewis, L. W. (2005). The pragmatic and ethical barriers to corporate social responsibility disclosure: The Nike case. *Journal of Business Ethics, 60*(4), 359–376.

Druskat, V. U. (1994). Gender and leadership style: Transformational and transactional leadership in the Roman Catholic Church. *The Leadership Quarterly, 5*(2), 99–119.

Fernando, M. (2007). *Spiritual leadership in the entrepreneurial business: A multifaith study*. London: Edward Elgar Publishing.

Fernando, M. (2011). Spirituality and leadership. In A. Bryman, D. Collinson, K. Grint, B. Jackson, & M. Uhl-Bien (Eds.), *The SAGE handbook of leadership* (pp. 483–494). London: Sage.

Fernando, M., & Gross, M. (2006). Workplace spirituality and organizational hypocrisy: The Holy Water-Gate Case. Australia New Zealand Academy of Management (ANZAM) Conference Proceedings, Queensland.

Fernando, M., & Nilakant, V. (2008). The place of self-actualisation in workplace spirituality: Evidence from Sri Lanka. *Culture and Religion, 9*(3), 233–249.

Fernando, M., Beale, F., & Geroy, G. (2009). The spiritual dimension in leadership at Dilmah Tea. *Leadership & Organization Development Journal, 30*(6), 522–539.

Fry, L. W. (2003). Toward a theory of spiritual leadership. *The Leadership Quarterly, 14*(6), 693–727.

Fry, L. W., & Cohen, M. P. (2009). Spiritual leadership as a paradigm for organizational transformation and recovery from extended work hours cultures. *Journal of Business Ethics, 84*(2), 265–278.

Fukushige, A., & Spicer, D. P. (2007). Leadership preferences in Japan: An exploratory study. *Leadership & Organization Development Journal, 28*(6), 508–530.

Geroy, G. D., Bray, A., & Venneberg, D. L. (2005). The CCM model: A management approach to performance optimization. *Performance Improvement Quarterly, 18*(2), 19–36.

Greenleaf, R. (1977). *Servant leadership*. New York: Paulist Press.

Guillén, M., & González, T. (2001). The ethical dimension of managerial leadership: Two illustrative case studies in TQM. *Journal of Business Ethics, 34*(3–4), 175–189.

Hersey, P., & Blanchard, K. H. (1988). *Management of organizational behavior: Utilizing human resources*. Englewood Cliffs: Prentice-Hall.

Hicks, D. A. (2003). *Religion and the workplace: Pluralism, spirituality, leadership*. Cambridge: Cambridge University Press.

House, R. (1971). A path-goal theory of leader effectiveness. *Administrative Science Quarterly, 16*, 321–338.

House, R. (1996). Path-goal theory of leadership: Lessons, legacy, and a reformulated theory. *The Leadership Quarterly, 7*(3), 323–352.

House, R., & Antonakis, J. (2014). Instrumental leadership: Measurement and extension of transformational-transactional leadership theory. *The Leadership Quarterly, 25*(4), 746–771.

House, R., & Howell, J. (1992). Personality and charismatic leadership. *The Leadership Quarterly, 3*(2), 81–108.

House, R., & Mitchell, T. (1974). Path-goal theory of leadership. *Journal of Contemporary Business, 3*(4), 81.

Jago, A. G. (1982). Leadership: Perspectives in theory and research. *Management Science, 28*(3), 315–336.

Karadag, E. (2009). Spiritual leadership and organizational culture: A study of structural equation modeling. *Educational Sciences: Theory and Practice, 9*(3), 1391–1405.

Kerns, C. (2015). Situational context: A core leadership dimension. *Journal of Leadership, Accountability and Ethics, 12*(1), 11–24.

Klau, T. (2010). Europe would welcome a surprise act of statesmanship. *The Independent*, p. 4.

Kriger, M., & Seng, Y. (2005). Leadership with inner meaning: A contingency theory of leadership based on the worldviews of five religions. *The Leadership Quarterly, 16*(5), 771–806.

References

Kuvaas, B., Buch, R., Dysvik, A., & Haerem, T. (2012). Economic and social leader-member exchange relationships and follower performance. *The Leadership Quarterly, 23*(5), 756–765.

Lewin, K., & Lippitt, R. (1938). An experimental approach to the study of autocracy and democracy: A preliminary note. *Sociometry, 1*(3/4), 292–300.

Luthans, F., & Avolio, B. (2003). Authentic leadership development. In K. S. Cameron, J. E. Dutton, & R. E. Quinn (Eds.), *Positive organizational scholarship: Foundations of a New discipline* (pp. 241–258). San Francisco: Berrett-Koehler Publishers Inc.

Madison, K., & Kellermanns, F. W. (2013). Is the spiritual bond bound by blood? An exploratory study of spiritual leadership in family firms. *Journal of Management, Spirituality & Religion, 10*(2), 159.

Malone, P., & Fry, L. W. (2003). *Transforming schools through spiritual leadership: A field experiment.* Seattle: Meeting of the Academy of Management.

Mayer, D. M., Aquino, K., Greenbaum, R. L., & Kuenzi, M. (2012). Who displays ethical leadership, and why does it matter? An examination of antecedents and consequences of ethical leadership. *Academy of Management Journal, 55*(1), 151–171.

Parry, K., & Kempster, S. (2014). Charismatic leadership through the eyes of followers. *Strategic HR Review, 13*(1), 20–23.

Phipps, K. A. (2012). Spirituality and strategic leadership: The influence of spiritual beliefs on strategic decision making. *Journal of Business Ethics, 106*(2), 177–189.

Reave, L. (2005). Spiritual values and practices related to leadership effectiveness. *The Leadership Quarterly, 16*(5), 655–687.

Sanders, J. E., Hopkins, W. E., & Geroy, G. D. (2003). From transactional to transcendental: Toward an integrated theory of leadership. *Journal of Leadership & Organizational Studies, 9*(4), 21.

Schriesheim, C. A., & Neider, L. L. (1996). Path-goal leadership theory: The long and winding road. *The Leadership Quarterly, 7*(3), 317–321.

Smith, J. A., & Rayment, J. J. (2007). The global SMP fitness framework: A guide for leaders exploring the relevance of spirituality in the workplace. *Management Decision, 45*(2), 217–234.

Tannenbaum, R., & Schmidt, W. H. (1973). How to choose a leadership pattern. *Harvard Business Review, 51*(3), 162–180.

To, M. L., Tse, H. H. M., & Ashkanasy, N. M. (2015). A multilevel model of transformational leadership, affect, and creative process behavior in work teams. *Leadership Quarterly, 26*(4), 543.

Vaill, P. B. (1998). *Spirited leading and learning: Process wisdom for a new age.* San Francisco: Jossey-Bass Publishers.

Walumbwa, F. O., Avolio, B. J., Gardner, W. L., Wernsing, T. S., & Peterson, S. J. (2008). Authentic leadership: Development and validation of a theory-based measure. *Journal of Management, 34*(1), 89–126.

Wang, B. X., & Chee, H. (2011). *Chinese leadership.* New York: Palgrave Macmillan.

Wofford, J. C., & Liska, L. Z. (1993). Path-goal theories of leadership: A meta-analysis. *Journal of Management, 19*(4), 857–876.

Yammarino, F. J. (1993). Transforming leadership studies: Bernard Bass' leadership and performance beyond expectations. *The Leadership Quarterly, 4*(3), 379–382.

Yukl, G. (1999). An evaluation of conceptual weaknesses in transformational and charismatic leadership theories. *The Leadership Quarterly, 10*, 285–305.

Zwart, G. A. (2000). *The relationship between spirituality and transformational leadership in public, private, and nonprofit sector organizations.* La Verne: University of La Verne.

Chapter 5
Responsible Leadership in Theory

Introduction

Despite the advent of various leadership theories based on the factors of leader, follower, situation and goals, calls have been made for a leadership style that is embedded in the often implicit notion of responsibility. The Asian century world is becoming more unsustainable: natural resources are rapidly depleting, and pollution levels, overpopulation and the divide between the rich and poor are in need of greater monitoring and control. The call is for a leadership approach that is driven by sustainable development and social responsibility. Such a new approach will recognize that the organization is not merely a profit-making operation, but that leaders have an integral responsibility to contribute to the good and protect and develop the resources entrusted to them by society. One could argue that leadership practice derived from Milton Friedman's (1974) view that the only function of business is to garner profit would fall short of the demand for a new leadership approach that is more responsible and inclusive.

What Is Responsible Leadership?

Responsible leadership lies at the intersection between the fields of social responsibility and leadership. It involves individuals, groups and organizations (Waldman and Balven, 2014). Responsible leadership is focused on individuals exerting leadership influence at its core, hence it is important to consider how individuals act and make decisions. When asked to define responsible leadership, one interviewee said:

> I think there's an expression, 'what is old is new again.' I'm sure if I spoke to my grandparents, they would look horrified at some of these concepts because isn't that what you're supposed to do? It's doing the right thing. And not quite a utopian view of the world, but kind of being ethically stable and I guess a lighthouse or foundation stone that provides the anchor point for how people operate.

When one traces the development of more-recent leadership styles such as transactional, transformational, Full Range Leadership, transcendental, authentic and spiritual leadership, it appears that the trend is to focus on a limited number of elements in the leadership process. Although not apparent in the simple leadership model in Fig. 4.1, the notion of responsibility appears to be an implicit requirement in the leadership process. The interaction between two groups of people—in other words, the relationship between the leader and the followers—seems to rest on the critical but invisible notion of responsibility. It can be thought of as representing a hidden layer of the leadership process, which is central to the smooth functioning of the process as a whole. The increasing importance placed on responsibility in leadership can be a reflection of society's evolution and need to rise against the apparent deterioration of moral values, both generally and in business.

The common understanding of responsibility assigns certain obligations and corresponding rights to parties in a relationship. The uprisings in the Middle East in 2013 (BBC 2013) were in large part motivated by the people's demands for leaders with better morals. From a political perspective, leaders were held to account for their actions, and when these leaders failed to uphold basic human values, the populace wanted them removed. In the corporate world, Ken Lay at Enron (New York Times 2006) and Ray Williams at HIH (Financial Review 2014) were held to account for their negligent actions, which caused harm to others, including shareholders. Why have leadership scholars and practitioners ignored the central role played by responsibility for this long? Why have leadership approaches and styles ignored such an essential element in the leadership process?

It can be argued that even though acting responsibly is so central and common to healthy human relationships, the increasing attention on profit maximization has meant that the importance of the concept has been lost. From every corner of the world come reports of irresponsible actions due to gross negligence on the part of those in power and authority. The basis for efficient and effective operation of a civilized society in large part rests on the due discharge of responsibility in the exercise of either official or informal duties.

There are several differences between general leadership and responsible leadership. First, general leadership is about the relationship between leaders and followers, whereas responsible leadership includes a broader set of relationships. A responsible leader is expected to develop a mutually rewarding relationship with followers, but also with other internal and external stakeholders (Maak and Pless 2006). Second, in responsible leadership the nature of these relationships is primarily values-based and ethical-principles-driven. However, for example in transactional leadership, each relationship is based on reward and punishment (carrot and stick), not on values, ethics or morals. Third, compared with the simple leadership model (Fig. 4.1), the goal in responsible leadership is not merely to achieve a business goal, but to pursue goals that add value for a wide range of stakeholders and are sustainable (Fig. 5.1). These sustainable, value-adding goals help generate social change (Maak and Pless 2006). For this reason, the concept of social innovation has a special relevance in responsible leadership.

What Is Responsible Leadership?

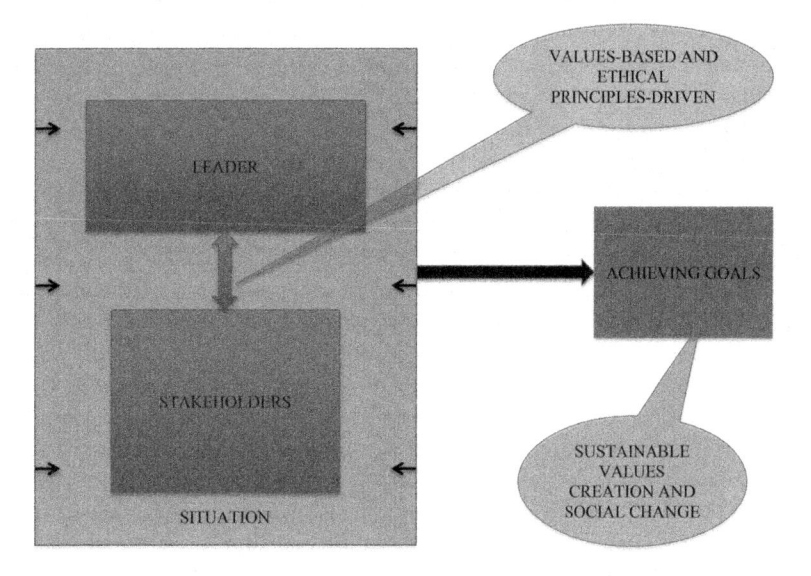

Fig. 5.1 Leadership as a process embedded in responsibility

Several scholars have attempted to identify the attributes of responsible leadership. Stahl and de Luque (2014) propose a conceptualisation of responsible leadership that is developed from "do good" and "avoid harm" perspectives. It highlights the influence of individual, situational, organisational, institutional and supranational factors on responsible leadership behavior and explains how these factors affect decision making. Doh and Quigley (2014) attempt to reconcile divergent approaches to responsible leadership that include strategic CSR activities. They explain responsible leadership using stakeholder theory through a psychological path and an informational path. Trust becomes an integral part of this exchange. The mere existence of another person in one's presence casts certain responsibilities on an individual. However, the performance of these responsibilities should not be detrimental to one's own well-being; the self should be preserved in discharging one's duties to another (Knights and O'Leary 2006).

What is trust within a leadership context? According to Ciulla (2001), trust is the glue that binds the disparate parts of leaders' personality so that there is little difference between their public and private faces. Although public and private worlds of leaders are different, leaders' unethical behaviour in private may erode the trust that others have in the leader when known in public. Doubt erodes the delicate fabric of trust (Ciulla 2001). According to Pless (2011), being held accountable for actions and being trusted and reliable are not just synonyms for responsibility. They are relational concepts that give meaning to responsibility.

While shared leadership has also been proposed as a viable approach to enact responsible leadership (Pearce et al. 2014), Filatotchev and Nakajima (2014) have proposed a link between corporate governance and responsible leadership to resolve

CSR issues. However, Waldman and Balven (2014) caution theorists to avoid using only normative approaches as the way forward, as there are multiple ways to conceive responsible leadership. They argue that the conceptualization of responsible leadership is still controversial and it would be futile to consider developing theory without considering individual leaders.

Responsible leadership has been identified as a "values-based and thorough ethical principles-driven relationship" of leaders and stakeholders (Pless 2007, p. 438). Responsible leaders ensure that the stakeholders of their organizations are linked by a purpose and shared meaning. This understanding is present to such an extent in the relationships, that it raises each other to levels of motivation and commitment to generate sustainable value and positive impact in their society (Pless 2007). She defines a responsible leader as someone who "reconciles the idea of effectiveness with the idea of corporate responsibility by being an active citizen, and promoting active citizenship inside and outside the organization." (Pless 2007, p. 450). The broader relationship with stakeholders that is the focus of responsible leadership somewhat limits the relevance of more prominent leadership styles such as transactional, transformational, servant, authentic, transcendental and spiritual leadership approaches (Pless 2011).

The theory of responsible leadership distinguishes the relationships with corporations and others, and what corporations actually owe in terms of responsibility to others.

Using stakeholder theory, Doh and Quigly (2014) demonstrate how organizational processes and outcomes are influenced by responsible leadership. They integrate the general leadership and responsible leadership literature with stakeholder theory to map out strategies for responsible leaders to influence outcomes at different organizational levels. They propose that leaders who consistently seek and consider numerous stakeholder views in their decision making are likely to generate a positive impact. Using psychological and knowledge sharing pathways, Doh and Quigley (2014, p. 255) claim that leaders can exhibit and project their responsible leadership behaviours. While noting that the psychological pathway consists of trust, ownership and commitment, the knowledge-based pathway consists of options, creativity and knowledge sharing, they assert that pathways stem from responsible leadership with a stakeholder approach. These pathways can lead to outcomes at individual, team, organisational and societal levels. Thus according to Doh and Quigley (2014), both pathways consist of process mechanisms that promote signals and messages, actions and outcomes at multiple levels; individual, team, organisational and societal levels.

Stakeholder theory is based on the assumption of a network of connections between the firm and its stakeholders (Doh and Quigley 2014). Scholars over the years have examined various attributes of this relationship, including its nature, antecedents, processes and outcomes. For example, Donaldson (1982, 1989) notes that a social contract is formed with stakeholder connections and consent. Legitimacy for corporate actions come through by securing stakeholder consent to a social contract. While there are benefits, Doh and Quigley (2014) observe that there are unresolved issues with applying stakeholder theory in practice such as the limitless list of potential stakeholders, prioritising that list and the complex and dense stakeholder relationships in a global setting.

According to Doh and Quigley (2014), knowledge-based pathways assume that an organisation is an open system. With a greater focus and care of the relationships with stakeholders, responsible leaders are more likely to easily operate within organizational contexts both internal and external. They will also be in a favorable position to promote knowledge flow within and across organizational boundaries. A responsible leadership approach needs to consider the demands of numerous stakeholder groups and it is likely to psychologically influence stakeholders at the individual level, leading to higher engagement with the organization (Doh and Quigley 2014). This holistic approach suggested by Doh and Quigley (2014) is of significant value to the socially innovative responsible model developed later in the book.

According to Freeman (2004), values are embedded in stakeholder theory as a necessary and explicit condition of conducting business. The theory integrates different stakeholders in a shared sense of value creation; it makes the leaders reflect on how they want to conduct business and the type of relationships they need to develop to conduct the business effectively (Maak and Pless 2006). Until recently, the social contract relationship between the corporation and society implied an embedded understanding that the corporation had an obligation to society to conduct business in a responsible manner. This relationship and the nature of the *quid pro quo* assumption has become explicit; leaders are constantly required to communicate the value they create, and what elements integrate stakeholders.

Maak and Pless (2006) view leadership as being values-laden. In the context of stakeholder theory and the CSR debate, leadership can be—and, some argue, should be—linked with both the concept of the triple bottom line (profitability, community benefit and minimal environmental impact) and the broader idea of sustainable development. For example, suppose a company is producing millions of units of bottled water, and transporting them thousands of kilometres per annum, by both air and ground, and that the current pallet configuration is wasting enormous amounts of space. Can the company use square bottles rather than round, so that every millimeter of a square palette is used? Organizations are now looking at issues like this, which appear simple but could make a significant difference to resource allocation and climate change initiatives over time. The challenge is to fulfill the present needs without sacrificing future generations' ability to satisfy their needs.

Antecedents of Responsible Leader Behaviour

Stahl and de Luque (2014) propose a theoretical model of antecedents of responsible leadership that focuses on the individual, situational, organisational, institutional and supranational influences on responsible leader behaviour. These researchers argue that classic economic constructs hold that business has no responsibility other than making profit for shareholders. On the other end of the spectrum it is believed that businesses have an obligation to make decisions to contribute to the common good.

Claiming that previous research has neglected a holistic conceptualisation of responsible leadership that includes all antecedents, they note that responsible leadership has been conceptualised either through an ethical/moral lens or through a citizenship perspective (enhancing societal wellbeing) (p. 236). According to these scholars, antecedents have inconsistently been emphasised as psychological, organisational and the broader national and institutional environment in which leaders operate.

Furthermore, Stahl and de Luque (2014) note that while the definition of responsible leadership is debated, there is a consensus that individual leader behaviour has an impact on social performance and long-term viability of their organizations. The unifying framework proposed by these scholars focuses mainly on ethical dimensions, but does acknowledge the influence of legal/economic perspectives.

The model distinguishes between two dimensions of responsible leader behaviour; "avoiding harm" (proscriptive morality) which includes decisions and actions taken to avoid negative outcomes for stakeholders and community (e.g. ensuring product safety or avoiding pollution) and "doing good" (prescriptive morality) which refers to activities aimed at promoting societal welfare (e.g. supporting community development and philanthropy) (Stahl and de Luque 2014, p. 238). "Doing good" behaviour is not required by society but has become a "might-do" action that is desired by society although not expected. "Avoiding harm" is a normative, "should-do" action that is expected by societal members.

The key contribution of Stahl and de Luque's (2014) model is the differentiation of "doing good" and "avoiding harm" behaviours and how they have different psychological bases and antecedents. There is little evidence of how the identified antecedents may differently affect the two dimensions. Thus the call is for more studies on the contextual conditions that moderate individual difference effects, particularly on the role of situational strength (Stahl and de Luque 2014). They propose that contextual influences and leaders' propensity to lead responsibly may be mediated by situational strength.

Responsible Leadership for Performance (RLP)

Responsible Leadership for Performance (RLP), proposed by Lynham and Chermack (2006), was one of the first attempts by scholars to explicitly link responsible leadership with performance. For these authors, leadership is responsible when it "demonstrates, and is judged to demonstrate, effectiveness, ethics, endurance" (2006, p. 77). This responsible leadership theory says that there is a contextual environment that includes a social, economic, cultural, technological, ecological and political environment within which the constituents and performance system reside and goals are achieved. For Lynham and Chermack, leadership is, therefore, "a focused system of interacting inputs, process, outputs and feedback wherein

The Contextual Environment
The Social, Economic, Cultural, Technological, Ecological, and Political Environment in which the Constituency and the Performance System Reside

The Performance System

Internal Environment of the Performance System
Cultural   Political   Technological

Input   Process   Output

The Leadership System-in-Focus

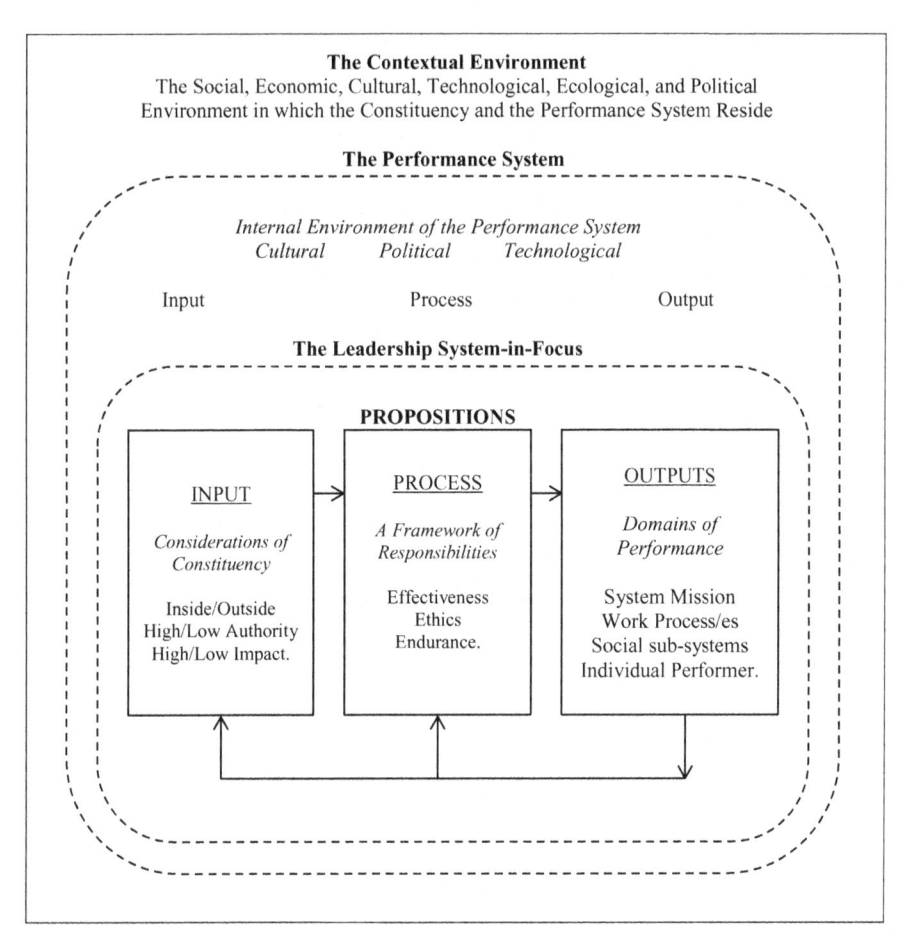

PROPOSITIONS

INPUT	PROCESS	OUTPUTS
Considerations of Constituency	A Framework of Responsibilities	Domains of Performance
Inside/Outside High/Low Authority High/Low Impact.	Effectiveness Ethics Endurance.	System Mission Work Process/es Social sub-systems Individual Performer.

Fig. 5.2 Responsible leadership for performance (Lynham, S. A., & Chermack, T. J., 2006. Responsible leadership for performance: A theoretical model and hypotheses. *Journal of Leadership & Organizational Studies, 12*(4), 73–88, Reprinted by Permission of SAGE Publications)

individuals and/or groups influence and/or act on behalf of specific individuals or groups of individuals to achieve shared goals and commonly desired performance outcomes, within a specific performance system and environment" (p. 75) (Fig. 5.2). They describe leadership as a system with intended inputs, outputs and boundaries operating in a performance system representing joint, coordinated and purposeful action.

According to Lynham and Chermack (2006), the need for a performance-based theory of responsible leadership fills an important void in the literature. The available theories do not simultaneously address the nature and challenges of leadership, focusing instead on effectiveness at the expense of examining responsibility. In contrast, RLP "is a general, integrative theoretical framework of leadership that addresses the nature and challenges of leadership that are both responsible and focused on performance" (Lynham and Chermack 2006, p. 74). The question this theory seeks to answer is not "How can leaders be more effective in increasing the bottom line?", but "How can leaders increase their bottom line responsibly, with due regard to other stakeholders' needs?" There is a constituency (followers) that defines the morality of leader actions. In the RLP approach, responsibility is linked to professional action. It concerns with thorough, reflective thought about what action is professionally right in a given context. This "right" is a very subjective term. It can be determined by several means; this is where moral frameworks such as utilitarian, Kantian or virtue ethics come into play. Lynham and Chermack (2006) take the example of leadership in the military to highlight how RLP works:

> In this context the military makes for the particular performance system in which the leadership system-in-focus occurs. From the perspective of the theoretical framework of RLP, the military performance system must therefore be used to inform, shape and evaluate the required leadership system in terms of considerations of constituency, responsibleness and multi-domain performance. The nature and value of the three units of the framework are therefore changed by the purpose and nature of the performance system to which the leadership system-in-focus is in service. Considering the military as the performance boundary of the leadership system-in-focus significantly impacts who could, and should, be included in the considerations of constituency, what makes for responsible leadership in that performance system and context, and what constitutes acceptable performance in that performance system. This integrated perspective of leadership, in turn, informs the leadership traits best suited to the particular performance system, and highlights the need to reconsider these traits when the nature and purpose of the performance system itself changes. Thus, it is unlikely that the leadership traits best suited to a military performance will be the same as those best suited to a non-military one (p. 84).

Thus RLP is a systems-based theory that is focused on context, working from eight strategic propositions (Lynham and Chermack 2006). First, unlike in other popular approaches to leadership, in RLP, leadership does not operate at the individual level, nor is it managed by the leader. Second, the purpose of the RLP system is to address the needs of what Lynham and Chermack call the constituency (in essence, followers): "those whom leadership in the performance system serves, and for whom the leadership produces desired results" (Lynham and Chermack 2006, p. 76). Leadership would not exist without a constituency; thus the constituency defines what is moral for RLP. Third, RLP operates on three units that must interact for it to manifest in action: considerations of constituency, a framework of responsibleness and domains of performance. RLP theory proponents suggest that considerations for constituency can be measured primarily by whether the group is internal/external of the performance system, the extent of authority on the performance system and the likelihood of impact on the performance system. Responsibleness is measured by constituents' perceptions of the effectiveness of leadership practices, ethical leadership habits and enduring leadership resources. Domains of performance (the output) are determined by constituents' perceptions of four dimensions: the system mission, work processes, social sub-systems and the individual performer.

Fourth, a framework for responsibleness is explained by Lynham and Chermack in terms of professional action. Reflection is key, and considered thought before action will lead to professionally right action to suit a particular context. The three key criteria that determine what is professionally right are effectiveness, ethics and endurance. Being only focused on effectiveness appears to be indelicate, even dangerous to stakeholders because a person can be effective whilst being unethical. The often-cited example in this case is that of Hitler. As Ciulla (2001) noted, leaders are "carved from the warped wood of humanity. This does not mean that humans are evil, rather that they are imperfect" (p. 313). Some leadership scholars consider forms of morally based leadership approaches such as transformational, and by extension transcendental, leadership to be value-neutral phenomena. "Even in the face of such obviously differing charismatic leaders as Adolph Hitler and Mahatma Ghandi" (O'Connor et al. 1995, p. 531), there is no way to distinguish the effectiveness of their leadership skills. This problem, which Cardona (2000) calls the Hitler problem (p. 201), has plagued leadership analysts who have tried to solve it, with varying levels of success. One approach has been to differentiate leaders' power needs as socialized versus personalized. In socialized charismatic leadership, leaders use their power to empower subordinates, in non-exploitative ways, and to motivate them to maximize gains for the organization without regard for their personal needs (O'Connor et al. 1995). These researchers claim that in personalized charismatic leadership, leaders use their power to further their own needs, often at the expense of the organization they belong to. Thus to differentiate between a good or bad transformational/transcendental leader one must look at how they use their power. This neat solution is hard to apply, because personalized charismatic leaders have a high ability to self-regulate and tend to conform to authority-based norms (O'Connor et al. 1995), and thus their motivations are hard to determine. To be responsible, a leader needs to consider the demands of all stakeholders and act accordingly, in a virtuous manner.

Endurance is a more complicated and controversial criterion for responsible leadership. It is the stamina to survive and persist in one's determination to lead despite challenging circumstances. It is related to drive, passion or hunger, despite challenges or what difficulties followers are presenting to the leader. All three must be present in the leadership process and action for the leadership to be considered responsible: "Leadership that is responsible is that which demonstrates, and is judged to demonstrate, effectiveness, ethics, and endurance (DePree 1989, 1997; Treviño et al. 2003; White-Newman 1993), and are necessary components of responsible leadership. What constitutes these three Es is determined by the constituency of the performance system in which the leadership occurs" (Lynham and Chermack 2006, p. 77). Performance is about executing an action and includes an underlying expectation that such action will be undertaken with due exercise of skill and care. According to Lynham and Chermack (2006), leadership is responsible with the reliance of agreed moral norms of the constituents, and is performance-based, aiming to achieve output agreed by the constituents.

Fifth, in RLP, there is an interdependent relationship between the considerations of constituency, a framework of responsibleness and domains of performance. A change in one element is expected to generate changes in the other two. The sixth proposition of RLP is that as the level of responsibleness of the leadership process increases, the system performance is expected to increase. The seventh and eighth propositions explain the importance of the constituency in the process of enacting RLP. The seventh stipulates that the existence of a constituency is a necessary condition for RLP. The eighth emphasizes the significance of the relationship between inputs of the constituency and outputs through multi-domain performance.

Taking the above eight propositions into consideration, Lynham and Chermack (2006) propose that RLP in action is more about leadership as a driver of a process rather than an outcome of performance. Within the RLP context, leadership needs to be understood as a "system-in-focus" in service to the broader performance system in the contextual environment. It means that the leadership system-in-focus will need to successfully negotiate and interact with the pressures and challenges of the broader cultural and performance systems. In this manner, RLP is a general theory explaining, and applicable to, a range of diverse contextual and performance environments.

Responsible Leadership for Relations (RLR)

In contrast to RLP, the attention in Responsible Leadership for Relations (RLR) shifts from performance to another dimension in the simple leadership process: understanding responsible leadership as a social-relational and ethical phenomenon, which occurs in social processes of interaction (Maak and Pless 2006, p. 99). These relationships are distributed to a broader set of stakeholders, not just between the leaders and their direct followers (such as employees). The contemporary leadership theories mostly focus on the relationship between the leaders and followers of an organization. The followers are usually subordinates residing inside the organization. Maak and Pless (2006) show "that leadership takes place in interaction with a multitude of followers as stakeholders inside and outside the corporation" (p. 99). Internal relationships include those among employees, managers and shareholders. External relationships include those among customers, competitors, community, creditors, suppliers, governments and environmental groups (see Fig. 5.3). The unique feature in this theory of responsible leadership is the emphasis on external relationships. Maak and Pless (2006) write, "In a stakeholder society, leadership has to reach beyond traditional leader-follower concepts. Here, the leader becomes a coordinator and a cultivator of relationships towards different stakeholder groups." (p. 100)

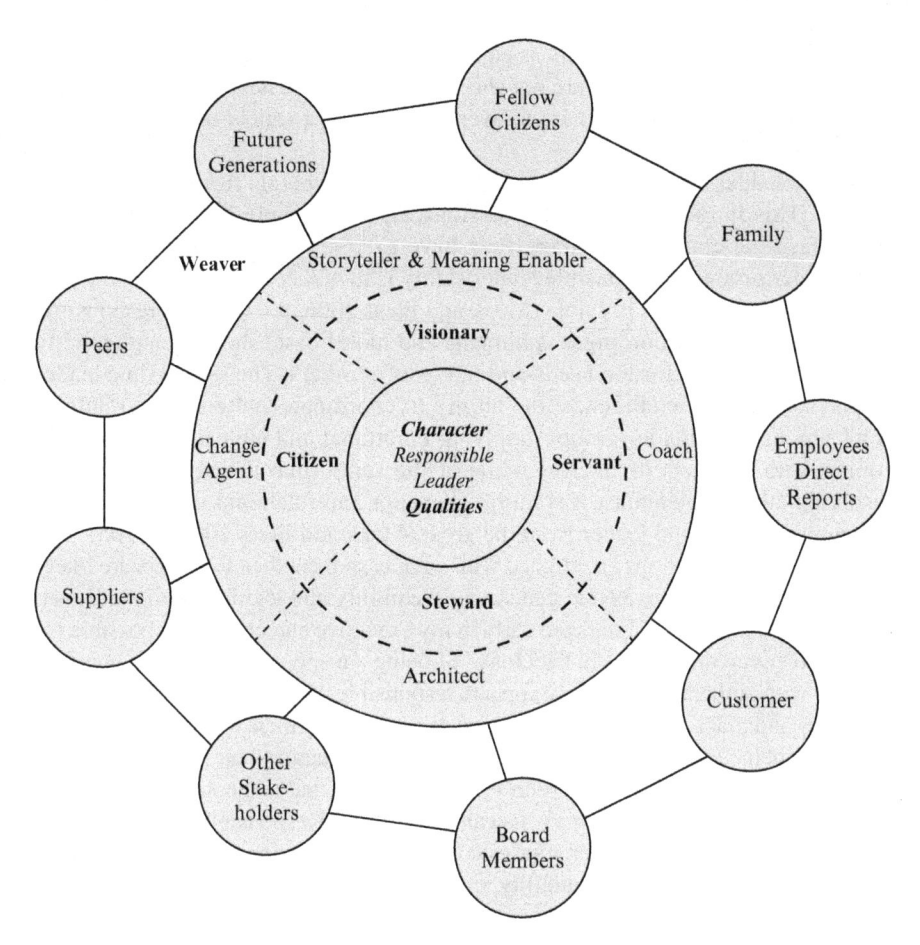

Fig. 5.3 Responsible leadership for relations theory (With kind permission from Springer Science+Business Media: Journal of Business Ethics, Responsible Leadership in a Stakeholder Society – A Relational Perspective, volume 66, 2006, p. 107, Maak, T. and Pless, N.)

Dame Anita Roddick can be seen in her pioneering leadership role at The Body Shop as an example of a responsible leader who embodied these key relationships (Pless 2011). Roddick championed the view of a responsible leader by creating a company that was firmly focused on benefiting society. Her first obligation was not to her shareholders, but rather to the wider stakeholder groups that she saw as vital to the success of her company. She concentrated on creating environmentally sustainable products, thus fulfilling her obligation to her customers. Roddick took her cause further by actively engaging with politicians in human-rights campaigns. In this way, she sought to build relationships with all stakeholders, and to use these relationships to advance the common good.

At the heart of RLR theory is the idea of the responsible leader (Maak and Pless 2006). Responsible leadership is about developing and maintaining healthy relationships with all stakeholders. A responsible leader's key task is to weave a web of inclusion and interact with others as equals. Maak and Pless (2006) note that Plato saw this quite clearly: people are not sheep and leaders are not shepherds (p. 104). Instead, leaders in this context are weavers, integrating a variety of people into the fabric of society.

All the leader's attributes are used to bring in viewpoints from diverse stakeholders. This introduces enormous tensions. If, for example, the directors want to increase the employees' salary, they have to take those funds from another stakeholder group. A responsible leader's duty is to make sure that these tensions are balanced as much as possible (Maak and Pless 2006, p. 104). The responsible leader seeks to act according to a humane and moral base, showing authenticity and integrity, caring for the needs and interests of others. The responsible leader displays relational intelligence: the ability to coordinate and cultivate relationships among stakeholder groups, applying emotional and ethical intelligence in coping with conflicts of interest while at the same time taking decisions and resolving ethical dilemmas. It is moral character and relational intelligence that distinguishes the good leader from the great (Maak and Pless 2006, p. 105).

A leader whose actions are aligned with what is spoken, then followers are likely to assign integrity to the leader, generating credibility and legitimacy to the leader. As recounted in Chap. 4, I realized early in my executive career that it is possible for leaders to "wrap themselves in the cloak" of being a responsible leader; in contrast, a leader with authenticity not only appears responsible, but actually acts in a responsible way and makes responsible decisions. It can happen, then, that one can observe from their behavior that one's leaders do not actually practice their principles. While one might be influenced to a certain extent to accept that someone is moral, over time it becomes obvious that this is just an appearance. Responsible leaders must be authentic and of good character, motivated by virtues and principles such as respect, care, honesty, accountability, humility, trust and active citizenship (Maak and Pless 2006).

Research on leadership has examined the significance of leadership roles sparingly, and the ethics of leadership to much a lesser degree. The focus has been on traits and personality attributes, leadership styles and the situational practice of leadership. However, according to Maak and Pless (2006, p. 107), leaders can play a dynamic mix of roles. A leader can act in a citizen-oriented role today, but as a servant tomorrow, next month a missionary, then suddenly drop everything and become a steward. Stewardship-based leaders are the custodians of values and resources, and can help shape their followers' values. Citizenship-based leaders are active and caring members of the community. Servant leaders do a great deal of groundwork behind the scenes to support their followers; they are hidden, rarely in the limelight—and are often worse off than their own followers. Visionary leaders provide inspiration and perspective to their followers with respect to a desirable future. Missionary leaders are the gatekeepers of values in their society, and must model these values in their behavior. Architect leaders build inclusive systems, processes and moral structures.

Within the framework of transformational leadership, change agents are responsible for initiating and supporting movement towards making the business value-conscious and sustainable in a stakeholder society (Maak and Pless 2006). Coaches place intensive emphasis on supporting their followers. Leaders who are storytellers and meaning enablers are the creators and communicators of moral experience and shared systems of meaning. Leaders tell stories, through which followers get an idea of the culture—the meaning system—of the organization. RLR will have a particular relevance to the thesis of this book and we will revisit this theory in Chap. 7.

Differences Between RLP and RLR

RLP and RLR have been developed partly in response to recent corporate scandals and increasing calls for top management to exhibit responsible action. These theories support an understanding of how responsible leadership can be used to mitigate future corporate scandals. Although the two theories have originated from the same catalyst, they differ on a number of points.

RLR views responsible leadership as a relationship-bound ethical phenomenon that occurs in the process of socially interacting with a range of stakeholders. It places the organization in the midst of key stakeholder groups and views the leader as a weaver of relationships between stakeholder groups. Contrary to the traditional views of a leader as a great individual leading a group of followers, RLR places the leader at the center of a web of inclusion that integrates relationships with all stakeholders. The role of the leader is thus to build and cultivate enduring and trusting relationships between related parties. RLP, on the other hand, is focused on performance rather than developing and maintaining relations. It views leadership as a system-in-focus, which in turn exists within a wider performance system. The leadership and performance systems are influenced by the internal and external contextual environmental systems. Leadership thus becomes a fluid and dynamic entity consisting of inputs, processes and outputs.

RLP is a multi-level approach to leadership that explains the varying organizational levels and the constant exchange of information and fluidity that occurs as a leader engages with stakeholders. The multiple levels in RLP's environmental system consist of cultural, technological, economic and legal systems. The performance system is where the internal performances of the organization are achieved.

RLR lists four key roles for a leader: citizen, steward, servant and visionary. Rather than listing the traits and characteristics of a leader, the theory contends that the relational aspects of roles to enact are more important. Leaders are able to undertake these roles by acting as a coach, architect, change agent and storyteller/ meaning enabler (Maak and Pless 2006). By weaving a web of inclusion, leaders can create dialogue through interaction, which promotes the development of sustainable relationships. On the other hand, RLP operates on three key units: considerations of constituency, a framework of responsibleness and domains of performance. All three units must operate and interact for RLP to manifest in action, and the goal is twofold: effectiveness and doing the right thing by the followers.

In RLP, the constituency consists of the stakeholders, and represents their level of authority and impact on decisions. They define the responsibleness of the leader: the ethical, effective and enduring resources that a leader will use to create social change. The performance level looks at mission, processes, subsystems and any individual performances that need recognition. In short, the critical difference between RLR and RLP theories is that the former is based on relations while the latter is based on performance.

Responsible Leadership and Social Capital

Maak's (2007) work on the link between responsible leadership and social capital remains the most comprehensive on the topic to date. This work linking the two concepts is discussed in detail here. Social capital has been explained as a resource generated from relationships between individuals, groups and organizations (Spellerberg 2001). For some, social capital is a micro level resource (e.g. Portes 1998) while for others it is a macro level property (Kawachi and Berkman 2000; Putnam 2000). Social capital refers to the stock of active connections and human networks such as trust, mutual recognition, shared values, beliefs and understandings (Adler and Kwon 2002). An investment in social relationships can generate returns in the marketplace, as active connections act to bind people, create mutual obligations and active communication networks. Maak (2007) notes that social capital consists of the social structures inherent to more or less institutionalized connections that facilitate active and beneficial relationships. Social capital stock depends on the likelihood for sociability, a capacity to form new associations and networks (Bullen and Onyx 1998). Maak (2007) argues that "social structures and resources, both internal and external to the organization…allow us to facilitate responsible action and…are inherent to more or less institutionalized relationships of mutual recognition" (p. 331). In the context of RLR, for example, it is through social capital that a leader acts as a weaver and broker (Maak 2007) to establish and nurture social relationships. According to Maak (2007), for responsible leadership to be enacted through social capital effectively, it must first meet several key elements.

The first element is "structure". The structure of social capital includes network ties, network configuration and adaptive organizations (Maak 2007). According to Nahapiet and Ghoshal (1998, cited in Maak 2007), "the fundamental proposition of social capital theory is that network ties provide access to resources" (p. 252). In other words, one's contacts determine who one is. It is in this context that the organization prepares its generation of social capital. Central to building social capital is the practice of two key concepts: bonding and bridging (Putnam 1993); these in turn are based on the concept of network configurations. There are network ties that sit within the structure of the social capital concept. Structure also includes bonding views, which are symmetrical ties that act as social glue that brings together desirable outcomes (Maak 2007, p. 333). These bonding views underscore warmer and more social ties. Bridging views, on the other hand, examine ties that are external to the organization and asymmetrical, enabling weaker and looser ties to make more stronger ties and provide access to resources. These views are important in social capital, as they help the leader combine and broker social relationships effectively. Additionally, bridging views are developed on the structural-hole theory (Burt 1997): the gap between people's knowledge. "The structural hole argument defines social capital in terms of the information and control advantages of being the broker in relations between people otherwise disconnected in social structure.... The structural hole is an opportunity to broker the flow of information between people and control the form of projects that bring together people from opposite sides of the hole" (Burt 1997, p. 340, cited in Maak 2007). In this case, the leader acts more from a point of centrality, as opposed to a top-down (or even a bottom-up) approach, which is critical for the functioning of the responsible leader from a centric point in the RLR theory. According to Maak (2007), from a central point of network ties, the responsible leader can be a broker of disconnected information, weaving differences together to create a common good or mutual understanding. This first element of structure in enacting responsible leadership through social capital is a critical step in the process, because if leaders cannot bring these disconnected views together and close the structural hole, they will fail to achieve either embeddedness throughout the organization or effective stakeholder engagement (Maak 2007).

The second element is "content". According to Maak (2007), content includes the cognitive dimension, which looks at the relationships and personal elements of social capital such as language and the stories used to create trusting relationships. He notes that it also includes the relational dimensions, which look at what values, norms and shared understandings can be used to connect stakeholders. Developing these parts of enacting social capital is troublesome, as the leader must first painstakingly establish with stakeholders the grounds for a win-win relationship, emphasizing the benefits of the proposed relationship. This is critical for the establishment, and subsequent durability and quality, of the relationship (Maak 2007).

Network ties are based on the concept that who one knows is who one is, and that one achieves success by knowing people. This links into the bonding view of the social-capital structure of network configuration, which emphasizes the desirability of both dense, symmetrical ties and the creation of relationships (see Maak 2007). The bonding view is one of a relationship between the individual and the community, and is part of a bottom-up tradition where relationships are formed through intrinsic goals and common agreements (see Adler and Kwon 2002).

The bridging view, on the other hand, is based on asymmetrical ties (Nahapiet and Ghoshal 1998; Maak 2007). Here various actors or groups of actors from varying contexts having equally different networks develop "bridges" to link their existing relationships. Maak (2007) notes that these bridges circumvent the weak ties that would ordinarily fill structural holes, leaving these holes for responsible leaders to use as a means to broker the flow of information between people who are disconnected within the social structure. In this way leaders can bring people together in the form of projects from opposite sides of the structural hole.

The third element in Maak's (2007) model of enacting responsible leadership through social capital model involves "opportunity, motivation and ability". With this element, he notes that the leader is in a position to work toward facilitating the critical relationships throughout the organization. Opportunity in this context refers to the leader creating an open, transparent environment of trust that provides stakeholders with the option to branch out. Motivation in this context refers to either the instrumental or normative means of motivation. Maak (2007) contends that "in contrast to the dominant assumption in social capital research that actors are driven by instrumental reasons in exploiting resources for individual benefit,...social capital as sketched above will emerge only if an organization and her leader engenders and communicates a moral motivation based on normative commitment to responsible business practices" (p. 338). This moral aspect of motivation differentiates the type of motivation required in generating responsible leadership through social capital. Abilities—"competencies and resources at the nodes of the network" (Adler and Kwon 2002, p. 26)—constitute the skills the leader requires in effectively navigating through the development and sustenance of the networks; how well the leader manages this task becomes relevant. Thus the third element represents a deeper level of understanding that leaders must have about their stakeholders.

Maak (2007) convincingly argues that it is by managing these elements that leaders can generate responsible leadership and realize the benefits of the mutual and active relationships, even as they increase the goodwill and reputation of a company and help reach performance targets. If these elements are not met, a leader runs the risk of important ties becoming redundant and having to allocate resources to reestablishing and nurturing the obsolete ties (Maak 2007). How social capital enacts responsible leadership can be demonstrated through its role in social innovation. The win-win relationships developed through painstaking work over the years can be put to good use by leaders through socially innovative initiatives.

Finally, Maak (2007) asserts that the advantage of implementing social capital is that it connects individuals and groups to different network systems, where goodwill and mutual connections are created and the stock of knowledge and information rises. This in turn generates greater quality and relevance of the information being captured and distributed. He notes that there is also an increase of reputation and goodwill with stakeholders as they perceive the leader as being responsible, trustworthy and authentic. This is critical to developing value-based relationships and stakeholder engagement particularly in the context of the thesis developed in this book. The strength in Maak's (2007) work on responsible leadership and social capital lies in the central as opposed to the hierarchical role of the leader, and its relational and structural dimensions, as they are directly embedded within the organization and amongst the stakeholders. Along with these, there must also be opportunity, motivation and the ability; technically one may try and do without one or the other, though one leads to the other, and all have continuous beneficial effects if implemented effectively.

In sum, better social capital helps develop the relationship the leader has with the stakeholders as partners, which increases the opportunities, abilities and motivation to create knowledge, successfully undertake projects and increase reputation and goodwill. With regard to RLP and RLR, social capital appears to more directly support the theory of RLR. Under RLR, the responsible leader is considered a weaver of relationships. Thus the concepts of bonding and bridging will have particularly useful roles to play when leaders attempt to successfully navigate the complex Asian century challenges and opportunities addressed later in the book.

Values and Responsible Leadership

Values are at the heart of responsible leadership; in business, values are generally discussed and applied through the realm of business ethics. Ethics involves asking: how should we live? From this perspective, ethics is practical. In simple terms, it deals with how we choose to act and do things in our professional and personal lives. Philosophers claim that ethics is normative; that it concerns about our reasoning on how we *should* act.

Business executives' actions speak for themselves: how they are living, how they are managing their organizations. But it is often difficult to understand—let alone predict—how a person would act in a given scenario. If a business executive were asked how they would act in an ethically challenging situation, they would give a socially desirable response. For example, if a business executive were asked whether she would harm a person to safeguard a pharmaceutical formula for curing cancer worth billions of dollars, she would likely say no. But there are inherent limitations to this kind of enquiry. What if the business executive were asked whether she would harm an individual who wanted to destroy the pharmaceutical formula so that there would be no hope of developing a cancer vaccine for the billions of cancer sufferers on the planet? The response could be expected to vary. The idea of others (cancer patients) dying because of the business executive's inaction might compel her to act, even if it meant harming an individual. Thus it's important to examine on what basis individuals enter into decisions in ethically challenging situations.

During the collapse of Enron, various stakeholders (including stockholders, employees, suppliers, Enron's accounting firm and its employees and families of employees) were harmed, and many of the Enron executives linked to the scandal have endured criminal and civil penalties, including imprisonment (Hartman et al. 2008). Why did the executives at Enron make the decisions that disastrously ended the company? The literature offers three decision-making models (Bazerman and Moore 2009). The most common is the rational decision-making model. If ethics are important in the business environment, the familiar common-sense, rational model of decision-making must have values embedded to make sure that the decisions are not only effective but ethical, and do right by the relevant stakeholders.

The rational model of making decisions, which stresses the process more than the content of the decisions themselves, is typically based on the following steps:

1. Identification of a problem. In this step, the decision-maker needs to be aware of a problem. In an ethical dilemma, ethical awareness should help the decision-maker identify the presence of a problem. A business executive without ethical awareness might not identify an ethical problem where another, acutely sensitive to ethically problematic situations, would.
2. Identification of decision criteria. In this step, a typical decision-maker examines the factors that are key to determining the best decision. For example, a decision to purchase a family house might incorporate an evaluation of public transport, neighborhood safety and the age of the houses in the neighborhood. When choosing a university, a prospective student might consider costs, fee structure, the duration of course or major, the exemptions the university would give based on prior qualifications and the quality of the institution. In this rational decision-making model, the typical decision-maker might allocate weight to these important criteria, consciously or subconsciously. In an ethically challenging situation, the decision-maker must evaluate the key criteria on which to prioritise the decision. This may involve issues like parties' competing interests, the likely outcome and harm the decision would cause and the principles the decision-maker should abide by.
3. Development of alternatives. Based on the first two stages, a rational decision-maker identifies alternatives that will help to solve the problem. The key question at this stage would be "Is there anything else that can solve my problem?" During this stage, the rational decision-maker again goes through an evaluation of the decision criteria to develop a suitable alternative. In an ethically challenging situation, an executive might ask, "What are the alternative ways of solving the ethical dilemma? What are the risks and harms associated with each of the alternatives to various stakeholders?"

Although the rational decision-making model explains a logical process for arriving at decisions, individuals do not always take the decision it recommends. For example, a student might ultimately select a particular university for study because of the extremely friendly emails the staff sent out, or how far the university staff went to accommodate the student's specific needs and requests. There can be a rational process, but that still doesn't explain every choice individuals make. Thus, in addition to the rational decision-making model, there are two other main styles of, or approaches to, decision-making (although it should be noted that in ethically challenging situations, any one or a mix of the three styles could come into play).

One is decision-making based on bounded rationality (Simon 1972), in which the decision-maker's logic is constrained by certain conditions; for example, by the information to which the decision-maker has access. A student might not have Internet access, and decides to enroll in the university based on personal visits to campuses; an investor is locked into using only one broker, and relies totally on their advice. Bounded rationality can limit the value in the decision-maker's preferences. This approach may not yield the best choice, but the decision-maker can make the best decision from the options they know about.

The other main type of decision-making is intuitive decision-making (Burke and Miller 1999). For example, a CEO may be provided with reports that clearly make option Y the rational and logical choice, but inexplicably, after sleeping over it, the CEO chooses option Z. Sometimes this is referred to as "gut-feel" decision-making, based on a hunch or intuition. Little is known about how intuition in decision-making works. Scholars have argued that intuitive decision-making is based on accumulated experience.

In decision making involving ethical dilemmas, values are useful to act as the foundation or driver to overcome ethical dilemmas. A values-based framework provides the foundation to reason before taking an action. Emotions, however, bring a different dimension to the issue. One important class of dilemmas is known as the trolley problem (see Klein 2011, p. 144); the category gets its name from a classic hypothetical dilemma of whether to switch a runaway trolley from a track with five workers onto a track containing only one worker. Most people will select the switch that saves five but kills one. The classic trolley problem could be made more complex (i.e. the footbridge problem) by adding the issue of forcing an innocent onlooker in front of the trolley to stall the trolley and save the five people. In this context, most individuals would not volunteer to act. The explanation is the conflict between reason and feeling. Reason demands from us that "one must die to save many", but when we are directly involved in the act, the sympathy we feel for the innocent bystander, or our unwillingness to personally assume culpability for the bystander's death, could override the judgment of reason.

Klein (2011) explains this point succinctly:

> The explanation just given is an example of a dual-track theory of moral cognition. Dual-track theories typically comprise four commitments: (1) that the apparent conflict in intuitions in dilemmas is genuine: so, for example, there is no way to reconcile our intuitions in the Trolley and Footbridge cases, (2) that the conflicting intuitions issue from two distinct cognitive mechanisms ("tracks"), (3) that the cognitive mechanisms differ in systematic ways, and these systematic differences explain why they occasionally issue conflicting intuitions, and optionally (4) that at least one of the tracks is systematically unreliable, and so the intuitions issuing from it are untrustworthy bases for moral theorizing (p. 144).

Although there has been much research on how and why people make decisions, research typically finds it hard to extract a reasonable, realistic response to the question of what someone would do in a particularly challenging ethical situation. When evaluating an ethical decision, one approach is to apply moral philosophies such as utilitarianism or Kantian ethics, but the intention of the decision-maker cannot be clearly known, other than by asking them. Consider for instance a company pioneering the relief efforts from a natural disaster. It cannot be known for certain whether any instrumental aspects, such as promoting the company image and reputation, crept into the decision-making process. However, in the case of corporate initiatives involving natural disasters, the corporate response could be more driven by "non-rationalized outpouring of action" (see Fernando 2007, 2010). Unlike in the case of normal day-to-day corporate events where leaders are able to develop a more rational and structured response, these initiatives could be taking the form of mostly emotional responses to a disaster, thus leaving little room for strategic maneuvering and thinking.

Thus one of the major challenges in responsible leadership and, for that matter, business ethics, is the issue of intentionality. The genuineness, or authenticity, of an action is extremely important in deciding whether the action is ethical or unethical. It is very easy for a leader to wear a cloak of ethicality. But it is very hard to see into the leader's actual intentions. A values-based inquiry into the problematic aspect of intention in decision-making in ethically challenging situations offers an important way out of this problem.

An example may help in considering the link between values and responsible leadership. A junior executive is ambitious to get to the top of the corporate ladder. To realize this ambition, the executive can work and live his or her life in a certain way. The inexperienced executive can be a loner, and not care about whose feet they're trampling, whose neck they're stomping on in their single-minded goal of climbing the corporate ladder as quickly as possible. But if they want to achieve their goals in a more humane manner, the value of ambition clashes with the value of respecting the other. In this manner, individuals' various values can have conflicting aims and can place them in ethically challenging situations. What are the sources of these values? What values do individuals actually live by and are driven by? On what basis do they prioritise values when these values conflict?

Perhaps acting on one's values is a good starting point for acting authentically. Freeman and Auster (2011) explore the interesting concept of authenticity in business ethics. In my former corporate life, I often struggled with living with an authentic life that both honored the profit-making goals of the corporation and allowed me to live honestly and with integrity in my personal and professional lives. When I was a senior corporate executive, a workaholic who was enjoying the materialistic comforts that come with a senior management job, I was neither happy nor content. I was lucky enough to be able to change what I was doing; now, as an academic, my values are aligned with what I want to be. Ambition and action are embedded extremely tightly. Life is more meaningful, and I have little or no conflict among the values in my life. In other words, I am living an authentic life. Authentic action involves the absence of instrumentalism. An authentic leader attempts to live and act according to his or her true self. Talk and action are closely aligned.

The Poetic Self

Based on Harold Bloom's (1997) contribution, Freeman and Auster (2011) introduced the idea of the poetic self, which is explained as a project of seeking to live authentically. The notion of the poetic self is not a pre-determined, stable phenomenon. It evolves; it changes; it is fluid and dynamic. The individual needs to acknowledge the regenerative capacity of the self and harness that capacity to lead an authentic life. In my view, Freeman and Auster's concept of the poetic self has tremendous potential to advance the field of values-based responsible leadership. Freeman and Auster (2011) view "being authentic" as a continuing process of conversation with several elements. Using authenticity and the notion of "Poetic Self", they develop a fascinating argument on how responsible leaders should be linked to their past, present and future. First, authenticity involves not only one's values, but one's history. When individuals are attempting to act authentically, they need to go back in time and consider and reflect on their actions. In similar circumstances, how did they act in the past; i.e., what is the precedent? Second, being authentic is influenced by the individual's relationships with others. Third, self is also about the future, the individual's aspirations. Freeman and Auster point out the futility of trying to live a value-laden life without aspiring to be something. When there are no aspirations, eventually one loses the passion for living. For example, once someone like an Olympian fulfills their early dreams by winning a gold medal, they often become "lost" until they find their next goal or ambition in life. Aspirations or ambitions are important for the poetic self.

For Freeman and Auster (2011), values are preferences at various levels (individual, organizational); a relatively stable set of permanent desires. However, they can actually be quite fluid, based on the individual's circumstances and stage of moral development. Even the word "preferences" has its limitations, because the question arises as to what is preferred, and to which standard. On what basis does one determine good versus bad values? Do good values become bad when used instrumentally, as in the case of a corporation helping tsunami victims for publicity and promoting its reputation?

When one considers that values essentially define who we are as people, how to act authentically could be a matter of how to know what one's values are (Freeman and Auster 2011). They note that, while for Aristotle the doing or the acting was more important, Plato emphasized that the act of knowing is all-important: individuals must know what their values are before they can act on them.

According to Freeman and Auster (2011), the underlying view of the self can be presented as a clay vessel that contains values. The self (vessel) does not show explicitly what the contents (values) are or whether the contents are good or bad. Only when the self "pours" out of the vessel can one "know" whether the contents, the values, are "good" or "bad". Similarly, consider the role of values in leadership. Effective leadership has no color in terms of its ethicality, its morality. So why are there good and bad values (the contents of the vessel)? Or why are individuals themselves (the vessel) good or bad?

Freeman and Auster (2011) point out two reasons an individual can be good or bad, based on a differentiation between internalism and externalism. Internalism is where actors do not know whether their actions are good or bad. When they engage in an unethical act, they think that they are being authentic, that they are, in fact, being true to themselves, because they don't have the capacity to know whether their values are good or bad. Take, for example, someone who has grown up in a city neighborhood with high levels of criminality. The aspiration of the young in these neighborhoods is often to emulate the feats of gang leaders, to acquire the possessions they have. The values that are created by the context, the way a person is recognised by the community as a valuable, contributing citizen to this particular community, mean that that person is not able to know whether their values are bad. "For the internalist, acting on one's values is problematic because of the uncertainty and complexity in the process of coming to know one's values" (Freeman and Auster 2011, p. 18). Problems arise with the internalist approach when individuals lack the ability to discern good or bad within themselves. For example, a contract killer might honor contract commitments honestly and authentically, within the context of honoring promises to their employer. They might be making an extremely professional job of it, but they are unable to understand that what they are doing is something bad.

Externalism is the opposite of internalism. Individuals know what their values are, but lack the motivation to carry them out. Problems arise with the externalist approach when considering motivation. Here the externalist cannot generate the effort needed to enact their values. In Stanley Milgram's (1974) experiment about obedience to authority (described in Chap. 3), a scientist in a white coat, someone in authority, instructs a volunteer to administer shocks to another person. Only one-third of participants had the motivation to say, "No, that's it, I'm not going to go through with this any further," and leave the experiment. Two-thirds of ordinary American participants did not have the motivation to leave. There are many examples that highlight the externalist problem: individuals know their values, what is correct, what is ethical, but do not have the motivation to stand up and say, "Right, this is it, and I'm going to blow the whistle" or "I'm not going to participate anymore in this unethical activity."

Freeman and Auster (2011) propose the notion of the "essential self" or "good self" as the starting point in overcoming the problems associated with internalism and externalism. They outline several techniques and processes for creating an "essential self". One of these is self-enlargement, which requires individuals to probe more deeply into their past to understand some of their history, which makes them unique. Use of reflexive practice is a key element in self-enlargement. The second element of creating a "good self" is self-connection, which recognizes that values and relationships in the past are embedded in current relationships. What someone is, why they love doing the things they do, is not because they chose to do those somewhere back in their youth. Freeman and Auster assert that the individual needs to ask what made them make those choices; only then will they know their own poetic, creative self. Third, to create the "good self", the individual needs to maintain the tension between the self and the Other. According to Freeman and Auster, if I am a subject, I have no value, no place, no worth, unless there is another subject. The self is nobody if there is no-one else recognizing that self. There is no self-worth if there is no Other. There is an inherent human need to connect with something else. This process gives individuals the appreciation that they exist, because someone is valuing them. It is an interchangeable, simultaneous process of mutual recognition. Many of the dilemmas in business ethics arise because of this constant tension between the self's interests and the Other's interests. As long as individuals are aware of this tension, that there is the Other who is demanding something different from what they would like to have—as long as they take that into account in their way of acting, living their lives and conducting their professions—then they are honoring this poetic self and being authentic to themselves. They are enlarging their self-capacity.

The other side of authenticity is when someone is disengaged from self. The more one does things that are inauthentic—totally different from what their values tell them is important—the more their two selves are, in a sense, ripping apart. Meditation and religious thought commonly refer to the concept of "centering oneself"; this refers to an individual trying to being who they essentially are. If one can picture oneself as connected to the past, the present and the future, the required three dimensions for creating the poetic self are covered. There also has to be the relationship with the Other. The self is informed by this relationship, and by the mutual relationships among the past, present and future (balancing one's values with aspirations or ambitions). Connection to the past is self-enlargement; connection to the present is self-connection. Between these two, Freeman and Auster (2011) bring in the Other, which can be the community as well as an individual or a group of individuals, and can, in some belief systems, be extended to all living beings. For example, a practicing Buddhist will extend the notion of the Other and the care of others to people and all sentient beings.

The argument so far has been that if one can think about self, and model oneself in this manner in an organizational context, responsible leaders have no reason not to act according to this model. In other words, they should be authentic to themselves, starting by looking at their past. How did they come to occupy their roles? What hard times did they suffer as junior executives? It's human nature to tend to forget the past once one reaches a position of power. Freeman and Auster (2011) assert that to be both authentic and responsible, leaders should be in constant touch with the past. As well, they should be in touch with the present, and with their aspirations and those of the organization, and should recognize and respect the tension between the self and the Other. Thus Freeman and Auster's (2011) concept of the poetic self requires one to take decisions based on the intersection of several elements: our values, our past, ourselves, our connections to others and our aspirations—ours and our community's. It champions the idea of concurrently developing self and community. The person engaged with the poetic self is improving not only the organization as self, but also the community as Other.

My research on CSR initiatives related to the Asian tsunami provides a good example (Fernando 2007, 2010). A number of Unilever executives said in interviews that they really missed what they did in the tsunami-relief efforts in the immediate aftermath of the tsunami, because they had felt good about going out to the affected areas and helping the victims, and now they didn't get the chance to do that. These executives had felt during the relief effort that they were more than just employees. When opportunities to volunteer gradually declined, these employees felt less capable; the self was deflated. Organizations need to recognize that giving employees the chance to volunteer enhances the individual self as well as the community (Fernando and Chowdhury 2010). The word "poetic" emphasizes the way an individual develops how they are going to act ethically. Developing the poetic self offers a process to act authentically: one can analyse, "Has the leader reflected on the past? Is there respect for the Other, the community? Does the leader have aspirations?" I add weight to Freeman and Auster's (2011) claim that the notion of a "poetic organization" certainly is a step forward to promoting a change of thinking in business from purely profit-oriented goals to a more common good driven agenda.

According to Freeman and Auster (2011), the notion of the poetic self in terms of responsible leadership means that leaders must think outside the box; that is not only safeguarding the wellbeing of followers but also assume responsibility for the stakeholders' needs. The ideal is to embrace everyone in an inclusive approach, and to do that with the common good in mind, not just the individual or organizational good. A poetic leader is someone who goes through that poetic-self process, connected to the past, present and future, and always has the presence of mind to acknowledge the tension between the self and the Other (including the community). A poetic leader will have similar characteristics to those of a responsible leader. It can even be suggested that a RLR-based leader will more closely approach the attributes of a poetic leader than will an RLP-based leader.

First, the servant role in RLR (Maak and Pless 2006) emphasizes the importance of the Other and the need to consider both the self and the Other in decision-making. Similarly, a strong attribute of a poetic leader would be the integration of the self and the Other in any action. Freeman and Auster (2011) say that the notion of poetic self promotes the idea of generating self and community concurrently; thus it is social and interconnected. Second, the meaning-enabling and storytelling attribute of the RLR approach is represented in poetic leaders through the self-enlargement process, one requirement of which is to connect with the past, the present and the future. In connecting with the past, for example, the important role of storytelling and meaning-enabling becomes clear. Third, the role of reflection in both RLR-based and poetic leaders can be seen. In RLR, building and maintaining relationships with all stakeholders is facilitated through reflective practice. For poetic leaders, reflective practice is essential to connect the past, present and future. Authentic behavior is the goal of poetic leaders, and being true to one's self is the starting point of the journey. Reflective practice serves as the vehicle through which the leader can center—be true to—their authentic self.

Links with Other Leadership Approaches

This section examines the extent of overlap between responsible leadership and other prominent leadership styles. Ethical leadership, shared leadership as well as several other leadership styles discussed earlier—including spiritual, servant and authentic leadership—have elements that overlap with responsible leadership.

Ethical Leadership

In essence, both ethical and responsible leadership promote doing the right thing in business. In Chap. 4, we noted that ethical leadership is about doing what is morally right, just and good. The ethical leader attempts to create awareness in followers to do the same (Ciulla 2013). Ethical leadership is concerned with the leader's ethical awareness, sensitivity and behavior (Ciulla 2013). In this sense, ethical leadership is more leader-centric. However, responsible leadership has a broader reach and relevance in business. For example, based on RLR, responsible leaders are driven to generate and maintain healthy stakeholder relationships both inside and outside the organization. They are considered weavers of relationships. And these responsible leaders can play several roles. For instance, a responsible leader's role can change between a citizen-oriented role to a servant role based on the situation. According to RLP theory as well, responsible leaders operate in different dimensions in a systems-driven context where ethics, effectiveness and endurance are at play. Thus, as opposed to ethical leaders, responsible leaders have to operate at several levels and with many different players in the environment.

Shared Leadership

Pearce et al.'s (2014) unique contribution linking shared leadership and responsible leadership deserves a detailed discussion here. They propose how responsible leadership can be supported by a shared leadership processes. Their thesis is based on both stakeholder perspectives and strategic/economic perspectives as integral elements to attaining sustainable corporate social responsibility. Pearce et al. (2014) use the stakeholder by engaging responsible leadership (i.e. in relation to the individual members and other stakeholders). Their view also addresses the strategic/economic perspective as without sustainable economic viability there can be little debate about stakeholders. They assert that shared leadership is recognised for promoting mutual accountability, and is a less contentious and provides more equal attention to the requirements of different stakeholders. As a result, they contend that shared leadership can lead to long-term performance that is linked to more socially responsible outcomes that meet both the stakeholder and strategic/economic views of responsible leadership (p. 285).

Shared leadership is defined as the serial emergence of both formal and informal leaders as a part of a simultaneous, ongoing, mutual influencing process (Yukl 2010, p. 504). Pearce and Sims (2001) define shared leadership as a form of leadership that projects from the team rather than from the formal leader. Shared leadership has also been defined more similarly to the general definition of leadership but specifying that the leadership sits with two or more members of a team rather than with a single leader (Bergman et al. 2012). Thus shared leadership can be any leadership approach, the only difference being the extent of "sharedness" in the leadership process. Shared leadership at its most extreme includes all the groups in the leadership process leading each other towards achieving organizational goals (Derue and Ashford 2010). When leadership is shared completely across behavioural influence approaches, across structural boundaries and across organisational forms, research shows profound positive organisational outcomes (Pearce et al. 2014).

According to Pearce et al. (2014), in the absence of shared leadership, irresponsibility is easier to grow and spread as a highly hierarchical and central influence from the more powerful to the less powerful. It does not have the benefit of integrating others views and balancing the power in the leadership process. Corporate social irresponsibility and irresponsible leadership have become a major challenge for management. In this context, Pearce et al. (2014) claim that shared leadership is not a substitute for a hierarchy, but that it is based on reciprocal relationships, and is systematically flexible and multi-layered.

They identify several forms of shared responsible leadership including rotated shared responsible leadership, integrated shared responsible leadership, distributed shared responsible leadership and comprehensive shared responsible leadership. There are specific shared leadership actions that leaders who are prone to central and hierarchical command can develop to avoid irresponsible leadership.

There are also different levels at which shared leadership can be effective. Individual-level actions must have the knowledge, skills and abilities for their tasks, have keen listening skills, show respect and be proactive leaders (Pearce et al. 2014, p. 284). These scholars point out that group-level actions include trust, transactive memory (i.e., knowing which member in the team possesses the required skills, abilities and knowledge), and driving creativity and innovation by clearly demonstrating team standards developed by critiquing each others' ideas. Organisational-level actions include using a common vision, engaging others in the vision, allowing knowledge to trump status, encouraging leadership and creating organisational support from the top. Pearce et al.'s (2014) contribution to the responsible leadership literature is novel and in the context of the Asian century where relationship building will be paramount, shared leadership is likely to have a key role to play in leading responsible organizations.

Spiritual Leadership

A clear consensus emerging among researchers is that a strong spiritual component is present in leadership (see Fernando 2011). In a chapter titled "Spirituality and Leadership" (2011), I observe that of all the leadership approaches, researchers most frequently link transformational leadership with spirituality. Compared with other leadership styles, the superior moral framework of transformational leadership is well established (Popper et al. 2000). As observed in Chap. 4, transformational leaders are considered more morally advanced than transactional leaders, as a transformational leader "raises the level of human conduct and ethical aspiration of both leader and led" (Burns 1978, p. 20). Transformational leaders are also more effective in inspiring followers to move from basic needs to needs for achievement and self-actualization (Bass 1995, p. 467). However, the moral basis of transformational leadership has been questioned. For example, Kanungo (2001) argues that transformational leadership lacks a clear ethical justification. Fernando et al. (2009, p. 528) note that "unless leaders are able to transform everyone and create absolute unanimity of interests, transformational leadership simply produces a majority will that represents the interests of the strongest faction" (citing Kanungo 2001, p. 258). That type of leadership will not be able to ensure the rights of the weak against the self-interest of the strong. Although transformational leadership appears to be linked to spirituality, researchers into workplace spirituality claim that there is a void in the leadership literature concerning a leadership style based on spiritual motivation that is moral and authentic (Fernando et al. 2009).

In this context, there are several ways in which spiritual leadership and responsible leadership intersect. At a theoretical level, spiritual leadership is focused on developing the spiritual well-being of the leader and the follower "through calling and membership, to create vision and value congruence across the individual, empowered team, and organization levels and, ultimately, to foster higher levels of organizational commitment and productivity" (Fry and Cohen 2009, p. 269). Fry (2003) writes that spiritual leadership is about developing spiritual survival through calling and membership. Spiritual leadership represents values, attitudes and behaviors required to intrinsically motivate oneself and others. The purpose of spiritual leadership is to create alignment between the vision and values in a team at the individual level, with a view to promote high levels of organizational commitment and productivity (Fry 2003). Thus two key attributes of spiritual leadership can be identified.

The first is *connection*. Spiritual leadership can be enacted through a connection with self, others and community. The second is *shared vision*. To enact spiritual leadership, a desire to motivate one's self and others to create a sense of community in the organizational culture is critical (Fernando 2011). When the organizational culture is based on a strong sense of shared community, popular management practices such as being engaged in meaningful charity, benevolence, social inclusion, global-citizen initiatives and corporate social responsibility practices become more authentic. A strong sense of shared community in an organization can reduce the likelihood of leaders irresponsibly exploiting their power to boost their egos and engage in self-interested activities, rather than engaging in initiatives that satisfy a broader set of stakeholders' needs.

Both these attributes are central to responsible leadership as well. Responsible leaders need to make connections with stakeholders to develop and maintain sound relationships for the benefit of the organization. These leaders also need to create a shared sense of their vision for the business both within and outside the organization. For some scholars, responsible leadership lacks the transcendental and faith-based element that they attribute to religion-based spiritual leaders.

At a practical level, the link between spiritual and responsible leadership can be seen in the often-cited case of Canadian Robert Ouimet, the chairman and CEO of Holding OCB Inc., Cordon Bleu International and Ouimet-Tomasso, a producer and marketer of frozen food products in Canada. Ouimet is recognized by spiritual leadership scholars for drawing on spirituality to achieve a balance between his organizations' responsibility to each employee and the responsibility to make profits. Ouimet (2003) believes that the two responsibilities are constantly in conflict, but that both are fundamental to the daily operation of his businesses.

Servant Leadership

Responsible leadership includes several aspects of servant leadership. In Chap. 4, we noted that Greenleaf (1977) describes servant leadership in terms of a process beginning with the "natural feeling that one wants to serve first", and next, by an aspiration to lead (p. 12). Servant leadership, like responsible leadership, is based on the idea that leadership is about the leader's constituencies (Pless and Maak 2011). We have seen that one of the roles of a responsible leader in RLR theory is to be a servant. Serving the constituents and developing relationships in that sense are expected from responsible leaders. In the systems-driven RLP theory, the constituency has a special role to play in determining what is ethical behavior. The constituents define what is moral, according to the negotiations of the individuals who form that constituency. Thus, in essence, at a fundamental level, through the focus on constituents, there are similarities between servant leadership and responsible leadership.

Authentic Leadership

According to Pless (2011), both authentic leadership and responsible leadership are concerned with the positive and negative organizational impact of leadership. This is possible through by assisting followers to develop meaning at work, leading to improved well-being. The fostering of followers' meaning-making at work leads to long-term growth and value-creation for stockholders. Responsible leadership introduces a notion that is broader than the usual economic-outcome goals. In addition to these goals, it adds the elements of value and social capital of internal and external stakeholders to seek positive social change. The entire idea is built on the purpose of effecting social change (Maak and Pless 2006). When leaders define meaningful work for their employees/followers, there are positive organizational outcomes; for example, people who have meaning at work are more productive than those who do not.

Conclusion

This chapter has considered theories of responsible leadership as a way to develop leadership responses to the Asian century challenges. In a field that is still in its infancy, most of the theory is prescriptive and based on claims; very little has been verified empirically. However, RLR and RLP theories offer solid foundations to further develop the field. These two theories capture the essence of responsible leadership and provide a framework to develop a thesis to address leadership challenges in the Asian century. It is suggested that future research should focus on process issues as the process that responsible leaders use to reach consensus is inconsistent with some leadership theory (see Doh and Quigley 2014). Research is yet to reveal the effectiveness of responsible leaders. More is yet to be known about how responsible leaders manage organizational processes, and perhaps more importantly, how they communicate with all stakeholders, and balance the tension between responsibility and profit-making. Future research also need to examine the best practices of responsible leaders in managing the flow of knowledge with critical stakeholders and how they prioritise stakeholder demands. The next chapter will move from theory to examining the practice of responsible leadership.

References

Adler, P. S., & Kwon, S.-W. (2002). Social capital: Prospects for a new concept. *Academy of Management Review, 27*(1), 17–40.
Bass, B. M. (1995). Theory of transformational leadership redux. *The Leadership Quarterly, 6*(4), 463–478.
Bazerman, M. H., & Moore, D. A. (2009). *Judgment in managerial decision making*. Hoboken: Wiley.
BBC. (2013). *Arab uprising: Country by country*. Available at http://www.bbc.com/news/world-12482315. Accessed 21 Aug 2014.
Bergman, J. Z., Rentsch, J. R., Small, E. E., Davenport, S. W., & Bergman, S. M. (2012). The shared leadership process in decision-making teams. *The Journal of Social Psychology, 152*(1), 17–42.
Bloom, H. (1997). *The anxiety of influence: A theory of poetry*. New York: Oxford University Press.
Bullen, P., & Onyx, J. (1998). *Measuring social capital in five communities in NSW: A practitioner's guide*. Sydney: Management Alternatives Pty Limited.
Burke, L. A., & Miller, M. K. (1999). Taking the mystery out of intuitive decision making. *The Academy of Management Executive, 13*(4), 91–99.
Burns, J. M. (1978). *Leadership*. New York: Harper & Row.
Burt, R. S. (1997). The contingent value of social capital. *Administrative Science Quarterly, 42*, 339–365.
Cardona, P. (2000). Transcendental leadership. *Leadership & Organization Development Journal, 21*(4), 201–207.
Ciulla, J. B. (2001). Carving leaders from the warped wood of humanity. *Canadian Journal of Administrative Sciences/Revue Canadienne des Sciences de l'Administration, 18*(4), 313–319.
DePree, M. (1989). *Leadership is an art*. New York: Bantam Doubleday Dell Publishing Group. Inc.

Depree, M. (1997). *Leading without power*. Holland: Jossey-Bass.
Derue, D. S., & Ashford, S. J. (2010). Who will lead and who will follow? A social process of leadership identity construction in organizations. *Academy of Management Review, 35*(4), 627–647.
Doh, J. P., & Quigley, N. R. (2014). Responsible leadership and stakeholder management: Influence pathways and organizational outcomes. *The Academy of Management Perspectives, 28*(3), 255–274.
Donaldson, T. (1982). *Corporations and morality*. Englewood Cliffs: Prentice-Hall.
Donaldson, T. (1989). *The ethics of international business*. New York: Oxford University Press.
Fernando, M. (2007). Corporate social responsibility in the wake of the Asian tsunami: A comparative case study of two Sri Lankan companies. *European Management Journal, 25*(1), 1–10.
Fernando, M. (2011). A social innovation based transformative learning approach to teaching business ethics. *Journal of Business Ethics Education, 8*, 119.
Fernando, M., & Chowdhury, R. M. (2010). The relationship between spiritual well-being and ethical orientations in decision making: An empirical study with business executives in Australia. *Journal of Business Ethics, 95*(2), 211–225.
Fernando, M., Beale, F., & Geroy, G. (2009). The spiritual dimension in leadership at Dilmah Tea. *Leadership & Organization Development Journal, 30*(6), 522–539.
Filatotchev, I., & Nakajima, C. (2014). Corporate governance, responsible managerial behavior, and corporate social responsibility: Organizational efficiency versus organizational legitimacy? *The Academy of Management Perspectives, 28*(3), 289–306.
Financial Review. (2014). *'Emperor' after the fall: The story of Ray Williams and HIH*. Available at http://www.afr.com/news/emperor-after-the-fall--the-story-of-ray-williams-and-hih-20140116-iy96c. Accessed 3 Feb 2015.
Freeman, R. E. (2004). The stakeholder approach revisited. *Zeitschrift für Wirtschafts- und Unternehmensethik, 5*(3), 228.
Freeman, R., & Auster, E. (2011). Values, authenticity, and responsible leadership. *Journal of Business Ethics, 98*(1), 15–23.
Friedman, M. (1974, March). Letter on monetary policy. *Federal Reserve Bank of St. Louis Review*.
Fry, L. W. (2003). Toward a theory of spiritual leadership. *The Leadership Quarterly, 14*(6), 693–727.
Fry, L. W., & Cohen, M. P. (2009). Spiritual leadership as a paradigm for organizational transformation and recovery from extended work hours cultures. *Journal of Business Ethics, 84*(2), 265–278.
Hartman, L. P., DesJardins, J. R., & MacDonald, C. (2008). *Business ethics: Decision-making for personal integrity and social responsibility*. New York: McGraw-Hill/Irwin.
Kanungo, R. N. (2001). Ethical values of transactional and transformational leaders. *Canadian Journal of Administrative Sciences, 18*(4), 257–265.
Kawachi, I., & Berkman, L. (2000). Social cohesion, social capital, and health. In *Social epidemiology* (pp. 174–190). New York: Oxford University Press.
Klein, C. (2011). The dual track theory of moral decision-making: A critique of the neuroimaging evidence. *Neuroethics, 4*(2), 143–162.
Knights, D., & O'Leary, M. (2006). Leadership, ethics and responsibility to the other. *Journal of Business Ethics, 67*(2), 125–137.
Lynham, S. A., & Chermack, T. J. (2006). Responsible leadership for performance: A theoretical model and hypotheses. *Journal of Leadership & Organizational Studies, 12*(4), 73–88.
Maak, T. (2007). Responsible leadership, stakeholder engagement, and the emergence of social capital. *Journal of Business Ethics, 74*(4), 329–343.
Maak, T., & Pless, N. M. (2006). Responsible leadership in a stakeholder society–a relational perspective. *Journal of Business Ethics, 66*(1), 99–115.
Milgram, S. (1974). *Obedience to authority*. New York: Harper & Row.
Nahapiet, J., & Ghoshal, S. (1998). Social capital, intellectual capital, and the organizational advantage. *Academy of Management Review, 23*(2), 242–266.

References

New York Times. (2006). *Enron founder dies before sentencing*. Available at http://www.nytimes.com/2006/07/05/business/05cnd-lay.html?_r=0. Accessed 2 Aug 2014.

O'Connor, J., Mumford, M. D., Clifton, T. C., Gessner, T. L., & Connelly, M. S. (1995). Charismatic leaders and destructiveness: An historiometric study. *The Leadership Quarterly, 6*(4), 529–555.

Ouimet, J. (2003). *The golden book: Reconciliation of human well-being with productivity and profits* (S. R. Bigham, Translated from the French). Montreal: Ouimet-Cordon Bleu Inc.

Pearce, C. L., & Sims, H. P. (2001). Shared leadership: Toward a multi-level theory of leadership. *Advances in Interdisciplinary Studies of Work Teams, 7*, 115–139.

Pearce, C., Wassenaar, C., & Manz, C. (2014). Is shared leadership the key to responsible leadership? *The Academy of Management Perspectives, 28*(3), 275–288.

Pless, N. M. (2007). Understanding responsible leadership: Role identity and motivational drivers. *Journal of Business Ethics, 74*(4), 437–456.

Pless, N. M. (2011). Women leading a responsible global business: A study of dame Anita Roddick, founder of the Body Shop. In P. Werhane & M. Painter-Morland (Eds.), *Leadership, gender and organisation* (pp. 245–258). Dordrecht: Springer.

Pless, N. M., & Maak, T. (2011). Responsible leadership: Pathways to the future. *Journal of Business Ethics, 98*(S1), 3–13.

Popper, M., Mayseless, O., & Castelnovo, O. (2000). Transformational leadership and attachment. *The Leadership Quarterly, 11*(2), 267–289.

Portes, A. (1998). Social capital: Its origins and applications in modern sociology. *Annual Review of Sociology, 24*(1), 1–24.

Putnam, R. D. (1993, Spring). The prosperous community. *American Prospect, 7*, 35–42.

Putnam, R. D. (2000). *Bowling alone: The collapse and revival of American community*. New York: Simon and Schuster.

Simon, H. A. (1972). Theories of bounded rationality. *Decision and Organization, 1*, 161–176.

Spellerberg, A. (2001). *Framework for the measurement of social capital in New Zealand*. Wellington: Statistics New Zealand.

Stahl, G., & de Luque, M. S. (2014). Antecedents of responsible leader behavior: A research synthesis, conceptual framework, and agenda for future research. *The Academy of Management Perspectives, 28*(3), 235–254.

Treviño, L. K., Brown, M., & Hartman, L. P. (2003). A qualitative investigation of perceived executive ethical leadership: Perceptions from inside and outside the executive suite. *Human Relations, 56*(1), 5–37.

Waldman, D. A., & Balven, R. M. (2014). Responsible leadership: Theoretical issues and research directions. *Academy of Management Persepectives, 28*, 224–234.

White-Newman, J. (1993). The three e's of leadership: A model and metaphor for effective, ethical, and enduring leadership. In *The annual conference of the Communication and Theater Association of Minnesota*.

Yukl, G. A. (2010). *Leadership in organizations*. Upper Saddle River: Pearson.

Chapter 6
Responsible Leadership in Practice

Introduction

This chapter will move beyond theories of responsible leadership to examine how responsible leadership can be enacted through a range of organizational processes. Responsible leadership action in various spheres of human endeavour could address some of the key global issues of the Asian century. In our economic pursuits, the threat of major global financial crises similar to the 2007/2008 global financial crisis remains. In managing our environment, nations have been called upon to mitigate their emission levels. The Chinese and US governments' agreement in November 2014 to reduce emission levels was a step taken in the right direction that directly impacts leading responsible business organizations. Climate change adaptation is vital and remains an opportunity for responsible leaders to address. For example, a single cow emits as much CO_2 in to the environment as a normal car during a year. There are significant opportunities to develop alternative sources to satisfy our meat-eating habits so that cattle farming is not necessary to fulfil our dietary needs. Water crises will increasingly feature prominently as a major challenge for responsible leaders due to mismanagement and intense competition for already scarce water resources. The river Nile has been Egypt's water resource for centuries, but originates in Ethiopia. Already China is accused of moving into Ethiopia with significant investments to build damns to exploit the Nile's water resources (Nisman 2012). These global issues point to the need for responsible leaders to develop well governed, fiscally healthy and more importantly sustainable organizations. In this chapter, we will examine the opportunities leaders have to enact responsible leadership. First we will look at what decision-making options are available for responsible leaders.

Responsible Decision-Making Options for Leaders

Based on Lowry's (2006) continuum of ethical choices for managers, a model can be developed to capture the range of leaders' options in acting responsibly (Fig. 6.1).

At one end of the continuum is the choice of "quietism"; for example, when a manager chooses not to act due to the pressure of organizational strategic decision-makers. Even when leaders themselves see quietism as irresponsible, they are forced to internalise organizational values and activity. The assumption in this level of responsible choice is that if the leader is not with the organization, then they are against it. Lowry (2006) cites Fisher (2000, p. 69):

> At this stage, in the dialectic of inactivity, tolerating an act while retaining the right to let your true feelings show, through the whispered aside, is not acceptable. Neither is an agreement to disagree and say nothing about the subject. The failure to take action against an unethical act must be reinforced by committing oneself to the act. The threat, real or implied, is that if they do not volunteer a positive compliance they will be punished (p. 177).

The second form of responsible choice, "neutrality" is a less extreme form of inactivity "since there is no requirement to internalise or offer voluntary positive compliance to an unethical act" (Lowry 2006, p. 177). A person at this point is still responsibly mute, still not taking any action. They are tolerating the irresponsible act, yet are keeping a bit of distance: fear of consequences may keep them from taking a stand, although this distance might, for example, take the form of them making jokes or sarcastic comments about the situation. In these instances, the leader decides to be mute due to a range of reasons such as lack of political power and fear of reputational harm.

The third level of responsible choice is the situation where a leader may accept irresponsible organizational activity, but will take steps to show disagreement in the workplace. In this case, leaders are forced to accept the business case for organizations to behave irresponsibly, but are still resolved to show personal disagreement with those actions to others at a personal level. In this instance, the neutral leader

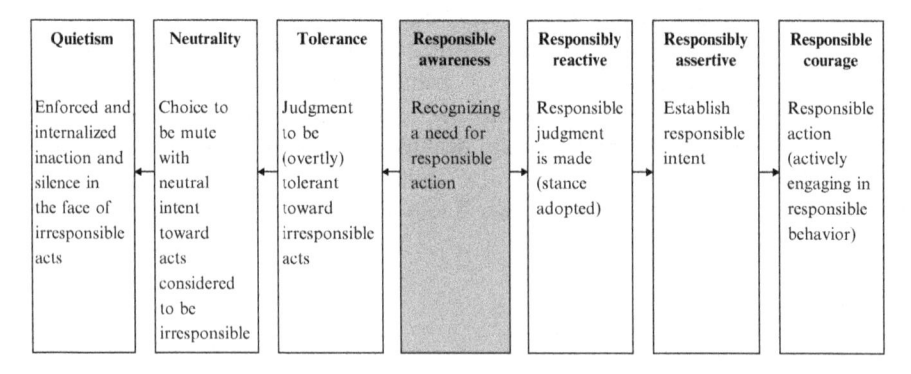

Quietism	Neutrality	Tolerance	Responsible awareness	Responsibly reactive	Responsibly assertive	Responsible courage
Enforced and internalized inaction and silence in the face of irresponsible acts	Choice to be mute with neutral intent toward acts	Judgment to be (overtly) tolerant toward irresponsible acts considered to be irresponsible	Recognizing a need for responsible action	Responsible judgment is made (stance adopted)	Establish responsible intent	Responsible action (actively engaging in responsible behavior)

Fig. 6.1 Continuum of Responsible Decision-Making Options for Leaders (Adapted with kind permission from SAGE Publications, Lowry, D. (2006). HR managers as ethical decision-makers: Mapping the terrain. *Asia Pacific Journal of Human Resources, 44*(2), 171–183)

gives way to needs of the bureaucratic context, which leads to a "separation or bracketing of personal values from the public domain" (Lowry 2006, p. 178).

According to the model, the responsibly active leader consciously attempts to address any deviation between the private and public domain. Using the case-study findings of Watson (2003), Lowry (2006) proposes that there are two options for responsible action. The first is responsible reactivity, where the manager may opt to act "because of a need to respond to pressures from the various resource-dependent constituencies with which their organization exchanges" (p. 178). In this case, the public domain is wider than the domain of the "interior" organization. Being responsibly reactive is to take a stand after the situation's negative consequences have already begun.

The next option that is open for leaders to act responsibly is "ethical assertiveness". In this case, there is no separation between the public and private domains. Being responsibly assertive is to be proactive: trying to prevent, not just react to, negative consequences. Leaders at Kohlberg's (1958) principled level of moral development, those who cannot tolerate an irresponsible action but must act to prevent or stop it, are at this point on the continuum. Responsibly assertive leaders are capable of successfully developing their private moral issues into a form of a business argument, and then negotiating on those issues. Leaders at the responsibly assertive extreme in the continuum potentially use various rationales for arriving at responsible decisions appropriate for different contexts. According to Lowry (2006), at this end of the continuum, the responsibly assertive leader is likely to demonstrate moral courage: "the capacity to do what one judges is ethically called for in spite of one's instinctive reaction to the perceived dangers and difficulties in which such action will result" (Mahoney 1998, p. 189). These leaders are also likely to show confidence, patience and perseverance in conducting their negotiations, and make their way to the last option, responsible action through showing courage.

These decision-making options can explain the challenges that responsible leaders have, for example, when sacrificing short-term profits for long-term climate change mitigation and adaptation measures. Taking responsible action through RLR or RLP processes would mean that a leader could take courageous responsible action on climate change that involves all stakeholders. In the Asian century, with cut-throat competition in global markets, however, this is easier said than done. At a pragmatic level, adopting an inclusive approach where there is a win-win outcome for all concerned is hard to achieve. The rest of the chapter presents some of the approaches available to make this outcome realistic. CSR is at the heart of these approaches.

Corporate Social Responsibility (CSR) and Responsible Leadership

The last three decades have continued to witness an intense discussion on the relationship between society and business (see Fernando 2007, 2010; Basu and Palazzo 2008; Godfrey and Hatch 2007; Jamali 2007; McWilliams et al. 2006). A

Time magazine special issue on what makes people good and evil highlighted that "[w]e face our biggest challenges not when we are being called on to behave ourselves within our family, community or workplace, but when we have to apply the same moral care to those outside our tribe" (Kluger 2007). An individual's morality and ethics are easier to discern and practice within the confines of their own family, group, culture or nationality. But when it comes to showing the same care to a stranger that they show to family members, there can be conflicts. Some scholars hold that social responsibility is something that an organization owes not just to its stockholders, but to other people as well. The duties emanating from the implicit social contract that exist between organizations and society may be represented and discharged through CSR.

Bowen is credited with one of the earliest definitions of CSR: as "obligations of businessmen to pursue those policies, to make those decisions, or to follow those lines of action which are desirable in terms of the objectives and values of our society" (1953, p. 44). Interest in CSR has exponentially grown so much so that it has become the public face of business (Lee 2008; Gibbons 2014). The purpose of CSR was to draw attention to the social impact of such rapid economic expansion. Several studies (e.g. Davis 1960; Frederick 1960; McGuire 1963; Walton 1967; Sethi 1975; Carroll 1979, 1991, 1994, 1999; Drucker 1984; Wartick and Cochran 1985; Swanson 1995; Moon et al. 2005; Scherer and Palazzo 2007; Basu and Palazzo 2008) demonstrate that organizations need to play a more engaging role for the common good of the society. The practice of CSR has been promoted through the implementation of CSR strategies in marketing, risk management and gaining strategic competitiveness (Murray and Montanari 1986; Porter and Kramer 2006; Varadarajan and Menon 1988). Yet, Mather et al. (2011) observe tensions between social justice considerations and profit-maximising objectives (see Gibbons 2014).

According to Nobel laureate Milton Friedman (1996), a company has its primary obligation to its stockholders; this is the classical view of corporate responsibility. The more Asian century view is that an organization needs to engage with its community, environment, supply chain and local and overseas communities. One of the classic debates in the academic literature is how a company can satisfy each of the stakeholders in its social responsibility endeavours. For example, to satisfy the community would mean to reduce the available dividend paid to stockholders. To pay the highest dividend to stockholders may mean short-changing employees in terms of higher salaries and working conditions. If a board of directors is planning to allocate a social responsibility budget of $2 million, they need to decide how they want to allocate this budget among various stakeholder initiatives, even though they are susceptible to the feeling of wanting to hold onto the money rather than give it away. Several scholars have proposed frameworks for the way to allocate these funds based on various social responsibility types. Some of these typologies include legal (i.e., the need to engage with a certain level of community involvement as mandated by law); philanthropic (i.e., voluntary initiatives that go beyond what is mandated by law); and ethical (i.e., where initiatives are linked to a particular ethical or moral philosophy). The CSR literature includes many such typologies.

Approaches to CSR[1]

Among the various approaches to explain and understand CSR, here I present four approaches. One of the first academic conceptions of social responsibility was put forth by Archie Carroll, a pioneering academic in the area of the social responsibility of corporations. In his now seminal article "The Pyramid of Corporate Social Responsibility: Toward the Moral Management of Organizational Stakeholders" (1991), Carroll depicts an organization's social responsibilities as a pyramid. At the bottom is economic responsibility: an obligation to make profits, pay employees, look after suppliers and so on. Next is legal responsibility, which represents obligations owed to society to obey laws; for example, those governing emission levels or the fair treatment of employees. Ethical responsibility is above that; according to Kant, intention does matter, and instrumentality (i.e., behaving in a seemingly ethical manner merely to obtain a benefit) is insufficient to meet this responsibility. Utilitarians, on the other hand, would argue that as long as the consequences are beneficial to the majority, an action is deemed ethical. Hence how a leader discharges his or her duties in relation to a complex issue like climate change, where the obligation to future generations conflicts with the obligation to stockholders to generate the highest profit in the short term, could determine the level of ethical responsibility. Discretionary responsibility is even nobler than ethical responsibility. There is no obligation to discharge discretionary responsibilities, but they come from the heart with no self-interest, such as when multinational corporations helped tsunami victims after the 2004 Asian Boxing Day tsunami. There are other, more recent approaches to CSR that reflect the changing times and demands of business activity.

Another typology of CSR is from Basu and Palazzo (2008). They use the concept of a CSR character based on the language-pragmatic reasoning of organizational sensemaking. Proposing that the CSR character reveals into cognitive, linguistic and conative dimensions, Basu and Palazzo attempt to explain how a company thinks CSR, behaves and talks CSR. In the first dimension, Basu and Palazzo (2008) argue that companies have mindsets, depicting orientations (or perceptions) of what is to be a responsible corporate. One such orientation in the cognitive dimension is the identity orientation. It is based on Brickson's (2005) claim that similar to individuals, organizations may show individualistic, relational and collectivistic identity orientations. According to Brickson (2005, 2007), the individualistic identity orientation demands that organizations perceive itself with a distinct entity whereas in the relational orientation, organizations are attempting to understand its partnerships (dyadic connections), and in the collectivistic orientation, organizations are attempting to work within a larger collective.

---

[1] This section includes an updated version of ideas first presented in Fernando and Almeida (2012).

Basu and Palazzo's (2008) thesis integrates the stakeholder approach into the corporate sensemaking process. They work on the assumption that "cultural definitions determine how the organization is built, how it is run, and, simultaneously, how it is understood and evaluated" (Suchman 1995, p. 576). Basu and Palazzo (2008) argue that external demands in the environment force organizations to satisfy different constituent needs based on pragmatic legitimacy. Legitimation strategies that aim for pragmatic legitimacy are "purposive, calculated, and frequently oppositional" (Suchman 1995, p. 576).

Basu and Palazzo (2008) also propose different postures of corporations—defensive, tentative and open—as paths to corporate responsibility (see also Zadek 2004). In defensive posturing, Basu and Palazzo (2008) outline that organizations attempt to cover up mistakes and/or mislead stakeholders (as in James Hardie). Shifting attention from firm's issues to other issues is a common tactic in defensive posturing. But a tentative posture is where when an organization shows both established behavior and new behaviors when confronted with emerging issues. On the other hand, an open posture adopts a more positive, learning approach with a long-term strategic view of CSR.

Basu and Palazzo (2008) also propose that organizations use various forms of justifications when confronted with corporate responsibility issues. The most common would be economic justifications—using economic reasons to justify various corporate actions. Thus typical reasoning in these types of arguments would include that organizations have a duty to maximise profits and achieve business success. These goals—argued in the classical Friedman approach—are beneficial to society (e.g. providing employment). In legalistic justifications, complying with the law is regarded as adequate for initiating corporate responsibility (e.g. meeting legal emission levels). Organizations that resort to scientific justifications use scientific or technical language to justify corporate actions while those organizations using ethical justifications refer to moral frameworks.

The third approach is based on corporate governance and institutional theory. Filatotchev and Nakajima (2014) develop a novel idea based on the interrelationships between organizations' corporate governance, responsible leadership and CSR. Accordingly, the role of corporate governance in an organization is an important precursor of strategic decisions on CSR. They claim that an organization's choice of a specific CSR approach is not random, and that it could be based on a set of corporate governance factors (Filatotchev and Nakajima 2014). In the corporate governance literature, the call is for business leaders to take strategic CSR decisions using the governance mechanisms available at the organizational level. These authors note that more research is required on the role of governance and control systems in CSR strategy and its implementation. Corporate governance factors underlie both financial and strategic controls (Aoki 2001).

Effective corporate governance relies on various mechanisms to ensure that leaders and managers safeguard the interests of stakeholders, and to hold them accountable for actions on the protection, generation and distribution of wealth of the organization (Aguilera et al. 2008). It is thought of as a set of organizational practices geared to monitoring and if required, limiting managerial discretion (Filatotchev and Nakajima 2014, p. 284).

Based on their corporate governance argument for CSR and responsible leadership, Filatotchev and Nakajima (2014) suggest that leaders need to recognise the significance of CSR for survival, profitability and growth. Without simply making changes to the board of directors, they argue that considered selection of external directors with professional and balanced mindsets is crucial for effective governance.

Filatotchev and Nakajima (2014) argue that as companies become global, leadership and CSR become even more important, and available CSR approaches promote organizations to transform their resources and knowledge to generate wealth for stakeholders. They note that systems and managerial incentives as key governance factors could work in alignment to shape the CSR outcomes. It is suggested that in order to add richness, further research should be conducted based on the multi-level examination of the multifaceted and interdependent relationships within organizations, the governance structure and CSR (Filatotchev and Nakajima 2014).

The fourth and last approach is based on strategic CSR, the idea that an organization cannot morally engage in social responsibility without having a win-win situation for all stakeholders; this idea has been receiving increasing attention. To promote strategic CSR, the social-responsibility process should be intentionally and explicitly incorporated in strategic planning. In this version of CSR, social responsibility and corporate profits go hand in hand, and this is more ethical than just "throwing money away" through some other forms of CSR. Instead, it will be in the company's best financial interest, and in the interest of all stakeholders, to engage in socially responsible behavior.

McWilliams et al. (2006) called for close examination of the strategic use of CSR activities. Jamali (2007) supported this call in the context of developing countries. Several scholars note that strategic CSR appears to be linked to an manipulative process and outcomes, using stakeholders other than the stockholders to achieve profit maximization goals (Graafland and Van De Ven 2006; Jamali 2007; McWilliams et al. 2006). Strategic CSR initiatives include forms of charity that are linked to profitability goals benefiting both the society and business. According to Jamali (2007), the challenge for leaders in developing strategic CRS programmes is to ensure that they produce win-win outcomes for all stakeholders. Consider for instance the case of an automobile company active in socially responsible production processes.

A hybrid model would be more environmentally friendly than a standard model. Thus it would attract the socially responsible consumer to pay a higher price (McWilliams et al. 2006). According to Brenkert (1996), enhanced reputation could flow from this type of differentiation. However, organizations taking a strategic CSR route are likely to be criticized for the apparent instrumental nature behind these initiatives. Hence, there is a critical need to explore the morality of strategic CSR initiatives (Bright 2006).

Some researchers assert the moral superiority of strategic CSR (see Fernando and Almeida 2012). For example, using Milton Friedman's (1996) claim that an organization's only social responsibility is its duty to maximize stockholder wealth while following the law and basic canons of ethics, Lantos and Cooke (2003) advance an argument in favor of the moral superiority of strategic CSR over altruistic CSR. Altruistic CSR, according to these researchers, infringes stockholders' property rights, unfairly taking ownership of stockholders' wealth and benefits at the expense of those for whom the organization should care for in relationship building (such as employees and customers). Consequently, Lantos and Cooke (2003) argue that altruistic CSR is unethical on several counts.

From a utilitarian perspective, altruistic CSR will compromise the stockholders, employees and consumers interests by stakeholders' such as society and local community. Deontological, or duty-based, ethics suggests that a leader's primary duty is to the stockholders, followed by a duty to employees and customers. According to justice theory, organizations should attempt to provide a stakeholder what he or she legitimately deserves. This theory promotes an anti-utilitarian argument; it is unjust to siphon off stockholder's dividends or employee pay or even raise product and consumer prices without the permission of these stakeholders. The ethics of care suggests that special and close relationships with particular stakeholders such as employees and customers should be prioritised over distant relationships (i.e. with people in distant communities or markets).

Thus Lantos and Cooke (2003) propose that strategic CSR is a morally advanced and more superior option to altruistic CSR; stockholders and other stakeholders both stand to benefit from it. Examining the moral dimension of strategic CSR in 111 Dutch organizations, Graafland and Van De Ven (2006) found the view that CSR is a necessary moral duty of organizations towards generating common good involved a stronger response and commitment than when CSR was used as a strategic element in the long-term planning of organizations. Furthermore, moral motivations could have a critical impact on clarifying organizational behaviour (see Etzioni 1988).

Strategic CSR in the Asian Context

Although there is a strong case for organizations that operate in Asia to engage in strategic CSR, there is little discussion on the topic in the Asian management literature. According to Porter and Kramer (2006), organizations in the Asian region have a significant opportunity to use the region's resources and unique competitive advantages to meet its social needs, promoting a union between society and business. However, Jamali (2007) and others (e.g. Fernando and Almeida 2012; Whelan 2007; Lee and Oh 2007) note that Asian based organizations due to various factors such as lack of resources are not able to fully engage in CSR practices in the conduct of their business. According to Chapple and Moon's (2005) study on various forms of CSR in the Asian region, they found that philanthropy-based social engagement was more prominent. However, organizations in Asia are coming to acknowledge that charity does not form the foundation for an effective CSR agenda.

Within this context, it is relevant to examine the instrumental use of strategic CSR. As with any other management concept, an organization can be perceived to be using CSR initiatives for instrumental purposes: to appear to adhere to the idea of sustainability to exploit the consumers and the public by creating a positive image. Even companies with good moral intentions are criticized for engaging in social responsibility. One of my conclusions from my research into corporate philanthropy, specifically after the 2004 Asian tsunami, is that company executives feel that if they engage in philanthropy, they will be criticized regardless because of others' inauthentic philanthropy. If companies do not engage in philanthropy, they are still liable to criticism for lack of community involvement and social responsibility.

For example, MAS Holdings (see Fernando and Almeida 2012), a Sri Lankan organization, makes it very clear that they are "doing good while doing well"—they are not engaging in philanthropy solely from altruism, but because it also results in economic benefit for the organization. MAS Holdings manufactures lingerie, and was the first to come up with the idea of the "ethical bra". They are unashamed of their spending on ethical activities in a strategic, profit-making sense. The company, which is Victoria's Secret's largest supplier, employs 45,000 people across 28 plants in eight countries, while avoiding sweatshop conditions. In 2007 MAS was selected as one of the 15 companies in the world to be cited in the first Global Compact report for engaging in exemplary labor practices. But some may ask whether it is right for an organization to exploit market conditions and use them strategically for CSR initiatives with a view to making profits. In MAS's case mostly rural, poor, female employees—92 % of MAS's total workforce—were selected for the CSR initiative called Women Go Beyond (Fernando and Almeida 2012).

Is it responsible for a company to exploit the vulnerability of a stakeholder group and use it to further its reputational and ultimately profits? There is a more extreme example. Eleven months after the 2004 Boxing Day tsunami disaster, I interviewed major Sri Lankan companies that engaged in CSR within Sri Lanka. One of these companies was Unilever Sri Lanka (part of the multinational corporation Unilever PLC). I interviewed the acting chairman at the time of the disaster, and asked why Unilever had contributed money to this initiative. I wanted to find out if the company was just using this as a public-relations exercise. I asked, "How would you answer all those critics who criticize you for merely engaging in a public-relations gimmick?" He said, "If you were here at that time and saw what we saw—we first had to be humans. I had to leave my corporate hat and first become a human. It was a spontaneous reaction that came from our hearts. Do you think that at that point we were wondering about what kind of mileage we would get from this particular exercise?" They decided immediately that the company would allocate quarter of the SLR 100 million received from the Head Office to the relief effort. I was intrigued by his response. The area of CSR related to natural disasters was at that time a relatively new area of research. However, he eventually admitted that Unilever had to be seen to be engaging in the relief effort.

Elaborating further, he said that the day after the tsunami, all the directors came in for an emergency board meeting. Most of the workers came in as well to demand immediate action, and were themselves willing to volunteer. They wanted Unilever to be seen to be out there helping the victims (see Fernando 2007). There had been increasing pressure from some of Unilever's stakeholders to have a better presence in the media in terms of the publicity for the company's pioneering work on tsunami relief, especially because Unilever (Sri Lanka) undertook the responsibility to channel various resources donated by some of its stakeholders' (e.g., ex-employees) to deserving victims. The company decided to embark on a focused awareness-building campaign targeting its stakeholders rather than a general public relations campaign. The company did not want to be seen to exploit the tsunami tragedy to enhance its image. But at the same time, the company owed an obligation to the stakeholders—they expected the company to be seen engaged in the relief efforts. So the leadership team had to ensure that their actions while targeting a limited stakeholder awareness campaign about company relief efforts did not seem to exploit the opportunity for publicity.

After this incident, eventually all the board members agreed that the company had an obligation to help, but that their heads had to have a role as well as their hearts. Their management of publicity wasn't about getting media coverage, but about focused awareness of the company's activities within Sri Lanka and among the Unilever companies internationally. They had to engage in limited stakeholder awareness of their relief efforts to satisfy stakeholder needs. This is an example of a corporations' dilemma (particularly based in Asia) in engaging in CSR: they are criticized if they engage in philanthropy, and they are criticized if they don't; moreover, they are criticized for publicizing their philanthropic efforts, and also for not publicizing them.

I went back 35 months after the Boxing Day tsunami and asked these questions again from the same corporations (see Fernando 2010). Many did not show the same passion about the tsunami-relief effort as they had in the immediate aftermath of the tsunami. For example, one had promised to build 450 houses, but had built only 75 due to cost rises and the war in Sri Lanka. What I observed was that the leaders had lost that emotional connection with the project (Fernando 2010).

It appears that CSR initiatives can be a practical and popular way to enact responsible leadership. However, the type of CSR approach adopted can play a key role in determining the extent of authentic responsible leadership. A leader opting to lead through more RLR attributes could engage the individualistic identity orientation of an organization (Basu and Palazzo 2008) which allows it to orient itself with a distinct entity but yet optimizing dyadic connections (Brickson 2005, 2007). RLR leaders prioritising partnerships could promote responsible leadership by attempting to meet organizational objectives within the larger collective of society. On the other hand, a leader opting to lead through more RLP attributes could use strategic CSR to employ the three Es (effectiveness, ethics and endurance) and focus on organizational performance through an integrated effort linking inputs, processes and outputs. With a more open posture (rather than defensive and tentative posturing), adopting a positive, learning approach with a long-term strategic view of CSR is likely to promote RLP. Enacting RLR and RLP approaches through CSR initiatives, however, are open for criticism (from the collective). As external demands in the environment forces organizations to satisfy different constituent needs, organizational strategies to overcome constituent needs can become calculated and oppositional (Suchman 1995). In summary, when enacting responsible leadership through CSR action, a responsible leader should plan to avoid defensive or tentative posturing and plan to operate more openly where long-term strategic use of CSR is enacted. CSR action leading to social innovation is one which is promoted in this book as a key path to a more balanced, open and engaging responsible action that integrates the individual, relational and collectivistic dimensions. Responsible leadership through social innovation is discussed later in the book.

Globalization impacts most aspects of human activity, and in the Asian century, responsible leaders are increasingly called upon to make decisions with a global mindset. Let us next examine how globalization could impact responsible leadership practise.

Responsible Leadership in Global Business

The principle of comparative advantage is perhaps one of the most important drivers of globalization. In this context, the closure of the Pacific Brands apparel factory in Australia provides an interesting example. In 2010 Pacific Brands, the parent company of Bonds, shed nearly 2,000 jobs across Australia to operate at much lower cost in China. At the micro level, from its workers' perspective, was the company acting ethically in moving their jobs overseas?

When looked from the macro perspective, the question is more complex than it appears. In the 2009/2010 period, enrollments at Australian universities by students from China, the largest contributor country of international students, increased by 6 % to reach 27 % of all international student enrollments (Australian Bureau of Statistics (ABS) 2011). On one hand, Australia lost jobs to China. On the other hand, Australia gained foreign income through international students from China because of raised income levels in the Chinese middle class due to employment in companies like Pacific Brands setting up operations in China. On the whole, over a period of time, globalization can act as a leveller. Then is it really unethical for a company to outsource jobs? Pacific Brands saved $150 million by outsourcing to China. A simple application of the utilitarian perspective would dictate that consequences do matter. If it benefits the majority, utilitarians would deem such an action ethical. On the other hand, from the Kantian perspective, intent matters: why did the company choose to outsource?

The context is also important in considering the ethical dimensions of a decision. Bangladeshi workers earn only a fraction from the price of the manufactured garment sold in affluent countries. This could be seen as exploitation. But this fraction goes a long way to feed the Bangladeshi worker and his or her family. From the workers' perspective, it's not exploitation: they're prepared to work under these conditions. They look forward to receiving something, preferring it to receiving nothing. The decision as to whether an action is ethical or not depends on from whose perspective one is looking as well.

Voegtlin et al. (2012) argue that globalization leads to an increased integration of value creation but at the same time it reduces the capability of a country to regulate the outcomes of the economic, political and social systems. The leadership challenges posed by increasing levels of globalization through the dilution of national boundaries is becoming an increasingly relevant topic. For example, when Kmart, Target and other major global retail brands place orders for garments made in Bangladesh, their reach goes beyond the national boundaries of the incorporated country's legal and governance frameworks, and enters other legal jurisdictions. Global retailers might exploit the lower-cost options available from countries like Bangladesh due to their lower safety and health standards, but from a moral perspective, should the standards they accept from their suppliers be any lower than those they accept for their own employees?

In 2013, a factory building collapse in Rana Plaza in Bangladesh killed over 1,000 people. After the collapse, the horrific circumstances these Bangladeshi workers were put through were discovered. The Australian Broadcasting Corporation's Four Corners program (2013) investigating the incident found that large Australian brands are ordering clothes from factories that operate far below international standards of workplace health and safety. In 2013, Australia's best-known retailers, such as Rivers, Coles, Target and Kmart, were accused of engaging in business with Bangladeshi factories that ignore international standards. There were accusations of physical abuse (Four Corners 2013).

The collapse in Rana Plaza was the latest of a number of deadly factory incidents. However, local operators claim that retailers place them under such enormous pressure that they cannot provide a safe working environment. Workers in Dhaka spoke of the unacceptable conditions, including long hours for little pay, threats of abuse if deadlines are not met and actual physical and verbal abuse. According to the Four Corners (2013) programme, workers were paid as little as $3 per day manufacturing products for top Australian brands. Some reported of appalling working conditions, including abusive language, and slapping on the face, head and neck.

China is the world's largest garment producer (CNGA 2013). However, Bangladesh will overtake them within a few years. Apparel manufacturing for Australian companies by Bangladeshi factories have increased by 1500 % since 2008 (ABC News 2013). Oxfam, a not-for-profit aid organization, conducted a survey that found almost 70 % of Australians would pay more for their clothes if workers making their clothes were paid a livable salary and given a safe environment to work. In addition, 84 % of Australian respondents said they want Australian companies to sign an accord ensuring that Bangladeshi factories improve safety standards (ABC News 2013).

The Rana Plaza collapse's devastating aftermath has caused many Australians to think carefully about where their clothes are produced. Oxfam research shows that Australian consumers support the apparel industry workers from being exposed to further disasters by the irresponsible action of Australian retailers (ABC News 2013).

According to ABC News (2013), the sourcing patterns of 34 Australian companies showed that 62 % of these failed to show a clear policy on labor and human rights on the supply side. Prevention of exploitation of children and forced labor policies were enacted only by one third of the companies. As Bangladesh approaches China's level of garment production, Australians are demanding that Australian companies bring their human-rights and labor policies up to international standards, even if it causes prices to rise.

Should major retailers owe a higher level of obligation to the thousand Bangladeshi workers who perished in the building collapse in 2013? Did they monitor the buildings and working conditions? Did they know that workers were forced to go back into a building that was already showing signs of structural deterioration? Or did they choose to ignore the situation, because that's where the cost savings were taking place? Was cutting corners on health and safety one of the contributions to those savings? These sorts of situations lead to governance gaps, and the public interest is insufficiently served. Did the retail firms that benefited from this relationship with the Bangladeshi manufacturer serve any public interest?

The issues within the Bangladeshi apparel industry highlight problems in a globalizing world; stakeholders and leaders are increasingly challenged by a diverse cultural context wanting of a common moral orientation or even a legal framework. Other than the relatively universal requirement of being humane (and even that is subject to interpretation), various nations' and organizations' moral and legal frameworks differ widely. The moral framework of most of the Bangladeshi population is based on Islam. Legal frameworks could be different as well: for example, minimum-wage requirements and occupational safety and health requirements could vary. In the pursuit of profits, business leaders when confronted with ethical dilemmas are without any support or guidance on what action to follow (Voegtlin et al. 2012). What should be done to maintain those minimum standards of humane behavior in organizations abroad? The only standard seems to be increasing profitability. When governance and legal frameworks, and even moral orientations, are diluted and fragmented across national boundaries, it is easy for those with power to ignore or manipulate the conditions. When supply of labor is ample, profit maximization becomes the guiding principle. Thus, it is appropriate to examine in detail how responsible leadership is relevant to global business operations.

Globalization and MNEs

The power that multinational enterprises (MNEs) can exert over economies, nations and individuals has been receiving increasing attention at all levels. There are four possible styles of decision-making in international contexts (Weiss 2014). The *foreign-country style* applies the values and norms of the local host; an example is McDonald's revamping its menu to fit in with the social norms of India when it began operations in that country. With the *imperialist* (or empire) style, the MNE is not prepared to change operational procedures or products or services. MNE representatives use their own home-country values, even though they are operating in an alien culture.

Between these two extremes are two grey areas. MNEs using the *interaction style* ask, "What are our competitors doing? Have they changed their operational systems to acknowledge the religious and cultural values of the host country?" In other words, the MNE matches its style of making ethical decisions to the one it sees its competitors using. While an MNE is prepared to accommodate local customs, it doesn't adopt them fully, but strives for a blend between the customs of its own country and those of the host country. Lastly, the *global style* applies a more integrated, specialised set of values and norms—in other words, a customised decision-making framework—for each country, even within the same region.

These four styles build heavily on the distinction between *ethical relativism* and *ethical absolutism*. Ethical absolutists can enter into a totally different culture or environment while dogmatically holding their own principles and values to be true, and neither adapt nor be willing to compromise on their values or set behavior patterns. On the other extreme are the ethical relativists, whose approach is, "When in Rome, do as the Romans do." However, experienced practitioners assert that when it comes to being ethically sound in one's judgment, it's best to operate in a middle ground, avoiding the extremes. Thus, the last two styles—interaction and global—would be quite helpful from a practical point of view for expatriate managers. This practical approach of striving to combine the insights of both relativism and absolutism is called *ethical pluralism*. The central challenge is how to live together with differing and conflicting values.

In 2011, the multinational chain Woolworths announced a collaboration with the American hardware manufacturer and distributor Lowe's to aggressively compete with the large Australian hardware chain Bunnings (The Sydney Morning Herald 2011). In this struggle, small hardware shops in Australian communities were threatened with being wiped off from the market because of their inability to compete in a market increasingly dominated by larger players. The effects of MNEs' activities span a number of different arenas. One is the political-environmental domain, where MNEs have to deal with governments, media and local laws. As noted earlier, of the 100 largest economic entities in the world, 51 are corporations (Anderson and Cavanagh 2000). General Motors, for example, was the first corporation, appearing at number 23. General Motors (company size measured in annual sales) was larger in size than Denmark (country size measured in gross domestic product). Wal-Mart (25), Exxon Mobil (26), Ford Motor (27) and DaimlerChrysler (28) were bigger than Poland, Norway, Indonesia, South Africa and Saudi Arabia. When an economic entity with the sort of power that an MNE possesses enters an economy or a country, the political power they wield and the influence and impact they could have on the government and its people could be enormous. For example, when BHP Billiton operated within Papua New Guinea without paying enough attention to worldwide standards in mining operations—specifically, by neglecting to erect dams to protect surrounding areas—the Ok Tedi River became seriously polluted, and communities that depended on this river for their livelihoods were drastically affected.

Another arena where MNEs generally have more expertise than their host countries is in the technological domain. Technology can play an enormous role in economies. For example, MNEs in the technological sector have affected countries' economies. In one country alone—the Congo—widespread suffering attaches to the mining of coltan, which is widely used in the manufacture of mobile phones and video gaming units (Hayes and Burge 2003).

MNEs can also have a great influence on stakeholders. For example, Nike was criticized in the early 1990s for its exploitation of child labor in Asia. MNEs also have a significant impact on the economic issues of a host nation. Just by moving their operations into a developing country, MNEs can boost investment and the general robustness of its economy. For example, McDonell (2013) reports on the mining giant Rio Tinto's new operations in Mongolia. Rio Tinto has negotiated with the Mongolian Government to develop one of the world's biggest copper mines, investing over $12 billion and building or bringing in all supplies, equipment and infrastructure to Oyu Tolgoi, in the South Gobi Desert (McDonell 2013). The mine is expected to be in production for 50–100 years. Even before the mine has become operational, Mongolia's GDP has been increasing at 12–17 %. Supporters are praising the job creation from spinoff industries. When operational, the copper mine will be one of the biggest in the world, and will comprise 30 % of Mongolia's total GDP (McDonell 2013).

Although there are supporters of the deal and the benefits it provides, many critics feel Mongolia should renegotiate the terms. Mongolia has agreed to retain only 34 % of control over the mine to secure this substantial investment (McDonell 2013). Dorjdari, a Mongolian member of the Responsible Mining Initiative, says the mining giant has taken advantage of the Mongolian government's inexperience at deals of this kind, and that such deals should be made completely public (McDonell 2013). Controversially, Rio Tinto has also been granted an exemption from the windfall-profits tax, as it is claimed that otherwise the mine could not develop.

According to McDonell (2013), a number of Mongolian MPs are pushing for renegotiation, but at present do not have the numbers to prevail. Rio Tinto has stated that it cannot renegotiate, as billions of dollars have already been expended, and the company is hoping that support from the Mongolian public will continue to grow.

Some MNEs hire convicts as laborers to sew clothes, pack software and so on. Do these convicts deserve jobs that should perhaps first be offered to the unemployed citizens in the society? But if a society deprives convicts of gainful employment, is it failing to treat them as human beings? Imagine the complications that would arise if an MNE were to employ prison labor in Indonesia or China or Vietnam. But does the practice present a problem if it is legal, and gives a comparative advantage to the employer? That's the essence of globalization: being able to cross national boundaries to take advantage of the increased profitability that is available by making use of each particular nation's specialisation. So how does globalization impact responsible leadership in the Asian century?

Impact of Globalization on Leading Responsibly

The Asian century work context influenced by rapid globalization brings particular leadership challenges. The modern workplace can be increasingly an "inter or rather multi-national and multi-cultural workforce with employees holding various cultural backgrounds" (Sackmann 2006, p. 122). For example, consider the career of a senior executive interviewed for this book. His 26 years with a steel company has exposed him to different cultures and leadership challenges.

> I started my career in human resources and principally that career started in industrial relations and negotiating with people like the maritime unions. I moved in to operations, which ran from the port of Port Kembla in Australia for BHP for a few years. Then, subsequently I went into management/sales/marketing for a few years. ...Then I was asked to lead the Malaysian steel business in mid 2005 to the end of 2007. That was a turn around for that business. From there I was asked to go to China for 3 years with one of our businesses there. That was successful. Then I went to a New Zealand pacific island business for 2 ¾ years and was leading that business. It was not a turnaround business, which was more about changing the culture and bringing the business into the 21st century. I then went off to the US leading an investment proposal for BlueScope and a joint venture business in the US. Then I was asked to come to Indonesia to try and lead a turnaround in our Indonesian business that has been in a steady decline for probably 4–5 years. That's my personal journey that brought me to Indonesia.

To add to the challenge, these leaders may be located within the boundaries of inter-, multi-national or global organizations. Thus the modern organizational structures can be composed of multiple cultures that co-exist simultaneously within organizational boundaries, making the modern organizational context very complex and consisting of members of several subcultural groups (Sackmann 2006). Sackmann (2006) claims that the "sensitivity and attention to cultural differences at the national level has dramatically increased both in the business and in the academic world over the past years" (p. 127). The national culture may only be one of several other cultural influences as a culture may emerge whenever a group of people works together over an extended period of time. Sackmann and Phillips (2004) note that these subcultures have been found to exist within sub-organizational level due to ethnicity, functional domain (such as among human resources or finance or operation divisions); at the organizational level as a single business culture; beyond organizational level as professions (see Kwantes and Boglarsky 2004), networks and race; and at the supra-organizational level such as a nation, industry, geographic region, ideology/religion.

Sackmann (2006) develops a dynamic model to understand leading across cultures and explains that due to the confluences of various cultural and subcultural baggage, leaders and constituents bring with them a set of cultural identities that are a product of socialization processes in their individual culture and subcultural groups. Thus leading in such instances where context influences behaviour (Zimbardo 1972, 2001), the interaction between leaders and their constituents may engage cultural influences at the group, divisional, organizational, industry, regional and national levels. Highlighting this point, one interviewee elaborated on the differences in responsible leadership challenges between the Malaysian, Singaporean, Chinese and Indonesian markets:

> There are very different challenges by markets from a cultural point of view, and I can come back to that in terms of differences. Malaysia is a mature market and it's history has helped shape some of that. So it's British colonial history has helped shape the way, at least the baseline of activity in a way that is quite British or even Australian in context because I guess Australia has also had a British colonial past and so some of the frameworks are similar. And equally some of the standards are very similar for both Singapore and Malaysia. So often, for instance, for building codes they will reference Australian standards.
>
> China is a very different beat. I certainly went to China thinking that it would be a homogeneous market, and clearly that is not the case. It's very regional with different dynamics. Weather, climate and topography in places can be a significant issue as well and there are substantive differences, north, south, east, west, across the markets. And again it's history lends itself to authoritarian rule again partly being the geography being so large and diverse. Indonesia is a mix of the two. It has a different colonial past with the Dutch being here and the Japanese for a short amount of time. Because the Dutch used Indonesia as a trading vehicle, they didn't leave any significant legacies in terms of institutions, so that's been an interesting differential. And again, backed by authoritarian rule, you could say Malaysia has been one party in power for 60 years, but there's at least a political process, whereas in Indonesia, up until the swearing in of the new President there hasn't really been a big successful democratic transfer of presidential power in 60 years. Corruption is an issue in all 3 countries, but in Indonesia its probably more public and more expected than it is in Malaysia or China.

Therefore, responsible leaders need to acquire knowledge of the cultural complexities and sensitives in a context. They need to be aware of their biases and how these influence their decision making. At the national (Hofstede 1994), organizational (Schein 1995; Sackmann 1991) and industry (Phillips 1994) levels, scholars have developed and empirically verified various types of models. However, Sackmann (2006) argues that these models fail to capture the nuances of leader/constituent interactions in "open perception, open interaction, and customized treatment of each individual interaction partner with his or her specific cultural socialization and related expectations" (Sackmann 2006, p. 132). From a cultural perspective, responsible leadership behaviour therefore could vary on (1) the extent of leader awareness of his or her cultural identity and biases, (2) the extent of sensitivity of the constituents' cultural identities and their expectations of responsible leadership, (3) the extent of importance of issues based on their relevant cultural perspective (particular of those who have multiple cultural values) and (4) the cultural specifics of the context involved.

Voegtlin et al.'s (2012) views on responsible leadership in global business and the application of Habermas's theory of deliberative democracy (1996) is particularly relevant to the thesis of this book. Next, we will examine these views in detail. With increases in the number of business activities conducted across national boundaries, the traditional national system of influence on the organization is fast being replaced by a more complex set of borderless economic, political and social influencing factors (Voegtlin et al. 2012). These multifaceted and complex cross-border influencing factors lead to governance gaps. This is likely to result in a lack of attention to serving the public interest. When we consider more recent leadership approaches based on moral dimensions, this void becomes quite clear.

Voegtlin et al. (2012) point out the key differences in these leadership approaches (p.1). Ethical leadership attempts to measure the ethical relevance of leadership, or the ethics in leadership in organizations. Transformational leadership, which is based on the moral dimension, attempts to develop a leadership style based on transforming the whole follower. Authentic leadership is where leaders display behavior true to their inherent moral values. This is in contrast to instrumentalist leadership, where although leaders may assume a cloak of ethical behavior, they are not acting from an internal, genuine concern for ethics, but from a desire to exploit situations by appearing ethical. Servant leadership understands leaders as people who are not necessarily perceived as being above their followers, but below, with the aim of meeting their needs. There are other contemporary leadership approaches, such as spiritual, heroic, visionary or charismatic leadership, that address leaders' ethical or moral challenges. Despite these contributions, Voegtlin et al. (2012) argue that there is a void in the leadership literature: conceptual limitations inhibit the growth of the field, because the causality of leadership challenges is not sufficiently explained. These challenges are engrained in the economic, social and moral implications of globalization. Furthermore, these authors argue that due to the pervasive impact of globalization in every aspect of the contemporary business operation, leadership should be discussed and understood at three levels: individual, organizational and societal.

Voegtlin et al. (2012) propose that studies such as those involving agency theory do not consider individuals' actions as being embedded in organizations and societies. For example, in the Dilmah Tea case study (Fernando et al. 2009), are the organization's structure and processes shaping the founder of the company, or is he shaping them? Which is having more influence on the other: the leader or the organization itself?

Voegtlin et al. (2012) claim that leadership research is not addressing this situation, which needs to be analysed on several different levels; the lack of an understanding of the organizational and societal inclusiveness in ethical decision-making presents a significant research gap, as current leadership theory remains primarily focus on the meso and micro levels (the interactions within the organization, and the leader as an individual), and not on the macro level (the interactions that are external to the organization and the impact of the organization on society). According to Voegtlin et al. (2012), only by integrating the organization level of corporate responsibility with the individual level of leadership responsibility can the pluralist and multifaceted tasks of leaders can be recognised. Their approach adds to the debate of leadership responsibility that reshapes the leaders' role in a truly globalized world through Habermas's theory of the deliberative democracy (1996).

The Asian century demands that responsible business leaders adopt a more inclusive approach to leading. Responsible leadership by definition includes a broader group of stakeholders beyond the traditional stockholders, and globalization in the Asian century infuses an added layer of complexity to the task. More diverse groups from a variety of ethnic, religious, cultural, business and ideological backgrounds have the opportunity participate in business. In the midst of rapidly changing business challenges and opportunities in the Asian century, their needs and aspirations have to be managed. One approach that business leaders could espouse to face this added layer of complexity is by following Habermas's communicative action theory (Voegtlin et al. 2012).

Habermas and Responsible Leadership

Voegtlin et al. (2012) propose a novel perspective to responsible leadership through the integration of Habermas's communicative action theory. In this section, we examine the key aspects of this contribution. The German philosopher Jürgen Habermas is a rationalist in that he believes in the power of logic and reason. Habermas's communicative-action theory (1984) is one of his key contributions to the field of linguistics (Raelin 2012). He emphasizes the free exchange of ideas, but status, power, authority and ethos (or character) need to be removed from the free exchange of ideas for it to be a truly free communication between equals. Good faith, which can only occur in these conditions, allows people to reach a consensus about truth. According to Habermas, truth does not reside "out there", but within the community. Truth is what people create subjectively as beings, as selves. This is a major epistemological belief, a belief about how the world operates, and is of special significance to responsible leadership in the Asian century. A positivist will tend to believe that there is a single answer to a question. In contrast, others would tend to believe that a question can have multiple truths, depending on the context and the perspective through which one understands and interprets the question. Habermas's views have distanced him from the positivist view. While his contributions may not be a major paradigm shift in researchers' understanding of the world, his ideas have a certain amount of traction because of the focus on communication based on humaneness, as well as on reasoning, which seem to be vital to enact responsible leadership in the context of the Asian century.

Habermas coined the term "communicative action" for communication that takes place in an authentic way to find out truth: in practice, this is interpersonal communication oriented toward a mutual understanding (Habermas 1984). If individuals have an extremely acute need to make sure that they communicate as equals, and that they have a mutual understanding on a sensitive and hotly debated topic, how does Habermas say they should restrain themselves and conduct the conversation? Participants are to treat each other as genuine persons, not as objects of manipulation. One cannot practice Habermas's guidelines in communicative-action theory if the intention is to manipulate the other. Instead, participants need to focus not primarily on their own success, but on harmonising their actions or action plans with the other. When there is mutual understanding and reciprocity in what each party wants, communicative action can take place. Status and hierarchy have no place in Habermas's communicative-action theory, but conversation as equals in a free exchange of ideas does (Habermas 1984). In an interview about leading responsibly in China, this aspect of Habermas's theory was well captured by one interviewee:

> The first thing about leadership is that you need to earn the confidence and trust of the people with whom you interact. I would certainly start with colleagues and employees; bosses of course; definitely customers; the people in the other functions of your business that need to cooperate with you for you to achieve what you need to in your job. ..... not letting politics be a distraction in a business, being open and honest about what you are trying to achieve, communicate effectively and broadly. And I think being very transparent is an important quality of a leader. I think establishing that trust with your colleagues, employees, customers, suppliers, all of the people that are essential to the success of your business, very early on to establish that trust, that the working relationship with those who influence the success of the business is the top priority.

In Habermas's communicative action, there is room for neither strategic thinking (in which participants primarily seek their own ends) nor manipulation of others, either openly or tacitly. Habermas uses the word "strategic" to indicate "instrumentalism" in communication. According to Habermas, action that is devoid of strategy and instrumentalism and is principled on mutual understanding is communicative action.

How, though, does one know if the other party is entering the conversation from a perspective of communicative action? Habermas would say that the moment one thinks about what the other party is planning, they themselves are strategizing. According to Habermas, that could be the foundation for manipulating the discussion. All one can hope for is to prepare oneself for conducting the conversation as an honorable human being based on rational thinking, and assume that the truth is between oneself and the other person. That is, one should have an expectation to lay everything on the negotiating table honestly, and to accept whatever the other gives as similarly being open and honest. So in a sense, the participant is actually placing him- or herself in a vulnerable position. The power and potential of this course of action in conducting negotiations in MNE dealings with host-country agencies can be significant. Responsible leadership within MNEs can be demonstrated at an individual level by adopting communicative action to project genuine honesty and integrity in one's intentions and dealings. This point was emphasised eloquently by an interviewee:

> Responsible leadership is really about sticking to the set of values that your company has and possibly not taking advantage or exploit the differences that exist in other economies. Even if you can, within the norms or regulations of a new investment venue, you should not compromise your value set. There are some things that will challenge you, some things that you may not be able to control, but keep to values wherever you can influence or control. Some foreign companies coming into China have possibly not managed closely to their values and some employees have engaged in business conduct that they would not otherwise use in other countries where they do business; and finally that has come back to bite them. Whether that has been deliberate or not it's hard to say. It's the responsibilities of leadership, and again this is right from the top of the company, to be very clear about what

it expects from its leaders in terms of how it conducts itself in the various communities in which it operates. It's almost like if you're not going to do a certain thing in Australia, then you're certainly not going to be allowed to do a different thing in China.

At an organizational level, Voegtlin et al. (2012) propose an understanding of responsible leadership in terms of "deliberative processes"; a view developed on Habermas's deliberative democracy (e.g., Habermas 1998, 1999, 2001). It refers to the idea of lawmaking in societies from public deliberation, and is based on the philosophical foundation of discourse ethics (Habermas 1993, 1996). Habermas's deliberative democracy represents a key element of political autonomy based on citizens' ability to reason. An individual adopts a deliberate, conscious approach to reclaiming the truth, to deal with the other as honestly as possible and on an equal footing. Essentially, this idea represents, albeit in a more collective sense, what is true of communicative action at the individual level: public engagement, discourse and dialogue are extremely important. As long as all stakeholders are consulted, and their views are considered genuinely in decision-making, the deliberative process is enacted (Raelin 2012). An excellent example of the deliberative process in action in the corporate world is how Jim Burke, the CEO of Johnson & Johnson from 1976 to 1989, conducted affairs during the 1982 Tylenol crisis (described in Chap. 2).

Some of the rare company video footage available in the public domain shows Johnson & Johnson's senior management discussing the organization's action plan during the crisis. Burke didn't know what would happen to the company or himself, but he did his best to communicate responsibly, without any compulsion from the board, shareholders or the wider community. This represents the notion of political autonomy generating from the practical reasoning of citizens. Throughout the next 18 months, citizens with the ability to reason grew to accept Burke's version of the events and continued to purchase Tylenol products, and it returned to its previous market share. However, according to one interviewee, President of BlueScope China, following this course of action could be more challenging if you are leading a business in China (see his interview in the appendix).

Voegtlin et al. (2012) point out that in a typical communicative-action scenario, the usual factors that disrupt systemic means of coordination (e.g., money and power) are replaced with solidarity as the premise of societal integration and coordination. The rise of Lech Walesa, pioneer of the Solidarity movement in Poland, is another example of the integrative power of the people. All individuals have a need to integrate, and thus tend to move toward thinking as one.

In this societal deliberation process, leaders hold roles in organizations which are well resourced and powerful in society. From this perspective, leaders are actors; they are required to develop morally legitimate decisions by engaging the societal self-determination process and stakeholders (Voegtlin et al. 2012). In other words, they have the opportunity to showcase and champion communicative action. A leader who makes a serious mistake, causing death to individuals, but comes out at the earliest available moment and says, "This is what I did, this is what happened," will likely be respected in the long term.

In sum, based on the above discussion on Voegtlin et al.'s (2012) views on responsible leadership and global business, the notion of Asian century business leaders using a deliberative and democratic process as the source for developing of responsible leadership offers to produce a more inclusive, normative direction and realistic approach. It's not a question of just sticking to the words; talk should be followed with action. This was Habermas's key contribution from his communicative-action theory: the integration of theory and practice to yield benefits for the community. The communicative-action theory is normative in the sense that leaders should think of the consequences of their actions and the impact these have on constituencies (Voegtlin et al. 2012). Leaders could then value the legitimate claims of the stakeholders (both internal and external), and use the resulting goodwill to develop and sustain meaningful connections with the stakeholders. Such interactions with all constituents promotes a process where the tension created by various stakeholders across the globe of diverse types of demands on the resources of the organization is given full consideration to generate a just outcome for all. For example, in the case of the Bangladesh factory collapse, the global merchandisers had the option to go to Bangladesh and meet with government officials and other stakeholders and come to a resolution about what needed to be done and how future disasters could be avoided. At the time of writing, only one major retailer—Benetton—has accepted culpability and agreed to pay compensation to the victims' families.

Through a deliberative process, responsible leaders could attempt to foster the open and public exchange of ideas. The process becomes pragmatic by engaging the affected constituents, and following an active stakeholder dialogue to achieve a win-win outcome for all by balancing the competing interests of the constituents.

Communicative Action and Responsible Leadership Outcomes in the Asian Century

Using communicative action, Voegtlin et al. (2012) propose a responsible leadership outcomes model. The outcomes of enacting responsible leadership are seen on three levels. The first is the macro level, where outcomes are beyond, or external to, the organization. The second is the meso level, between micro and macro: shaping organizational culture and performance within the organization. The third is the micro level, which involves personal interactions among individuals. At each of these levels, Voegtlin et al. (2012) suggest that relationships of responsible leadership and other variables can be considered, and several propositions to further understanding of the responsible leadership field can be developed.

At the macro level, by definition, responsible leaders could engage with external stakeholders. Voegtlin et al. (2012) assert three propositions at the macro level. First, responsible leadership helps build and maintain the legitimacy of the organization (proposition 1). The notion of legitimacy is related to someone else's opinion or perception of one's credibility—in this case, the community's perception. Legitimacy usually has a positive connotation. That does not imply that the concept of legitimacy necessarily represents legality. But legitimacy is more about conforming to predetermined community norms or standards. The community's role becomes central in building legitimacy. If leaders are responsible, the community will view their organizations in a positive light.

Second, responsible leadership has a positive effect on building trusting stakeholder relations (proposition 2). Trust involves a sense of vulnerability in a relationship, but it can also be misused. Trust is also a major tool in product marketing and advertising. The case of Johnson & Johnson discussed earlier can be cited as a good example of the community's trust in a company's ability to properly produce a product that is fit for its purpose and will not harm them.

Third, along with enhancing trust, responsible leadership also enhances the social capital inherent in stakeholder relations (proposition 3). The difference between the two is that trust is usually not assigned an economic, political or social value, whereas high social capital can be relied on and drawn on in adversity, just as financial capital is. A company can call on its high social capital to help negate any bad publicity and protect its legitimacy and level of trust with its stakeholders.

Communicative action at the meso level shapes the culture and performance within the organization. At the meso level, which is still concerned with the community, but from an internal perspective, Voegtlin et al. (2012) put forth five additional propositions. Responsible leaders act as role models, visionaries, change agents and stewards, and can, over time, change their organization's ethical culture. Responsible leaders will thereby encourage a culture of discursive conflict resolution and deliberative practices (proposition 4). Responsible leaders can treat everyone as an equal in a process of authentic, genuine communicative action, devoid of the use of power, authority, character/ethos and status.

Based on the level of influence leaders have on internal organizational cultures, responsible leadership can positively affect the perceived importance of corporate social responsibility (CSR) in an organization (proposition 5). It is important to note the emphasis on "perceived importance". For instance, I highlighted the role played by corporations in pioneering the tsunami relief effort in Sri Lanka after the 2004 Boxing Day tsunami:

> International Alert's (2005) study reveals that while businesses regard the practice of CSR as a genuine gesture, the public views it as self-interest. The majority of businesses say the main reason for their CSR policies is genuine concern for society, but a minority cites publicity as the primary purpose. The majority public view, by contrast, is that businesses practice CSR policies for motives of publicity and only a minority believe that they have a genuine concern for society (Fernando 2007, p. 3).

Similarly, it is important to note the importance managers place on CSR initiatives in their work. Leaders can use their influence to responsibly inculcate a culture where managers value CSR. The importance of CSR in responsible leadership leads to the next proposition. Responsible leaders are more likely than non-responsible leaders to act as social entrepreneurs; to bring about social innovation (proposition 6). Their many worthwhile stakeholder relationships can help them find new ways of manufacturing products, through innovations in process, product or service.

Responsible leadership contributes directly and indirectly to an organization's performance, under the conditions of ethical or moral norms (proposition 7). Responsible leaders by definition are expected to be more ethical and moral than non-responsible leaders. If a leader adopts a morally sound public dialogue, and is transparent, vulnerable, trusting and trustworthy, as in the case of Johnson & Johnson in the Tylenol incident, this type of behavior introduces morality and humaneness. In contrast, for example, in 2009 executives of the Toyota automobile-manufacturing company began, under compulsion, to reveal information about brake failures, and after more than a month many senior executives resigned. Why couldn't they have been forthcoming with all of the information far earlier? These types of behavior erode the trust stakeholders have in corporate leaders. In another example, in 2013, Sydney University extended an honorary professorship to a Chinese professor, Huang Jiefu, who had pioneered a government-supported scheme in China whereby the organs of executed prisoners were harvested without a donor-consent procedure for organ transplants (Robertson 2013). Immediately there were strong calls for this award to be rescinded. The honor given to Huang, who had been China's vice-minister for health and is now overseeing its organ-transplant committee, split Sydney university staff and transplant experts (Harvey 2013). A university representative told the press that it was the university's position that the program should continue for two more years (Robertson 2013); a dissenting professor at Sydney University, Maria Fiatarone Singh, contended that if the Sydney University were to act ethically, they should stop the program immediately (Robertson 2013).

The micro level involves the leader's personal interactions with followers, and the impact these actions could have on followers' attitudes, cognition and understanding. One outcome might be enhanced levels of organizational citizenship behavior: an attitude of being prepared, as a member of the organization, to go over and above the call of duty. Responsible leadership enhances motivation, and creates an environment in which people can be happier and more satisfied because they perceive they are working with people who are ethical. This suggests a further proposition: responsible leadership will have a positive effect on followers' attitudes and cognitions (proposition 8).

In summary, Habermas's theory is centered on the free exchange of ideas, and many of the communicative-action principles are already present in responsible leadership. Thus it makes perfect sense to integrate communicative action with responsible leadership. Voegtlin et al.'s (2012) eight propositions offer hope for further refinement and development of the responsible leadership field.

Significant opportunities also lie in the practice of sustainability for enacting responsible leadership. The need for sustainable business operations have been emphasised by both scholars and practitioners for some time now (Gibbons 2014). According to Thomas and Cornuel (2012), sustainability is rapidly influencing corporate agendas in a significant way. However, in real terms, the growth of sustainable business practices in industry is not reaching expectations of society. One of the key contributing factors is that implementing sustainable practices in business impacts the bottom line and erodes competitiveness in the global market. In the Asian century, where energy inefficiencies, natural resource shortages and climate change issues dominate almost every aspect of business decisions, responsible leaders will be called to use sustainability as a foundation to drive their responsible leadership initiatives.

Sustainability and Responsible Leadership

The link between sustainability and responsible leadership in the Asian century can be examined through Szekely and Knirsch's (2005) much cited article on the metrics for sustainable performance. Sustainable performance is about building an organization in which "a proper balance is created between economic, social and ecological ends" (Szekely and Knirsch 2005, p. 628). The concept is similar to Elkington's (1998) idea of the triple bottom line: it is not enough now to merely account for a company's economic profits; the company also needs to account for its social obligations and actions and its environmental or ecological obligations and actions (Moody-Stuart 2014). Essentially, a corporation must ask what it has done to meet the obligations placed on it in these three dimensions.

According to Szekely and Knirsch (2005), achieving a proper balance between economic, social and environmental dimensions (or the three Ps: profit, people and plant) is important, but it is not an easy task. If an organization siphons some of its profits into a social purpose, its shareholders will apply pressure to use the profits to pay dividends, not to benefit the community or improve solutions to an environmental problem, and employees will apply pressure to use them for pay increases. Given the range of stakeholders that can exert pressure on an organization, attaining the optimum balance is difficult. Responsible leadership in this context involves maintaining and promoting "economic growth, shareholder value, prestige, corporate reputation, customer relationships and the quality of products and services" (Szekely and Knirsch 2005, p. 628). For corporations, it's not enough just to sustain economic growth: they need to expand it as well. In this process, corporations also seek after prestige by safeguarding their brand value, and are thus reluctant to admit their errors openly. They want to guard their customer relationships and the quality of the goods and services they provide, as these affect profitability. So "sustaining and expanding" should apply to the economic, social and environmental dimensions. Certainly, economic growth cannot be sustained over the long term without attention to the social and economic aspects.

While the current hype about sustainability has come about mainly due to climate change, the implementation of sustainability values is expected to bring about benefits and changes to how an organization operates in a variety of ways. A persistent and detailed integration of sustainability measures at the core of business decision making usually generates a ripple effect of change across the organization (Szekely and Knirsch 2005). They claim that when implementing sustainability measures, aiming for attitudinal changes will be key to effective process innovation and interdepartmental collaboration, giving rise to new collaborative partnerships with a diverse set of external stakeholders. Integration of sustainability measures is likely to offer responsible leaders an opportunity to internally, initiate a conversation across the organization about the mission and objectives, and help the organization to stay relevant in the Asian century. Introducing sustainability at every level of the organization offers a great platform for systemic change across the organization.

Externally, adoption of sustainability measures increases the visibility, legitimacy and trust worthiness of the organization (Szekely and Knirsch 2005). They note that sustainability initiatives offer a great platform for responsible leaders through benchmarking to develop new and unique external partnerships to promote socially innovative initiatives. In light of the dramatic excesses that management theories such as the agency theory and the theory of the firm have brought about, it is time to review and reformulate these to develop new theories that integrate sustainability parameters to gain relevance in the issues confronting industry and academic scholarship in the Asian century.

It is commonly said that sustainability can be effective only when there is a top executive championing the approach. "Good sustainability is heavily influenced by the full and honest commitment of management and by the adoption of a management incentive scheme" (Szekely and Knirsch 2005, p. 631). The senior executives of the organization must promote sustainability and "walk the talk"; specifically, through process and product innovations. Key executives should lead from the top by showing passion and commitment to set objectives, and clearly communicate the sustainable goals through corporate level strategy-making (Szekely and Knirsch 2005). One interviewee at Unilever (see Fernando 2007) told how the employees wanted him to close the plants and let all the workers go out and help in the tsunami relief efforts, but how he couldn't do that, because he had obligations to customers and suppliers. The economic aspect ("nurturing the golden goose") is important, because it determines to what extent the corporation can survive. But at the same time, unless the community is robust and prosperous enough to purchase the corporation's goods or services, it's difficult for the corporation to expect economic growth, or even just sustained returns.

Several factors determine sustainability within a company (Szekely and Knirsch 2005). Internal factors include organizational structures and managerial procedures. For example, Unilever (Sri Lanka) did not have a designated CSR division before the 2004 Boxing Day tsunami; instead, the function was incorporated under the public-relations division (Fernando 2007). The disaster gave birth to several dedicated divisions within subsidiaries of multinational and other small to medium-sized organizations in Sri Lanka. According to Szekely and Knirsch (2005), another internal factor is the creation of incentive mechanisms to foster new sustainability initiatives and thereby promote organizational performance.

The extent of sustainability-led CSR activities in the organization can be shaped by the early identification and formulation of business opportunities. This may, and often does, cross the line into instrumentality, but this is useful to convince the organization's leaders to agree to sustainable action. Kantian ethics demands that one's intentions be altruistic; such a motivation would violate this principle. However, it could be argued that this is a systemic failure of the global economic system, not a organizational-level issue.

According to Szekely and Knirsch (2005), another key internal factor that determines the level of sustainability initiatives in the firm is the recognition of emerging risks, potential threats and management failures. For example, a company in the fast-food field can realize that it will lag in the marketplace unless it offers more healthful choices, and can portray its response to this risk as doing something good for the community. For most large companies, degradation of the environment is an unavoidable part of their process. The community needs their goods and services, and some environmental degradation will occur; however, most of these corporations highlight their efforts to minimize harm to the environment.

External factors, such as changes in customer values, can also affect companies' sustainability initiatives (Szekely and Knirsch 2005). Fast-food chains such as McDonald's have been responsive to these external factors by increasingly responding to customers' demands for more-healthful eating options. However, the tobacco industry missed a major opportunity to change in response to changing customer values when they failed to explore and offer alternative ways to provide cigarettes or substitutes that did not cause health-damaging smoke. Other external factors such as access to new markets (for example, China and India), industry competition and increased consumer interest in ethical and social business conduct can all influence companies' sustainability initiatives (Szekely and Knirsch 2005). I agree with these scholars that regulatory intervention in corporations' handling of environmental issues and stakeholder expectations—for example, legislation mandating full transparency and access to information—could pose challenges to sustainability initiatives. One interviewee notes:

> It's very clear that some things get done differently in Asia compared to other parts of the world. There are different regulations; different ways that employers tend to treat their people, different approaches to environmental management. A lot of those, a lot of those constraints are probably more relaxed than Western society in some ways. Now I think this is changing, particularly in China where the general population is very concerned about things like water safety, quality of the air that they breath, occupational health and safety, payment and conditions all that sort of stuff.

Other challenges could include internationalization of negative externalities (such as pollution and waste, as in the Ok Tedi case discussed earlier). In the past, internationalization allowed companies to operate in countries with less stringent regulatory regimes, and thus circumvent the demanding standards of their home countries (Szekely and Knirsch 2005). However, opportunities to exploit developing economies in this manner are becoming fewer as global standards and conventions demand reduction in material consumption and adoption of international labor codes such as the UN's Global Compact initiative. According to Szekely and Knirsch (2005), the "investment rationale for including environmental, social and governance criteria lies in the growing importance of intangible assets, such as management skills, reputation, human and intellectual capital, brands and the ability to work in partnership with stakeholders" (p. 630). A major challenge in measuring sustainability is the often long time lag between action and outcome. It's extremely hard to report on results in the same financial year as the initiative: projects can take at least three to five years to reach a point where either qualitative or quantitative results can even be detected.

When initiating sustainability measures, companies will create a better image if they can be proactive in protecting their customers. Shell Oil Company had a large oil rig (Brent Spar) off the coast of England that they wanted to decommission and sink into the sea. Among others, Greenpeace activists and the German environmental minister at the time opposed this, and called for a boycott of Shell products. Shell asserted that it had done nothing illegal, but consumer outrage compelled its senior managers to relent, and to dismantle the rig in a much more environmentally friendly way. The power of the marketplace is a factor in sustainability as well.

Szekely and Knirsch (2005) claim that adopting a sustainability approach requires continuous effort, investment and adaptation. Key challenges in this process include aligning sustainability activities with the purpose of the business, clarifying the board's level of involvement and ensuring the commitment of key staff (p. 631). The power of the arguments to convince top management to adopt sustainable practices is greatly enhanced by aligning these initiatives with the company's core business so that they can be incorporated into the company's overall business strategy and policies.

To promote a common understanding of approaches and expectations across the organization, all key stakeholders must be engaged. When humanity's footprint (that is, the effect of human activity, including resources consumed and environmental impact) is "within the annual regenerative capacity of nature, this footprint is sustainable" (Szekely and Knirsch 2005, p. 642).

Responsible leaders in the Asian century have a wonderful opportunity to enact their humane leadership style through sustainability initiatives. While sustainability as an idea that should be pursued has already been recognised by influential sectors in industry, sustainability is now part of the mission statements; some organizations are already reporting on sustainability performance measures. However, for many, sustainability is still not a central driver of the organizational processes. In the Asian century, responsible leadership offers a way to "make the implicit more explicit". It can help organizations to move from merely paying lip service to the concept to actually implementing key sustainability parameters and promoting social innovation as a result (the *how* of which is explained in the next chapter). The bridging of the gap between recognition and implementation of sustainability is hard and complex, requiring transforming the organizational culture. It requires a long and sustained effort at prioritising goals, getting all key actors aboard and mapping what organizational changes are required (Szekely and Knirsch 2005).

The adoption of sustainable initiatives through whatever mechanism in organizations could trigger innovative ways to meet the Asian century challenges in the economic, environmental, geopolitical, societal and geopolitical arenas. Organizations that integrate sustainability by making the implicit more explicit could experience a transformation of the organizational culture and impact the day-to-day operations of the organization. To holistically implement sustainability in organizations, two broad approaches could be adopted. One is to integrate sustainability initiatives as a matter of principle, based on an ethical perspective.

The other approach involves a more pragmatic approach to implementing sustainability, based on how organizational processes impact global issues of the Asian century such as scarcity of natural resources, exploitation of labour standards, corruption, climate change and piracy, just to name a few. The process of integrating sustainability at the heart of business strategy-making either way could generate novel and unique business arrangements promoting social innovation and social entrepreneurship. In the Asian century, this could offer responsible leaders particularly through RLR to establish a variety of mutually rewarding partnerships with stakeholders and establish tripartite social purpose business arrangements with non-governmental organizations. When executed with a high level of accountability and transparency, a responsible leader's actions could increase the organization's reputation. Taking the ethical approach to sustainability, next we will look at climate change and responsible leadership.

Climate Change and Responsible Leadership[2]

October 2015 was the hottest month on the globe since records started in 1880 (Newsweek 2015). Compared to the twentieth century, the average Asian century global land and ocean surface temperature rose by 1.76° (CNBC 2015). Integrating virtue into climate-change initiatives—what is now known as "climate ethics" (Singer 2002; Gardiner 2004)—is receiving growing interest in academia. National leaders at various times have attempted to reach a consensus on climate change mitigation and adaptation measures. These attempts have been at national (e.g., UK's Stern Report, Australia's Garnaut Report) and intergovernmental levels (e.g., the Kyoto protocol). However, these attempts to enact climate change measures pay little or no attention to ethical reasoning as a justification for accepting these measures. See for example, Australia's 680-page, key climate change review report (Garnaut Report 2008), which refers to "ethics" or "ethical" only once in the body and the reference list. Even some policy documents that explicitly acknowledge the importance of an ethical perspective in evaluating the consequences of policies and balancing the rights of agents, such as the UK's Stern Report, appeal by turning to conflicting moral arguments, and thus threaten their own credibility as effective policy instruments. Clearly there must be a higher moral standard to which to appeal in assessing climate-change initiatives, which could allow a clearer examination of what appear to be contradictory moral arguments in developing climate change policy. Such a standard would allow the equitable consideration of multiple interests, and ultimately promote justice among governments, organizations and populations around the world. The concept of virtue may provide this standard.

Virtue goes beyond merely ensuring the absence of unethical behavior. Instead, it acts as a foundation to develop personal and communal excellence (Bright et al. 2006). An ethos of virtue transcends the specifics of a given situation and "enables behaviors and decisions that rise above what is merely expected in ethical conduct" (Bright et al. 2006, p. 250); thus it is well suited to offering robust and flexible responses to the myriad of ethical dilemmas that will inevitably arise in managing climate change. Cameron (2003) asserts a continuum of behavior that ranges from harmful, unethical or dishonest behavior at one end, to normal or ethical behavior at the center, and active virtue or "flourishing" (Bright et al. 2006) at the other end; this last is climate change policy should aim for. The Kyoto Protocol provides a case study in the application of virtue to international climate-change

---

[2] This section includes an updated version of ideas first presented in Fernando (2009).

decision-making. As explained in Fernando (2009), Gardiner (2004) outlines three main phases in the Protocol's development. The first phase included the development of the UN Framework Convention on Climate Change at the Rio Earth Summit (1992). The understanding at this meeting was for leading industrialized nations to cut emissions levels and developing nations to show commitment to take action in the future. Although a number of industrialized countries announced voluntary stabilization levels, the increase in their emissions showed no sign of slowing. Thus, at a meeting in Berlin in 1995, member countries agreed to accept formally binding obligations on their emission levels. These levels were agreed through the Kyoto Protocol in 1997, in Japan (the second phase). Although the Kyoto Protocol first appeared to be successful, its promise, as Gardiner (2004) has pointed out, was "short lived" (p. 591). In a meeting in 2000 at the Hague, the Kyoto Protocol broke down, and the US withdrawal in 2001 seemed to constitute its decisive end. However with the meetings at Bonn and Marrakesh—the third phase—saw a full agreement. Since then, a number of nations, including Australia, have ratified it, and its survival, however improbable, has kept efforts to combat global climate change on track. However, Gardiner (2004) claims that the Kyoto Protocol is deeply flawed. Substantively, although the Protocol is useful as a first step (Gardiner 2004), it does very little to actually limit emissions. Because some industrialized countries were offered concessions as incentives to ratify the protocol, even if all signatories fully comply, their emissions at the end of the first commitment term would have been recorded at 9 % above the year 2000 levels. Between this increase and emissions growth in developing countries, the data was expected to show another substantial global increase by 2012.

Moreover, while the Protocol is not binding on any countries that fail to ratify their participation (Barrett 2003, p. 386), penalties are included through higher level targets in the forthcoming decade's commitment period. However, parties are free to negotiate these penalties in determining the targets for the forthcoming period (Gardiner 2004).

Although its substantive flaws certainly require attention, what may prove to be the most significant flaw in the Protocol is its assumption that without considering international justice issues, an agreement can be arrived on climate change. In other words, in its focus on cost-effectiveness, the Kyoto Protocol has marginalized ethical issues; specifically, the question of what constitutes not just ethical, but virtuous action in this context. Peterson and Seligman (2004) propose a set of common virtues across most cultures. Bright et al. (2006) have asserted that virtue is the perfection of character, and that it can be attributed to organizations as well as individuals (p. 251), and propose a three-element model to determine the extent of virtue inherent in a given action. The first element is human impact, which suggests that, in the specific case of the Kyoto Protocol, strategies to control emissions should be based on the extent to which they improve resilience, well-being and livelihood, and maximize positive outcomes for all generations.

Second, climate change mitigation and adaptation measures should also meet the moral goodness test: whether particular strategies are motivated by a search for human excellence that transcends instrumental reciprocity (Peterson and Seligman

2004), and actions are based on "the right thing to do", not because of an expectation of benefits. The evaluation of the moral goodness test is difficult because of the critical role played by intent.

The third test that mitigation and adaptation strategies should meet is the generation of unconditional social benefits. Based on Aristotelian ethics, this concept requires any mitigation and adaptation strategy to be implemented with an intention in the first place to generate first order goods (goods of first intent). These are inherently good. Unconditional social benefit also requires these strategies to wisely generate second order goods (goods of second intent). These goods (e.g., power, prestige and profits) have an instrumental element in them, and therefore pursuing them solely is amoral (Bright et al. 2006). However, if the second order goods are produced as a by-product while intending to produce first order goods, it is considered virtuous. For example, instrumental motives, such as political advantage or economic leverage, might come into play when allocating or agreeing to greenhouse-gas emission-reduction targets, thereby destroying any inherent virtue the action may originally have had.

This discussion highlights the practical challenges of assessing the virtue inherent in a given action. Bright et al. (2006) identify two types of virtue: tonic and phasic. Tonic virtue is present in a general and continuous way, taking forms such as integrity, hope, kindness and virtuous purpose. In contrast, phasic virtue—the type relevant to climate-change initiatives—generates as a response to an event. Bright et al. (2006) propose that responsibility, being a main element of phasic virtue, is connected to both social justice theory and empathy. According to these scholars, it would be expected that individuals who are ready to undertake responsibility usually have a sense of identity with the other. When the offenders readily accept guilt and responsibility, forgiveness follows. At the collective level, this process takes place when governments accept responsibility for climate policy violations.

Therefore, modeling involving mitigation and adaptation could consider integrating virtuous action. The three-attribute framework of Bright et al. (2006) provides some first steps. It could be applied to assess how aspects of virtue are demonstrated by different intergovernmental and governmental mitigation and adaptation strategies. In ensuring that such strategies actively undertake virtuous actions, these models incorporating ethics in the mitigation and adaptation modeling could produce more equitable and just outcomes for both developed and developing nations.

Challenges to Practicing Responsible Leadership

With the rising affluence of the Asian middle class and the resulting rise in consumer demand, the Asian century poses several challenges to enacting responsible leadership. The prevalence of opportunities for corruption is identified as a common challenge for responsible leadership by interviewees. But Asian governments are now taking steps to eradicate corruption from their societies. One interviewee commented:

> And leadership needs to be supported with the right governance processes to ensure that those things that you can control business practices to the best of your ability. It is very interesting sitting in China now just how much attitudes have changed even in the space of one year, since the new Chinese government leadership has come in and it has actually set some clear expectations of what appropriate business conduct looks like. There are now changes evident in areas such as the standard of entertainment, the standard of gifts people give to one another, in a business context; a lot of that has taken a much, much more conservative turn in the last 12 months or so. There have also been several high profile anti-corruption actions against government officials and also some foreign companies.
>
> Corruption is certainly something, as well as the things I've mentioned before, that the community over here value very highly as well as clean air, clean water, good food, safety, a safe environment. They don't want to see their leaders enriching themselves through corrupt business practices. So over time the community pressure will start to have a greater impact over here, I think.

Another observed:

> There are German companies that have been successful in the short term in China that have been held to account. In Asian countries it is politically/publicly easy to hold foreign companies up as the pariah.
>
> Ultimately, Asian governments will start to crack down on corruption, particularly as the country becomes more developed and greater separation of certain powers starts to occur. And the other part of that is they will not be able to attract foreign direct investments if they cannot deal with the issues of corruptions. If companies are going to be held to account for their behavior of making sure they operate responsibly, be it safety, environment, dealing with employees, dealing with customers and/or issues of corruptions, and others are not held to account then eventually, if we are not being successful, we will exit and say one of the reasons we are exiting is because we don't feel we can be successful because others are not being held to account on responsible leadership. The more foreign companies do that then the more the Asian governments will have to crack down.
>
> You can see it in China now. The new leadership in China is saying that this is an issue. Not just an economic issue but also a political issue. Corruption isn't just people taking money, but also turning a blind eye to certain activities or not meeting regulations, etc. But I think you see it in Korea with similar announcements about larger organizations being pursued for not following appropriate behavior. It's going to be an ongoing push from countries on business to start holding them accountable, and the GFC has been part of that. Business has been tainted by the actions of some businesses pre GFC. The pressure will continue to be on us to show we are a responsible member/part of society.

In terms of implementing sustainability measures, the time dimension in responsible leadership challenges leaders to sacrifice short-term gains for long-term, sustainable benefits. The typical short-term myopia in the current dynamic and competitive business climate can drive leaders to behave irresponsibly. Beale and Fernando (2009) note that "shareholders are motivating their most senior managers to put their needs, as defined by short-term movements in the share price, above the interests of the other stakeholders such as employees and the broader community, and arguably the long run interests of the firm" (p. 27). This corporate agenda is created by the constant pressure of the need to increase shareholder returns and the resulting management obsession on short-term profitability (Jensen 2004).

In the 1980s, a debate began about the nature, antecedents and possible responses to short-termism, which is explained as, "a systematic characteristic of an organization that overvalues short-term rewards and undervalues long-term consequences" (Laverty 2004, p. 949). As the incidents of corporate collapses continue across the globe, executives must balance the organization's long-term interests with its short-term necessities (Beale and Fernando 2009). Short-termism is linked to the "fundamental characteristics of an organization" (Laverty 2004), notably its structure and culture as the main reasons for favoring the short-term over long-term. Through short-termism, organizations stand to benefit only limited instrumental outcomes such as promotion of reputation and legitimacy.

> At its worst, this process has resulted in corporate pathology and managers who maximize short-run value and capitalize their options gains, quitting before the crash. It is argued that the short-term focus on share prices has been counterproductive for long-run economic growth as well as social cohesion and environmental sustainability. Furthermore, the short-term focus has discouraged other ways of viewing and thinking about how a company should be run. The short-term focus is arguably damaging to individual companies and the economy as a whole. Public suspicion and mistrust of large companies in particular is due to their lack of long-term responsibility or social conscience (Beale and Fernando 2009, p. 27).

An example can be found in the climate-change measures companies are expected to undertake to reduce their carbon footprints. In this case, the requirement is that companies forgo short-term gains to secure a sustainable future for an unknown generation. Thus to be a responsible leader, one has to connect not only with shareholder needs, but also with the needs of a variety of stakeholders, including future generations. This is an almost-impossible task, because to satisfy the needs of one stakeholder (e.g., to offer higher wages for employees), the leader of the company needs to sacrifice those of another stakeholder (e.g., to offer reduced dividends to shareholders). The requirement to connect with, and balance the needs of, a wider set of stakeholders is a formidable challenge to any responsible leader. One interviewee described this aspect well:

> A responsible leader would say, if anything that could give you a short-term benefit but does so at the expense of your long-term aspirations and credibility, they wouldn't take that short-term opportunity.
> It would be easy to take shortcuts and to deviate from our standards for short-term benefit, but that will ultimately give you longer-term pain.

Another challenge to enacting responsible leadership in the Asian century is to maintain the same level of responsibility to those who are distant in either time or space from the decision-making as to those who are closer (Pruzan and Miller 2006). For example, in the case of preserving the environment by cutting carbon emissions and implementing environment protection measures, the beneficiaries of such action are an unknown human generation. At this stage it is not known whether there will be a human race 50, 75 and 100 years from now, but leaders are still expected to take bold measures to safeguard the environment.

According to Pruzan and Miller (2006), the larger the corporation grows, the more distant the decision-making is from those affected by those decisions. For example, in the early 1990s, when Nike was charged with using sweatshop labor conditions in South East Asian countries, CEO Phil Knight was challenged by film-maker Michael Moore to visit Nike's Indonesian factories to see the labor conditions for himself (The Big One 1998). In the course of this discussion, Knight said that he had never visited these factories in Indonesia. While it is not reasonable to expect the CEO of a global manufacturer like Nike to have visited every global operation around the world, Knight's comment shows how decision-making is not concerned with real places or, more importantly, real people, but is reduced to a set of numbers and statistics. Under these circumstances, responsible decision-making is limited to what the numbers report and predict, taking away the context of the situation. One interviewee also drew attention to the issue.

> In Asian and developing countries, regulations are opaque. I think sometimes that is done deliberately to potentially give advantage to certain companies that might air on the lower side of standards. But I think typically in developing countries, it's actually because they are not quite sure the way to frame the regulations. Rather than phrase it in a way that copies a particular country or particular standard, it becomes loose or is framed loosely. As a result, that could lead you to "we can do this legally" but if you are very clear about your standards that you operate to globally, you can say you aren't prepared to take such actions regardless of what the regulations say.

Lastly, contextual pressures pose a key challenge for enacting responsible leadership in the Asian century. As an increasing number of Western countries become more heterogeneous with Asia's rising influence, leaders will need to be aware and better equipped to deal with a range of values in the workplace. One interviewee working in Singapore for over 20 years aptly described his leadership challenges:

> The biggest challenge is understanding people's emotional make up and unspoken social norms. In many Asian cultures, people often don't voice their opinions or differences openly. Sometimes it is out of respect for the other person's culture and sometimes out of fear of consequences.
>
> In Asia, the environment is far more complex than in the West because there are a lot of unsaid social norms and expectations, often unique to local culture, which a good manager has to keep in mind. Besides requirements of the Western model of responsible leadership, the Asian context requires additional sensitivity and capabilities to manage these unspoken norms. For instance, if an employee has violated some procedure and is removed within agreed contractual agreement and local law, it still may not be perceived as fair by the workforce and may lead to resistance.

The Chinese culture is linked to long-term orientation, high risk avoidance and medium femininity. According to Hofstede and Bond (1988), the ratings are different in Western cultures. For example, the general US population projects short-term orientation, low risk avoidance, medium masculinity and strong individualism. In contrast, the Chinese followers accept task-orientation more with their leaders. This could be a result of Chinese people's greater dependence on, and loyalty to, groups or institutions to determine their actions. For example, an interviewee said:

> It's recognizing that you don't have all the answers. Particularly in the Asian context, there's an expectation that the leader has the answer. So it's balancing that and making sure you can actually draw out of people their very best of who that person is without them feeling like you're just giving them the answer. I think that's one of the challenges of leading in

Asia. I think the challenge is not only reminding yourself that you don't have all the answers, but that every minute of every day people are observing what you do more so than what you say and will be making judgments on you every minute of the day.

The Chinese place more emphasize on personal relationships. In a study comparing Chinese vs English speaking followers' perceptions of their leaders, Fernando and Yang (2006) found that the former assign people-orientation to their leaders to a lesser extent than the latter. The Chinese have a culture in which people place great importance on personal relationships. In contrast, learning from others in a group context will be preferred by Westerners rather than through building personal relationships (Sosik and Jung 2002). Key cultural differences like these need to be taken into account in developing strategies to implement responsible leadership. The particular contextual challenges posed by the Asian century and the opportunities available for responsible leaders in this context are more fully explained in Chap. 7.

Conclusion

This chapter has moved beyond theory to examine how responsible leadership can be implemented through a range of organizational processes. The chapter examined the role of responsible leadership in the context of global business, CSR, sustainability and climate change issues. It was noted that the rising affluence of the Asian middle class and the resulting rise in consumer demand in the Asian century pose several challenges to enacting responsible leadership. In the Asian century, the community is set to become more diverse, more complex in its wants and needs; a deliberative and democratic process as the source for developing of responsible leadership was identified as a way to produce a more inclusive and realistic approach to enacting responsible leadership. The next chapter moves on to the central theme of the book: leading responsibly in the Asian century.

References

ABC News. (2013). *Australian retailers rivers, coles, target, Kmart linked to Bangladesh factory worker abuse*. http://www.abc.net.au/news/2013-06-24/australian-retailers-linked-to-sweat-shop-abuse/4773738. Accessed 23 Aug 2015.

ABS. (2011). *Australian social trends*. http://www.abs.gov.au/AUSSTATS/abs@.nsf/Lookup/4102.0Main+Features20Dec+20112013. Accessed 25 Apr 2015.

Aguilera, R. V., Filatotchev, I., Gospel, H., & Jackson, G. (2008). An organizational approach to comparative corporate governance: Costs, contingencies, and complementarities. *Organization Science, 19*(3), 475–492.

Anderson, S., & Cavanagh, J. (2000). *The rise of corporate global power*. Washington, DC: Institute for Policy Studies.

Aoki, M. (2001). *Toward a comparative institutional analysis*. Cambridge: MIT Press.

Barrett, S. (2003). *Environment and statecraft*. Oxford: Oxford University Press.

Basu, K., & Palazzo, G. (2008). Corporate social responsibility: A process model of sensemaking. *Academy of Management Review, 33*(1), 122–136.

Beale, F., & Fernando, M. (2009). Short-termism and genuineness in environmental initiatives: A comparative case study of two oil companies. *European Management Journal, 27*(1), 26–35.

Bowen, H. R. (1953). *Social responsibilities of the businessman*. New York: Harper.

Brenkert, G. G. (1996). Private corporations and public welfare. In R. A. Larmer (Ed.), *Ethics in the workplace: Selected readings in business ethics*. Minneapolis/St Paul: West Publishing Company.

Brickson, S. L. (2005). Organizational identity orientation: Forging a link between organizational identity and organizations' relations with stakeholders. *Administrative Science Quarterly, 50*(4), 576–609.

Brickson, S. L. (2007). Organizational identity orientation: The genesis of the role of the firm and distinct forms of social value. *Academy of Management Review, 32*(3), 864–888.

Bright, D. (2006). Virtuousness is necessary for genuineness in corporate philanthropy. *Academy of Management Review, 31*(3), 752–754.

Bright, D., Cameron, K., & Caza, A. (2006). The amplifying and buffering effects of virtuousness in downsized organizations. *Journal of Business Ethics, 64*(3), 249–269.

Cameron, K. S. (2003). Organizational virtuousness and performance. In K. S. Cameron, J. Dutton, & R. E. Quinn (Eds.), *Positive organizational scholarship* (pp. 48–65). San Francisco: Berrett-Koehler.

Carroll, A. B. (1979). A three-dimensional conceptual model of corporate performance. *Academy of Management Review, 4*(4), 497–505.

Carroll, A. B. (1991). The pyramid of corporate social responsibility: Toward the moral management of organizational stakeholders. *Business Horizons, 34*(4), 39–48.

Carroll, A. B. (1994). Social issues in management research experts' views, analysis, and commentary. *Business & Society, 33*(1), 5–29.

Carroll, A. B. (1999). Corporate social responsibility: Evolution of a definitional construct. *Business & Society, 38*(3), 268–295.

Chapple, W., & Moon, J. (2005). Corporate social responsibility (CSR) in Asia: A seven-country study of CSR web site reporting. *Business & Society, 44*(4), 415–441.

CNBC. (2015). Climate change: October was the hottest on record. Available from http://www.cnbc.com/2015/11/18/climate-change-october-was-the-hottest-on-record.html. Accessed 19 Nov 2015.

CNGA. (2013). *An overview of China's garment industry*. Available at http://www.cnga.org.cn/engl/about/Overview.asp. Accessed 10 Feb 2014.

Davis, K. (1960). Can business afford to ignore social responsibilities? *California Management Review, 2*(3), 70.

Drucker, P. F. (1984). The new meaning of corporate social-responsibility. *California Management Review, 26*(2), 53–63.

Elkington, J. (1998). Partnerships from cannibals with forks: The triple bottom line of 21st-century business. *Environmental Quality Management, 8*(1), 37–51.

Etzioni, A. (1988). *Moral dimension: Toward a new economics*. New York: The Free Press.

Fernando, M. (2007). Corporate social responsibility in the wake of the Asian tsunami: A comparative case study of two Sri Lankan companies. *European Management Journal, 25*(1), 1–10.

Fernando, M. (2009). Going beyond climate ethics: Virtuousness in climate change initiatives. http://www.nccr-climate.unibe.ch/conferences/climate_policies/working_papers/Fernando.pdf. Accessed 12 Apr 2014.

Fernando, M. (2010). Corporate social responsibility in the wake of the Asian tsunami: Effect of time on the genuineness of CSR initiatives. *European Management Journal, 28*(1), 68–79.

Fernando, M., & Almeida, S. (2012). The organizational virtuousness of strategic corporate social responsibility: A case study of the Sri Lankan family-owned enterprise MAS holdings. *European Management Journal, 30*(6), 564–576.

References

Fernando, M., & Yang, Y. (2006). Transformational leadership in a cross-cultural setting. *Proceedings of the 20th annual Australia New Zealand Academy of Management (ANZAM) conference*. Queensland: Central Queensland University.

Fernando, M., Beale, F., & Geroy, G. (2009). The spiritual dimension in leadership at Dilmah Tea. *Leadership & Organization Development Journal, 30*(6), 522–539.

Filatotchev, I., & Nakajima, C. (2014). Corporate governance, responsible managerial behavior, and corporate social responsibility: Organizational efficiency versus organizational legitimacy? *The Academy of Management Perspectives, 28*(3), 289–306.

Fisher, C. M. (2000). The ethics of inactivity: Human resource managers and quietism. *Business and Professional Ethics Journal, 19*(3/4), 55–72.

Four Corners. (2013). *Fashion victims*. Available at http://www.abc.net.au/4corners/stories/2013/06/25/3785918.htm. Accessed 28 Aug 2015.

Frederick, W. C. (1960). The growing concern over business responsibility. *California Management Review, 2*(4), 54–61.

Friedman, M. (1996). The social responsibility of business is to increase profits. In S. B. Rae & K. L. Wong (Eds.), *Beyond integrity: A Judeo-Christian approach* (pp. 241–245). Grand Rapids: Zondervan Publishing House.

Gardiner, S. M. (2004). The global warming tragedy and the dangerous illusion of the Kyoto Protocol. *Ethics & International Affairs, 18*(01), 23–39.

Garnaut, R. (2008). *The Garnaut climate change review: Final report*. Cambridge: Cambridge University Press.

Gibbons, B. (2014). *Design, development, implementation and evaluation of a web-based systems approach to teaching and learning responsible decision making in undergraduate business education*. Ph.D. thesis, University of Wollongong, Wollongong.

Godfrey, P. C., & Hatch, N. W. (2007). Researching corporate social responsibility: An agenda for the 21st century. *Journal of Business Ethics, 70*(1), 87–98.

Graafland, J., & van de Ven, B. (2006). Strategic and moral motivation for corporate social responsibility. *Journal of Corporate Citizenship, 2006*(22), 111–123.

Habermas, J. (1984). *The theory of communicative action. Vol. 1: Reason and nationalization of society*. Beacon Press.

Habermas, J. (1993). Remarks on discourse ethics. In J. Habermas (Ed.), *Justification and application* (pp. 19–111). Cambridge: MIT Press.

Habermas, J. (1996). *Moral consciousness and communicative action*. Cambridge: MIT Press.

Habermas, J. (1998). *Between facts and norms: Contributions to a discourse theory of law and democracy*. Cambridge: Polity Press.

Habermas, J. (1999). Popular sovereignty as procedure. In J. Bohman & W. Rehg (Eds.), *Deliberative democracy: Essays on reason and politics* (pp. 35–66). Cambridge: MIT Press.

Habermas, J. (2001). *The inclusion of the other: Studies in political theory*. Cambridge: MIT Press.

Harvey, A. (2013). *Organ harvesting links pressure*. Australian University. http://www.abc.net.au/7.30/content/2013/s3747778.htm

Hayes, K., & Burge, R. (2003). *Coltan mining in the democratic Republic of Congo: How tantalum-using industries can commit to the reconstruction of the DRC*. Available at https://www.isf.es/ee/pdf/FFI_20Coltan_report.pdf. Accessed 8 Aug 2014.

Hofstede, G. (1994). Cultural constraints in management theories. *International Review of Strategic Management, 5*, 27–48.

Hofstede, G., & Bond, M. H. (1988). The Confucius connection: From cultural roots to economic growth. *Organizational Dynamics, 16*(4), 5–21.

Jamali, D. (2007). The case for strategic corporate social responsibility in developing countries. *Business and Society Review, 112*(1), 1–27.

Jensen, M. (2004). Who gets Wall Street's attention? How alliance announcements and alliance density affect analyst coverage. *Strategic Organization, 2*(3), 293–312.

Kluger, J. (2007). What makes us moral. *Time Magazine*, pp 54–60.

Kohlberg, L. (1958). *The development of modes of moral thinking and choice in the years 10 to 16*. Ph.D., The University of Chicago, Ann Arbor.

Kwantes, C. T., & Boglarsky, C. A. (2004). Do occupational groups vary in expressed organizational culture preferences? A study of six occupations in the United States. *International Journal of Cross Cultural Management, 4*(3), 335–354.

Lantos, G. P., & Cooke, S. (2003). Corporate socialism unethically masquerades as 'CSR': The difference between being ethical, altruistic and strategic in business. *Strategic Direction, 19*(6), 31–35.

Laverty, K. J. (2004). Managerial myopia or systemic short-termism?: The importance of managerial systems in valuing the long term. *Management Decision, 42*(8), 949–962.

Lee, M. D. P. (2008). A review of the theories of corporate social responsibility: Its evolutionary path and the road ahead. *International Journal of Management Reviews, 10*(1), 53–73.

Lee, S.-H., & Oh, K. K. (2007). Corruption in Asia: Pervasiveness and arbitrariness. *Asia Pacific Journal of Management, 24*(1), 97–114.

Lowry, D. (2006). HR managers as ethical decision-makers: Mapping the terrain. *Asia Pacific Journal of Human Resources, 44*(2), 171–183.

Mahoney, J. (1998). Editorial adieu: Cultivating moral courage in business. *Business Ethics: A European Review, 7*(4), 187–192.

Mather, G., Denby, L., Wood, L. N., & Harrison, B. (2011). Business graduate skills in sustainability. *Journal of Global Responsibility, 2*(2), 188–205.

McDonell, S. (2013). Rio set to open mammoth Mongolian mine. ABC News. http://www.abc.net.au/news/2012-11-20/rio-to-open-mammoth-mongolian-mine/4381178. Accessed 26 Apr 2015.

McGuire, J. W. (1963). *Business and society*. New York: McGraw-Hill.

McWilliams, A., Siegel, D. S., & Wright, P. M. (2006). Corporate social responsibility: Strategic implications. *Journal of Management Studies, 43*(1), 1–18.

Moody-Stuart, M. (2014). *Responsible leadership: Lessons from the front line of sustainability and ethics*. Greenleaf Publishing.

Moon, J., Crane, A., & Matten, D. (2005). Can corporations be citizens? Corporate citizenship as a metaphor for business participation in society. *Business Ethics Quarterly, 15*(3), 429–453.

Moore, M. (Director). (1998). *The big one* [Motion picture]. United States: Mayfair.

Murray, K. B., & Montanari, J. B. (1986). Strategic management of the socially responsible firm: Integrating management and marketing theory. *Academy of Management Review, 11*(4), 815–827.

Newsweek. (2015). This October was the hottest ever recorded, marking six months of record-breaking heat. Available at http://www.newsweek.com/october-was-hottest-ever-recorded-marking-six-months-record-breaking-heat-noaa-395915. Accessed 19 Nov 2015.

Nisman, D. (2012). *China's African water scramble*. http://www.huffingtonpost.com/daniel-nisman/chinas-african-water-scra_b_2248874.html. Accessed on 30 May 2015.

Peterson, C., & Seligman, M. E. (2004). *Character strengths and virtues: A classification and handbook*. Washington, DC: American Psychological Association.

Phillips, M. E. (1994). Industry mindsets: Exploring the cultures of two macro-organizational settings. *Organization Science, 5*(3), 384–402.

Porter, M. E., & Kramer, M. R. (2006). The link between competitive advantage and corporate social responsibility. *Harvard Business Review, 84*(12), 78–92.

Pruzan, P., & Miller, W. C. (2006). Spirituality as the basis of responsible leaders and responsible companies. In T. Maak, & N. M. Pless (Eds.), *Responsible leadership* (68–92). London: Routledge.

Raelin, J. A. (2012). Dialogue and deliberation as expressions of democratic leadership in participatory organizational change. *Journal of Organizational Change Management, 25*(1), 7–23.

Robertson, M. (2013). *Honorary professor was an organ harvester, say critics*. http://www.theepochtimes.com/n3/31214-honorary-professor-was-an-organ-harvester-say-critics/

Sackmann, S. A. (1991). Uncovering culture in organizations. *The Journal of Applied Behavioral Science, 27*(3), 295–317.

References

Sackmann, S. A. (2006). Leading responsibly across cultures. In T. Maak & N. Pless (Eds.), *Responsible leadership* (pp. 122–137). Oxon: Routledge.

Sackmann, S. A., & Phillips, M. E. (2004). Contextual influences on culture research shifting assumptions for new workplace realities. *International Journal of Cross Cultural Management, 4*(3), 370–390.

Schein, E. H. (1995). The role of the founder in creating organizational culture. *Family Business Review, 8*(3), 221–238.

Scherer, A. G., & Palazzo, G. (2007). Toward a political conception of corporate responsibility: Business and society seen from a Habermasian perspective. *Academy of Management Review, 32*(4), 1096–1120.

Sethi, S. P. (1975). Dimensions of corporate social performance: An analytical framework. *California Management Review, 17*(3), 58–64.

Singer, P. (2002). *One world*. London: Yale University Press.

Sosik, J. J., & Jung, D. I. (2002). Work-group characteristics and performance in collectivistic and individualistic cultures. *The Journal of Social Psychology, 142*(1), 5–23.

Suchman, M. C. (1995). Managing legitimacy: Strategic and institutional approaches. *Academy of Management Review, 20*(3), 571–610.

Swanson, D. L. (1995). Addressing a theoretical problem by reorienting the corporate social performance model. *Academy of Management Review, 20*(1), 43–64.

Szekely, F., & Knirsch, M. (2005). Responsible leadership and corporate social responsibility: Metrics for sustainable performance. *European Management Journal, 23*(6), 628–647.

The Sydney Morning Herald. (2011). *Hardware price war 'unlikely'*. Available at http://www.smh.com.au/business/hardware-price-war-unlikely-20110707-1h4oj.html. Accessed 22 June 2014.

Thomas, H., & Cornuel, E. (2012). Business schools in transition? issues of impact, legitimacy, capabilities and re-invention. *Journal of Management Development, 31*(4), 329–335.

Varadarajan, P. R., & Menon, A. (1988). Cause-related marketing: A coalignment of marketing strategy and corporate philanthropy. *The Journal of Marketing, 52*(3), 58–74.

Voegtlin, C., Patzer, M., & Scherer, A. G. (2012). Responsible leadership in global business: A new approach to leadership and its multi-level outcomes. *Journal of Business Ethics, 105*(1), 1–16.

Walton, C. C. (1967). *Corporate social responsibilities*. Belmont: Wadsworth Publishing Company.

Wartick, S. L., & Cochran, P. L. (1985). The evolution of the corporate social performance model. *Academy of Management Review, 10*(4), 758–769.

Watson, T. J. (2003). Ethical choice in managerial work: The scope for moral choices in an ethically irrational world. *Human Relations, 56*(2), 167–185.

Weiss, J. (2014). *Business ethics: A stakeholder and issues management approach*. San Francisco: Berrett-Koehler Publishers.

Whelan, G. (2007). Corporate social responsibility in Asia: A Confucian context. In S. May, G. Cheney, & J. Roper (Eds.), *The debate over corporate social responsibility* (pp. 105–118). New York: Oxford University Press.

Zadek, S. (2004). The path to corporate responsibility. *Harvard Business Review, 82*(12), 125–132.

Zimbardo, P. G. (1972). Comment: Pathology of imprisonment. *Society, 9*(6), 4–8.

Zimbardo, P. G. (2001). Opposing terrorism by understanding the human capacity for evil. *Monitor on Psychology, 32*(10), 48–50.

Chapter 7
Responsible Leadership in the Asian Century

Introduction

The premise of this book has been based on a major shift in economic, cultural and political power from the twentieth "American century" to the twenty-first "Asian century". Significant changes are likely to take place, and business leaders are challenged to adapt to the dawn of a new era. The most obvious challenge involves the need to identify key competitive opportunities and threats in the Asian century. Despite China's stock market problems during 2015, it surpassed the US as the country with the largest number of billionaires (CNBC 2015). Producing nearly five billionaires a week for 2014/15, China has 596 billionaires as opposed to 537 billionaires in the US (CNBC 2015). China has also dethroned the US as the leading automobile manufacturer (Meredith 2009). China is the largest energy consumer, the world's largest new car market and has the largest foreign currency reserves (Bloomberg 2013). While the US struggles to resolve budget-deficit issues, China and India in particular are steadily growing as economic and political superpowers. Asia is home to 60 % of the global population, and by 2028, India is set to overtake China as the most populated country (Population Reference Bureau 2014). In the last 20 years, China and India have tripled their output into the global economy (Australian Government White Paper 2012). It is estimated that by 2025, Asia will produce almost half the world's output, and will be the largest consumer and producer. In 2012, based on the sum of exports and imports of goods, China has become the world's biggest trading nation, displacing the US (Bloomberg 2013).

In this context, based on the theme developed in previous chapters, this chapter looks at how the contemporary responsible leadership discourse needs to integrate Asian-century influences, and proposes a socially innovative virtuous responsible leadership model. Using the need for developing sustainable businesses as a core duty of a responsible leader, this chapter integrates social innovation and virtuousness in a unique way to offer a responsible leadership approach based on RLP and RLR theories. We start by examining the features of Asian management styles.

Asian Management Styles

The most quoted work on cross-cultural management is that of Hofstede (1998, 2003, 2010). His work has also been tested and largely validated (Sondergaard 1994). He identified five dimensions (or orientations) to compare and contrast the similarities and differences between national cultures: power distance, individualism, uncertainty avoidance, masculinity and short- and long-term orientation. Briefly, a high power-distance country projects imbalances of power. It portrays the average citizen less prominently. In contrast, a low power-distance country projects more equality among its citizens. In the individualism dimension, cultures high in individualism have a concentration of citizens with a larger number of loose relationships. Cultures with low individualism on the other hand have a concentration of citizens with very close ties in relationships. Uncertainty avoidance refers to the tolerance of a people to ambiguity. Masculinity refers to the gender roles of a culture rather than the physical attributes of genders. Cultures high in masculinity, for example have high levels of segregation based on traditional gender roles. Lastly, short-term and long-term orientation refers to the extent of a culture's focus on commitments and respect for tradition. Most Asian nations project long-term orientation cultures; for example, it takes longer to develop relationships and business in these societies.

According to Hofstede (1993), Asian cultures are generally moderate-high in power distance, moderate-low in individualism, moderate-high in masculinity, moderate-high in uncertainty avoidance and high in long-term orientation. Western cultures are generally low in power distance, high in individualism, moderate-high in masculinity, moderate-low in uncertainty avoidance and moderate-low in long-term orientation (Hofstede 1993). An interviewee highlighted some of these differences as Asian century challenges for a Western leader.

> I think people here in China do approach their daily work and the way they make decisions in a different way. So if I summarise the Western way of management is, give me lots of data, give me lots of facts, I want the black and white story, I want all the information in front of me to make a decision, I expect everyone to be on board, I expect you to be very clear in your communications and to tell me what's going on in the business, tell me what the opportunities are for improvement, be very open, very frank. [In China], …probably it is a little bit more of a challenge to get people to respond to you that way. They expect the boss to make the decisions a lot of the time, they look to the boss for leadership, they look to the boss to be right, and they look to the boss to take care of them. And probably they accept the consequences of poor performance a bit differently from what we would in a Western context. Because there's this tendency about 'saving ones face' particularly in China.
>
> Being from a Western background I actually want people's input, I'm using the same model I just described, I say "please tell me, I'm thinking out loud here, tell me if my ideas are stupid or otherwise" and they won't tell you, they're reluctant to tell you in a group if your idea is a poor one. The ones that really do know you and whom you've established a relationship will come up to you outside the meeting and say "boss well you asked for this

feedback, I didn't want to give it to you in the meeting but here it is, that was a stupid idea". So it's a lot more difficult to draw people out, particularly in a group situation, in a team situation. So you have to think about how you actually extract people's opinions and their recommendations to get the best out of what they have to offer. In my experience, after a time, and if the team has been together for a reasonable period of time, you can get them to act the way you want them to, but it's not a natural tendency.

Studies have suggested that Asian-style management can be subdivided into two main management clusters: Confucian Asian and Southern Asian (Gupta et al. 2009). The Confucian Asian cluster is characterized by the influence of China and the Confucian ideology, as well as a strong performance and family orientation (Gupta and Hanges 2004). The Southern Asian cluster shows a strong family and humane orientation combined with a strong future and collective orientation (Gupta et al. 2009). These researchers conducted a comparison of Anglo management and the two Asian clusters with regard to family businesses, finding that Anglo businesses have a far more distinct family boundary, whereby businesses are not obligated to take care of families in their times of need. Southern Asian clusters present moderately regulated family boundaries, where the family and business are separate but the livelihood of the family is expected to be supported by the business. Confucian Asian clusters show weak family boundaries, where the family and business are strongly connected and obligated to support each other (Gupta et al. 2009). But this trend could be changing, as highlighted by a Chinese internet entrepreneur interviewed for the book:

> Ten years ago, most companies were family businesses. Nearly all of the top executives were relatives. The issue with the leadership of family business were trust. How could I trust professional managers, who are not my family members, to manage my money? However, with more family business leaders going to business schools in US or Europe, they know how to manage their businesses without hiring relatives. As a result, nowadays, most successful family businesses hire professional managers to manage their companies.

Other differences between the three clusters include bridging relationships and organizational professionalism, which are highest in Anglo cultures, lowest in Confucian clusters and moderate in Southern Asian clusters. Another difference is family power, which has the highest presence in Confucian clusters, a moderate presence in Southern Asian clusters and the weakest presence in Anglo cultures (see Gupta et al. 2009). It is important to note that despite these differences, all three management styles are contextually embedded. Confucian and Anglo management are presented as contrasting approaches, with Southern Asian clusters as a hybrid between the two (Gupta et al. 2009).

Hofstede's (1993) research of ten countries, including four from Asia; China, Japan, Hong Kong and Indonesia shows a noticeable difference between some Asian cultures in certain dimensions (p. 91). China is considered to have the highest power distance of the four Asian countries, followed by Indonesia and Hong Kong. Alternatively, Japan is ranked as having a moderate power distance. At moderate, Japan has the highest ranking of the Asian countries on the individualism scale. Indonesia has the lowest ranking, followed by China and Hong Kong. Japan is by far the highest ranked on the masculinity scale, although Hong Kong is also given a high ranking. Both China and Indonesia are ranked low in this dimension, with Indonesia slightly lower than China. Indonesia and Hong Kong are both ranked as low in uncertainty avoidance, China as moderate and Japan as high. Indonesia is the only one of the four to be ranked as low in long-term orientation. China shows the highest long-term propensity, followed by Hong Kong and Japan. From Hofstede's (1993) research, Japanese management, while differing from American, is still the most similar to it. China and America are almost polar opposites, and Indonesia is presented as somewhere in between. It is important to note these differences when focusing on Asian management styles as a whole.

A senior executive interviewed for the current study with work experience of over 20 years in Asia noted:

> Each Asian country has a very strong culture of its own and people are very fond of their culture. There is a certain degree of resurgent pride in Asian culture. There was a time when Asians were quite in awe of the West, but now are more mature in balancing international norms with their own Asian culture. Hence some of the peculiar social norms and challenges of leadership are likely to remain.

In the Chinese context, another interviewee noted;

> I think that one positive thing is that it is a bit easier to get alignment here in China; because as I said, they look to the boss. So as long as you are very clear with what you want and you explain the context and they believe in what you are saying is right and they agree with the direction, they can come on board pretty quickly. On that point, I think there is little difference between Western society and China, people like to get clear directions, they like to know that the path that they are heading on.

Hofstede (1993) suggests that Japanese management is largely peer-controlled, in contrast to the Western style of management control. Hotta (2009) showcases this through the example of a large Japanese IT company attempting to overhaul the Japanese-style management they had in place. The idea was to replace it with a more clearly targeted Western style. Due to the differences between Western and Asian management styles, the organization could not simply implement Western systems without adapting them for the environment; "adjustment of the method to the culture is necessary." (Hotta 2009, p. 71). This implementation was not successful, as the cultural influence was not considered. In the implementation process organization's major strengths—flexibility and ambiguity—were lost and the new management culture did not synergize with Japanese culture (Hotta 2009).

Research shows further differences between American and Japanese management cultures. The core of the Americanized enterprise is the managerial class, whereas in Japan the core of the enterprise is the permanent worker group (Hofstede 1993). The Japanese are largely controlled by their peer group rather than the manager (Hofstede 1993). Hofstede (1993) describes this difference through research conducted in preschools in America and Japan, each with an ill-behaved child. When a Japanese teacher, who was responsible for 28 students, learned about the child's behavior from another child, this child responded by telling the misbehaving child to do something about the behavior. In a similar situation in America, a teacher who was responsible for nine children responded by having a long talk with the child and isolating him until his behavior changed. According to Hofstede (1993),

American styles of management are not suitable to the group-controlled nature of the Japanese culture.

As the quality of information influences the quality of decision-making, one explanation of the differences between Western and Asian cultures focuses on the lack of information in some regions (Haley and Tan 1999, 1996). Although since these views were presented there has been some improvement in what we know about these regions, these researchers claim of an informational black hole in South East Asia. This lack of information creates more complexities for decision-makers and leads to a management style that varies from that of the west (Haley and Tan 1996). They suggest that a holistic, intuitive decision-making style is well suited to environments with scarce information resources. Holistic information processing, action-driven decision-making, extensive knowledge and experience and experience-based intuition can combat the complexities found in low information contexts (Haley and Tan 1996).

Overall, strategic decision-making varies between Asian and Western management styles (Haley and Tan 1999). Several explanations are suggested for the differences in management style. The two most prominent are cultural influence and quality of information (Hofstede 1993; Haley and Tan 1996). While Western and Asian management styles differ, there are also noticeable differences between culture clusters within each style (Tixier 1994; Haley and Tan 1999). Culture is a forceful influence on management style.

Thus the diversity of management styles in Asia could pose several challenges to a responsible leader in the Asian century, particularly when the leader has been exposed to a Western management style. Generally, the best approach to effective leadership in Asia involves providing clear direction. One interviewee said:

> What makes a leader…is certainly giving your people the direction and confidence in you, making sure that the direction is clear, making sure that people not only know what the direction is but they know what their role is in helping the organization deliver against the objectives and strategy that it has; and also giving honest clear open feedback to the people about their performance.

However, despite the market attraction, for many a Western business leader, the biggest challenge to moving business into China is dealing with the cultural difference. For example, according to the CEO of PricewaterhouseCoopers (PwC) in Australia, Luke Sayers (2014), only a minority of large Australian companies have moved into China, and of these, only a handful have Australian employees "on the ground", located in China. In the next section, we move onto identifying some of the key cultural attributes of Chinese society that could influence responsible leadership in the Asian century.

Chinese Cultural Influences on Responsible Leadership

This section is developed on the key aspects of Chinese business and culture highlighted by Gallo (2011). Leadership when translated to Chinese is "leading ability", referring to a series of strategies and personal skills for mangers to develop (Wang and Chee 2011). China represents an array of diverse ethnic, linguistic and religious groups of people spread over a large geographical area. For example, Chinese provinces to the north border Russia and communism-influenced states like Kazakhstan and Mongolia. To the west, China's neighbors include Pakistan, India and Nepal. To the south, the predominantly Buddhist Myanmar (Burma) and Vietnam are neighbors, and to the east, Russia and South Korea. It is fair to expect a certain level of influence from these bordering nations on adjoining Chinese provinces.

Referring to the rapid economic growth of China in the Asian century, Beeson (2014) notes, "[e]ven if this is a more of a *re-emergence* than an entrance on to the world stage, it is a development of long-term global significance, the consequences of which will reverberate throughout the twenty-first century." (p. 150). In this context, it is well established that more business leaders are required in China (Gallo 2011). One key reason for this need is the 1960s Chinese Cultural Revolution, which promoted agriculture and discouraged business (Teiwes and Sun 2007). When China's centrally planned economy began to shift to a market-based economy in the late 1970s, foreign investment was allowed in for the first time in modern China. The country was on an upward growth trend in terms of productivity. However, businesses had a severe short-term focus, as foreign entrepreneurs expected quick gains out of their investments. There was lack of effective transfer of leadership skills within the Chinese cultural context. As a result, Chinese business leaders today are commonly 10 years younger than their Western counterparts (Gallo 2011).

Is there any value in examining the historical records of the Chinese civilization to develop a Chinese managerial theory? Based on the origins of a managerial system found in the Chinese Middle Kingdom labelled as proto-management, Warner (2014) examines whether it is time to develop a specialist Chinese managerial theory. However, after considering several scholarly contributions to the idea, Warner (2014) claims that the case for a Chinese management theory may be too premature. This conclusion is further strengthened by finding evidence of achievements of past civilizations prior to the formulation of management theory (see Witzel and Warner 2013). Certain features in Chinese business would be key to understanding leading responsibly in the Asian century. The first is the importance of relationships. One interviewee, a Chinese entrepreneur explained how difficult it was to let go of employees in his company:

> The greatest leadership challenge I have is with managing people. For example, I had to shut down the Beijing office because of business downturn. But I didn't know how to explain to the employees who have worked so hard. For many, it was their first job. And my personal preference was that I like to work with friends, that's my personal preference.
>
> My co-founder said that he would talk to the employees. But I said no, that's my decision, that's my team, I have to face them during this tough time. I think this is the most difficult time of my entire career. There is a conflict of my interest into people you have worked with and trained and the goal of sustaining and growing the business.

It is now well established that the academic literature on Chinese culture positions it as collectivist (Hofstede 2010). As opposed to the Western view, in collectivist cultures, people are treated as born into extended families or clans that protect them in exchange for loyalty. In the West, the individualist view holds that each should look after oneself. In individualist cultures, task prevails over relationship; in collectivist cultures, relationship prevails over task (Hofstede 2011). Thus in a collectivist culture, day-to-day activity and decisions are based on the collective: relationships with family, friends and other groups, or *guan xi*. It is most likely the first Chinese concept that a westerner would be encountering in China (Redding 1990; Warner 2014). An interviewee noted:

> Guan xi, or the forming of mutually rewarding relationships in business, is a deeply entrenched characteristic of the business culture in China. For example, the people you went to university with are still the guys you're doing business with 25 or 30 years later, that is very real and there is nothing wrong with that. Having strong networks and long-standing relationships and longevity of business are all very strong in the Chinese value system, so that can be very hard to compete with if you're relatively new to the country and you're at an early stage of forming your relationships. So that I think is a challenge.

While *guan xi* literally translates as "relationships", these are of a long-term nature, running into multiple generations, and have a reciprocal quality. Guan xi is "a tool to achieve the impossible"; it circumvents or neutralizes the bureaucratic system (Wang and Chee 2011, p. 59). They provide an excellent account of how to develop strategies for building and sustaining *guan xi* (p. 58). People in China use *guan xi* as a necessary element in engaging in business. It is used in most situations where knowing another would be advantageous and generate benefits. However, from a Western perspective, *guan xi* is often thought of from a negative sense; often frowned upon as another system for promoting bribery (Gallo 2011, p. 230).

Power is an essential factor in examining *guan xi*. But according to one interviewee, the significance of *guan xi* in Chinese business is changing:

> Ten years ago, if you ask a CEO in any company, "what makes you successful?", the answer normally will be "relationships". But right now they will tell you about 60 % is about relationships, 40 % is about management.

Second, according to Gallo (2011), the Chinese way of life is influenced greatly by Confucianism, Daoism and Buddhism. Much has been written about the impact of the philosopher Confucius on the Chinese way of life. His ideas have even been integrated into the statutes and in the Asian century, Confucianism has become a major ideological force in China (Wang and Chee 2011). According to Confucius, everyone has a role to play in society, and conforming to one's role according to a hierarchy is important (Gallo 2011). Confucians believe of the inherent goodness of people (Wang and Chee 2011). These scholars note that having an ethical and moral system that educates and develops people on how to act ethically is important. During the Cultural Revolution in China, Confucianism was shunned. All people were (in theory, at least) considered of equal status; for example, the status of women was elevated, to the point where billionaire property tycoon Zhang Xin could plausibly claim—and be a personal example—that in China, women have a fair chance to succeed as much as in any other country (Gallo 2011). However, there has been a resurgence of Confucianism-style state patronage in modern China. Although Confucianism is focused on providing guidance for ruling a country, the leadership skills and styles it explains are relevant to modern Chinese business organizations (Warner 2014). The Confucian Doctrine of Humanity is a core element of a leader's ideology. The goal is to deliver peace and happiness to everyone in the organization (Gallo 2011, p 43).

> When the Great Way is practiced, humanity thrives. Those with virtue and ability are chosen and used. People value trustworthiness and cultivate harmony with each other. They treat all old people as their parents, and all children as their children. As a result, the aged have appropriate last years, those in their prime have appropriate employment, and the young have appropriate growth and development. Elderly people with no spouses or children, the handicapped, and the ill are all provided for.... People don't engage in intrigue or trickery, nor do they engage in robbery, theft or rebellion. When people leave their houses they don't lock their doors. This is called The Great Harmony.
>
> "The Great Harmony" (dà tóng) from the Book of Rites, cited in Wang and Chee (2011, p. 26)

This emphasis on societal hierarchy has had a great influence on modern business leadership in China, making Western concepts such as empowerment difficult to practice in Chinese organizations. The Chinese subordinate is likely to think, "Why is my boss asking me for an opinion? Is it a way to get me to make a mistake and fire me?" Chinese leaders are expected to be courteous, of which a key element is being kind and benevolent. Other leader qualities include humility, patience and loyalty, and an authentic desire to foster corporate harmony.

Daoism is less clear and practical than Confucianism. The Dao is "the way": proper and natural choices and actions for living one's life (Wang and Chee 2011). It has very few rules and relies on a holistic explanation of life. The balance of yin and yang—dualities of light and dark, forceful and yielding, and so on—is a central concept in Daoist thinking, as is the importance of nature and one's environment in seeking harmony (Redding 1990). In contrast, Confucian thinking relies mostly on individuals' correct behavior. Applied to organizations, Daoism requires no hierarchy. The leader is expected to be invisible, having little interaction with the external environment (Wang and Chee 2011, p. 38). As in RLR, a leader influenced by Daoism is more likely to look at the leadership process as a holistic experience than an outcome- or goal-based process. Friendship is important in Daoist-based leadership. Developing the right context is believed to lead to the right balance and harmony in any endeavour. Rather than a top-down or bottom-up leadership approach, Daoist-based leadership focuses on leadership from the middle, similar to RLR. According to Gallo (2011), in Daoist-inspired leadership, leading by doing nothing is also a key element. Daoism-influenced leadership is perhaps the most difficult for a Westerner to master. It is most effectively learned from living in China and growing up with the experiences of interacting with Chinese people within the Chinese cultural context. Another challenge according to Gallo (2011) is the non-linear thinking involved in the decision-making process. Western decision-making is based on a linear, step-by-step approach. In Daoist-based decision-making, the decision-maker attempts to make a decision based on win-win outcomes for all by involving the context to a larger degree in each iteration of this reflective process. In leading, friendship comes first. Leading from the top is not important; Chinese lead from the middle. The founder of Daoism, Lao Zi, used water as a metaphor to demonstrate the qualities of leadership. "Water is altruistic because it supports life; water is modest and humble because it always takes the lowest ground; water is adaptable and flexible because it can stay in a container of any shape; water is transparent and clear" (Turnbull 2011, p. 180).

The last of the three major religion-based influences into Chinese culture is Buddhism. Similar to Daoism, Buddhism embraces the metaphysical. Self-reflection, or *wu*, is a key concept (Warner 2014; Gallo 2011). It implies deep insight gained by reflecting on the world and oneself. Both leader and employee expect that the other will try to understand them. The term is represented by a Chinese character that shows the heart on the left, the five senses on the right and the mouth at the top (Gallo 2011). This indicates that a person is expected to first use the mouth to ask questions and then to engage all of the senses and the heart to comprehensively understand an issue (Gallo 2011). Most Westerners find practicing *wu* difficult because of their lifelong orientation toward thinking linearly.

Another key Chinese cultural concept linked to Buddhism is *zhong yong*: expecting individuals to avoid extremes and to operate from a comfortable middle path (Gallo 2011). The preference under *zhong yong* is to hide one's intentions and capabilities (and hence one's weaknesses), as this is considered the safest way to operate in a group. A flow-on effect is that risk-taking is not promoted. There is a saying that while Westerners drive people, companies and goals, the Chinese prefer to build a canal to attract water (Gallo 2011). The preferred option is to attract by operating in the middle path. This idea of attracting rather than pushing signifies an important difference in the theories of RLR and RLP. RLR is about relationships and attracting people through using relational intelligence. RLP, on the other hand, places little emphasis on relationships; instead, performance is a key driver. In this context, RLR seems to be more relevant and more easily aligned with the key Chinese cultural traits.

According to Gallo (2011), the collectivist trait in most Asian societies is linked to a stronger sense of social mission than most Westerners tend to have. He asserts that whatever the Chinese engage in involves a clear sense of patriotism. As a result, Chinese business leaders operate on the basis that goals and objectives should be achieved not only for the company but for the community and country. The thinking process of the Chinese is also different from Westerners'. One main factor is the Asian process of holistic thinking. While Westerners tend to divide a problem into people, processes and systems, the Chinese understand problems holistically, and mostly pictorially (Gallo 2011). Chinese would look at the whole over and over again to identify the problem and come up with the solution. Also, *ren* (benevolence), as a Chinese concept applied in business means to be people-driven (Wang and Chee 2011). It includes people internal and external to the business, similar to RLR. It demands respect to authority figures, and care for peers and colleagues.

In summary, the major drivers from the Chinese cultural perspective that need to be taken into account are the importance of relationships, collective orientation, patriotism and the influence of a middle-path orientation. It was noted earlier that in the Asian region, organizations discharge their responsibilities in an environment with little motivation for engaging in CSR (Fernando and Almeida 2012; Jamali 2007; Lee and Oh 2007; Whelan 2007). As strong contextual factors that shape the 'responsibility' of responsible leadership, the Chinese cultural drivers can help identify and develop opportunities for Asian century leaders. Leaders who recognize these drivers have the opportunity to use their unique attributes to address responsible leadership opportunities in the Asian century. Although philanthropy-based community involvement was the most established form of CSR in the region (see Chapple and Moon 2005), Asian companies' recent responsibility initiatives show that charity alone does not form the basis of a firm's responsibility agenda.

Based on the Chinese cultural drivers, this book promotes the idea of leading responsibly through a convergence between business and society, particularly by using a social innovation approach to responsible leadership. We begin by examining the idea of a social purpose business.

The Importance of Social-Purpose Business in the Asian Century

Both popular and academic literature are showing a growing interest in social-purpose business activity. The idea of social-purpose business advances a position—although with little theoretical basis—where businesses are required to align profit-making with social engagement. Creating social change is at the heart of social-purpose business. Social entrepreneurship is also concerned with creating social change. As a practice, it aims to achieve meaningful social changes through generating social value (Perrini and Vurro 2006; Dees 2001; Dees et al. 2002; Boschee 2001). Social entrepreneurship can also take place through innovation in various private and public sectors (Hockerts 2010; Austin et al. 2004). According to Mort et al. (2002), social entrepreneurship seeks to develop social-change initiatives that can have a widespread impact on the community. As social entrepreneurship is mostly defined and practiced within a not-for-profit context (Martin and Osberg 2007; Thompson 2002), achieving social change while meeting organizational profit-making ideals requires special leader attributes.

In practice, social business seems to encompass several social-engagement initiatives. It can include any corporate activity promoting social responsibility, social innovation, social entrepreneurship, social performance and community engagement. It essentially attempts to apply Aristotle's ideas about the tension between excellence and success (MacIntyre 1998). Excellence in any activity promotes the internal goods of the activity, while success promotes instrumental goods such as power, profits and reputation. The idea behind social business is to ensure that organizations seek excellence over success.

Social business is not only a buzzword but is embraced by major players in the global market. For example, Grameen Danone Foods (GDF) was set up in 2007 in Bangladesh to operate a fresh dairy product company (Rodrigues and Baker 2012). A joint venture between Groupe Danone and Nobel laureate Muhammad Yunus's Grameen Bank, GDF produces yogurt from milk collected through small dairy farmers. Dannon yogurt has long been a Grameen Danone key product. Danone was launched in 1919, and is the global leader in fresh dairy products.

For Yunus, the social purpose business idea started in 1974 (Grameen Bank 2015). Yunus and his students were on a field trip in a rural village. They met a woman who manufactured bamboo stools by borrowing 15 pence to purchase raw bamboo shoots for each stool (Grameen Bank 2015). As a consequence she would make only a minute profit each week, as she had to pay back the middleman at rates higher than she could afford. It occurred to Yunus that there must be something wrong with traditional economic models. He found that by giving just $27 to 42 women in the village, it was possible for the women to not only survive but also pull themselves out of the poverty cycle, as they did not have to pay the money back with interest; this inspired the idea of microfinancing (Knowledge@Wharton 2009).

In 1976, enthused by his experiment and disturbed by the 1974 famine in Bangladesh, which he had witnessed firsthand, Yunus secured a loan from the government to lend to the poor, much to the disapproval of the state bank (Ekbal 2009). By 1982 the project was flourishing, with over 28,000 members, and the first Grameen Bank was established in 1983 (Ekbal 2009).

According to Ekbal (2009), at first, Yunus was ridiculed for his ambition to successfully lend money to the poor (with no collateral and low interest rates). During the establishment of the Grameen Bank, Yunus and his colleagues encountered a range of protests, including a backlash from the conservative clergy, who told women that if they borrowed from the Grameen Bank they would be denied a traditional Muslim burial (Ekbal 2009). Today, however, the Grameen Bank is considered a global success, and has since spawned a number of trusts, funds and projects, all of which are aimed at alleviating poverty through restructuring the economic system to support the financially disadvantaged, with a particular emphasis on women and those living in rural areas.

The thinking behind the current understanding of social-purpose business is well captured by Bull et al. (2008). They assert that social-enterprise literature has ignored how the classic tension between economic value creation and social value creation is managed, and more importantly, how social-purpose businesses are led. They suggest that a special form of capital, ethical capital, can help leaders of social enterprises. To develop and nurture ethical capital in an organization, special leadership qualities are required. By definition, responsible leaders are ideally suited to take on this demanding role and achieve a balance between economic and social rationality.

Based on Alter's (2004) social-enterprise typology, Bull et al. (2008) attempt to deconstruct the ethics of social enterprises. Alter developed the typology to represent the demands of social and economic sustainability. The traditional for-profit organization is at the economic-sustainability end of the spectrum, while the traditional non-profit organization is at the social-sustainability end. Alter places traditional for-profit businesses as well as organizations practicing corporate social responsibility and socially responsible business in the economic-sustainability category because the profit motive is primary for these organizations. They are driven by economic rationality. In contrast, traditional non-profit organizations, including those with income-generating and market-trading activities, are grouped under the social-sustainability heading.

Bull et al. (2008, 2010) note that various organizations can have a mix of different types of capital in varying degrees. Capital is normally accepted as consisting of physical (natural resources), economic (financial resources), human (labor resources), intellectual, social (civil-society resources) and ethical (moral values) components. Ethical capital represents the collective morality asset of the organization. It can bring long-term benefits to the organization, including fostering a loyal following of stakeholders who value doing the right thing. Wagner-Tsukamoto (2005) suggests:

...once morality is transformed into an economic asset, corporate moral agency yields competitive advantage, increases profitability and increases survival prospects of the firm. In this respect, insufficient corporate moral agency can be analysed not as a systemic, rule-based condition of defective incentive structures but as a capital utilisation problem in firm-stakeholder interactions (p. 77).

In this context, responsible leaders have a real opportunity to build ethical capital through RLR and RLP. Alter's (2004) typology consists of three levels of ethical capital; they represent the ethics of businesses driven by economic rationality that are primarily aiming for economic value creation. In the case of organizations driven by social rationality, Bull et al. (2008) extend these three levels to five. Level 4 includes social enterprises that are aligned with the argument that good must not be done solely for reasons of profit. Level 5 includes those organizations undertaking social initiatives with a pure charity mindset. In this level of ethical capital, economic thinking is absent from decisions on social-change initiatives. The whole purpose of the organization is socially driven. Economic aspects become a by-product rather than a driver. In the responsible leadership literature, little work has been done on building ethical capital through responsible leadership. This book proposes a social-innovation approach for responsible leaders to build ethical capital.

The theoretical void in the academic literature on what type of leaders might be ideal to run social businesses is more pronounced. The need to identify such leaders and leader attributes is essential, given the growing instances of unethical corporate behavior.

In the literature, social business is often defined as consisting of both for-profit and non-profit initiatives; in either case, the aim is to generate social wealth. Social business is sometimes defined in the context of social entrepreneurship as well (Mair and Marti 2009; Martin and Osberg 2007). Social entrepreneurship is primarily concerned with not-for-profits, while social-business initiatives are concerned with balancing the need to create social wealth with the need to generate economic profits for the company. In other words, the social-business leader has a responsibility to operate a profitable business while being sensitive to the social needs in the operating environment, and to align the interests of the two. A particular challenge is championing the cause for a social-purpose business in and out of the organization. Implementing the ideals of social-purpose business requires a higher degree of dedication.

The leadership style required for a successful social business can be expected to be somewhat different from the traditional leadership role. A leader who is passionate about social business is willing to champion a social cause while maximizing shareholder profits—and to place the social cause first (Yunus 2007).

Just as social enterprises can be presented in a continuum representing various forms of social and economic rationality (Alter 2004), from purely philanthropic to purely commercial (Dees 1998), this book proposes that socially innovative responsible leaders can also exist in a continuum. This continuum (Table 7.1) compares the attributes of RLR and RLP. RLR-based leaders are well suited to lead socially responsible business, whereas RLP-based leaders are better suited to leading economically responsible businesses. The distinction between economic and social rationality in leadership decision-making is at the heart of the difference between these two leadership styles. RLR is relationship-centered while RLP is performance- and efficiency-centered.

Table 7.1 Social-Purpose Business Attributes of RLP and RLR

Attributes	RLP	RLR
Rationality	Economic	Social
Motivation	To increase profitability with ethics, endurance and efficiency	To create and nurture strong stakeholder relationships
Method	Using interdependent inputs, processes and outputs to the leadership approach	Using the web of relationships developed and nurtured by the leader
Goal	To produce organizational outcomes that are profitable	To produce organizational and social outcomes that are profitable for the firm and society
Mission focus	Performance efficiency and effectiveness within ethical limits	Leadership that is based on relational intelligence
Social impact	Lower	Higher

Performance efficiency and effectiveness within ethical limits is the mission focus of RLP, while leadership that is based on relational intelligence is the mission focus of RLR. In the Asian century, with the growing Chinese influence on the global economy, more significance can be expected to be placed on developing relationships in all spheres of the economy. Responsible leadership necessarily involves a broader set of interacting parties (Sackmann 2006) or constituents (Maak and Pless 2006), both internal and, more importantly, external to the organization. Therefore, responsible leadership outcomes generated through RLR are more likely to make a higher social impact. It is the contention of this book that in the Asian-century leadership landscape, social innovation offers a significant opportunity for leaders to enact responsible leadership. A paradigm shift in the discipline of innovation underscores a focus on and need for social, as opposed to technological, innovation. This shift is broadly representative of the transformation from an industrial to a knowledge- and services-based society (Franz et al. 2012), as one that is taking place in the Asian century. There is increasing evidence in theory and practice to suggest the significant role social innovation can play in addressing economic, environmental, geopolitical, societal and technological issues through the promotion of equal opportunities, social integration, and also developing stronger relationships between innovative organizations and communities. This claim is further examined in the rest of the chapter.

Social Innovation[1]

Social innovation in business remains a largely neglected area of study in the social sciences despite calls for more attention to the concept (Mulgan et al. 2007; Dawson and Daniel 2010; Howaldt and Schwarz 2010). Social innovation has been defined in a multitude of ways (Table 7.2, also see Choi and Majumdar 2015). To some it is

---

[1] This section includes an updated version of ideas first presented in Fernando (2011).

Table 7.2 Key attributes and aims of social innovation from a sample of definitions

Social innovation			
Mumford (2002)	Dawson and Daniel (2010)	Pol and Ville (2009)	Heiskala (2007)
Social	People	Institutional change	Technological
Cultural	Problem	Social purpose	Economic
Economic	Process	Public good	Regulative
Environmental	Goal	Excludes business innovation	Normative
			Cultural

merely another management fad, to others a buzzword, while some others consider it a core aspect in a progressively developing society (Pol and Ville 2009). For example, Caulier-Grice et al. (2012) define social innovation as "new solutions (products, services, models, markets, processes etc.) that simultaneously meet a social need (more effectively than existing solutions) and lead to new or improved capabilities and relationships and better use of assets and resources. In other words, social innovations are both good for society and enhance society's capacity to act" (p. 18). Mumford (2002) defines social innovation as "the generation and implementation of new ideas about how people should organize interpersonal activities, or social interactions, to meet one or more common goals" (p. 253). To Kesselring and Leitner (2008), social innovation is a product of an interaction between sociological reflection and social action: it is "the interface point between sociological reflection and social action because it requires reflection on societal problems and targeted action" (p. 14). Social innovation has also been defined as a product of reflecting on social-relationship structures (Hochgerner 2009). A common theme running across most social-innovation definitions is that better social innovations are aligned with promoting social goals while also generating profits. An example is a social company in London that produces a magazine commercially run by the homeless (Howaldt and Schwarz 2010, p. 25). The requirement of commercial success is a moot point; not all researchers agree that it is necessary.

Social innovations vary in their ability to deliver positive outcomes. As opposed to traditional, financially motivated innovations, social innovations arise from a desire to help people or communities. Dawson and Daniel's (2010) definition of social innovation, "the development of new concepts, strategies and tools that support groups in achieving the objective of improved well-being" (p. 10), suggests that social innovations lead to the betterment of society as opposed to a narrower profit goal. However, social innovations can champion both the social and profit goals of businesses.

While Porter and Kramer's contributions do not specifically refer to social innovations, Dawson and Daniel (2010) indicate that many of Porter and Kramer's (2006) elements do in fact relate to social innovations in business. This suggests that social innovations can be beneficial for various stakeholders, including the community (Porter and Kramer 2006). This view is also supported by Auriac (2010), who suggests that social innovations created by business in conjunction with non-governmental organizations can benefit a wide range of stakeholders, including the business itself.

The literature on social innovation contains several key debates. One is on the nature of the "social" aspect of social innovations. For example, Baregheh et al. (2009) claim that their broader definition of innovation was more "biased toward economic innovation". Considerable debate has also taken place about the extent and nature of novelty required for social innovations. The consensus seems to be that the level of innovation required in social innovation is not the same as in innovations in a technical or scientific sense. Furthermore, the novelty of the social innovation is not required to be applicable universally, to all of humanity (Taatila et al. 2006). A social innovation is deemed sufficient if it is novel and relevant to the immediate community under consideration. However, even within the local community, a social innovation must include both internal and external stakeholders throughout its development and implementation process (Pot and Vaas 2008).

Pol and Ville (2009) critique the social-innovation literature and identify definitions, as well as overlaps between them. To simplify the understanding of the concept, they group the definitions under three perspectives in relation to institutional change. Heiskala (2007) presents five "ideal types" of innovations: technological, economic, regulative, normative and cultural:

> Technological innovations are new and more efficient ways to transform the material reality, and economic innovations put the technological innovations to the service of the production of surplus value. Taken together these two classes form the sphere of techno-economic innovations.... Regulative innovations transform explicit regulations and/or the ways they are sanctioned. Normative innovations challenge established value commitments and/or the way the values are specified into legitimate social norms. Finally, cultural innovations challenge the established ways to interpret reality by transforming mental paradigms, cognitive frames and habits of interpretation. Taken together these three classes form the sphere of social innovations (Heiskala 2007, p. 59).

Dawson and Daniel (2010) provide a useful explanation of social innovation: that it is not significantly different from technical innovation in the analytical sense of an examination of the relationships and behavioral practices of actors. On the contrary, "social" is used normatively, as a concept aimed at the common good. Dawson and Daniel (2010) identify four key elements to social innovation:

1. People: An initiative must be conceived by people and be useful for the people.
2. Problem: As looked at from an opportunity point of view—"What is the challenge?"—as opposed to a negative point of view—"What is wrong that needs to be fixed?"
3. Process: The approach and stages in which the challenge is negotiated and understood. In other words, how is the challenge to be addressed?
4. Goal: This stipulates the solution towards the increased well-being of the beneficiaries.

These four elements will be examined in detail later in the chapter.

Social Innovation and Responsible Leadership

At this stage, it is logical to ask (i) whether responsible leadership can help enact social innovation and (ii) if so, how? As noted in Chap. 5, responsible leadership has been defined as a "values-based and thorough ethical principles-driven relationship" of leaders and stakeholders (Pless 2007, p. 438). One of the key attributes of responsible leadership is that responsible leaders and stakeholders (not only followers) are linked by a sense of purpose and meaning that is shared to such an extent that leaders and stakeholders raise each other to "higher levels of motivation and commitment for achieving sustainable values creation and social change" (Pless 2007, p. 438). This larger, socially driven purpose for value creation and change, extending beyond the mere limits of the organizational boundaries, distinguishes responsible leadership from other leadership styles.

It was also noted that responsible leadership includes a broader set of relationships. A responsible leader is expected to develop mutually rewarding relationships with followers, but also with other internal and external stakeholders. The nature of the relationship in responsible leadership is different from that in general leadership, in that it is primarily values-based and driven by ethical principles. Compared with the simple leadership model, in responsible leadership, the goal is not only to achieve a business goal, but sustainable, value-adding goals for a wider group of stakeholders. Such goals help generate social change. For this reason, social innovation gives a special significance to responsible leadership. The question of how it does this can be answered by separately considering social innovation through responsible leadership for performance (RLP) and responsible leadership through relationships (RLR). In the following sections, this idea is explored in detail through the socially innovative responsible leadership model (Fig. 7.1).

Social Innovation Through Performance

For RLP proponents Lynham and Chermack (2006), leadership is "a focused system of interacting inputs, process, outputs and feedback wherein individuals and/or groups influence and/or act on behalf of specific individuals or groups of individuals

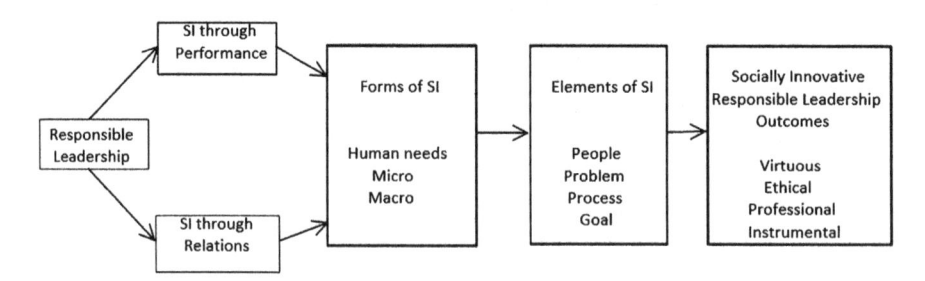

Fig. 7.1 Socially innovative responsible leadership

to achieve shared goals and commonly desired performance outcomes, within a specific performance system and environment" (p. 75). The inputs are the considerations of the constituents (in other words, the demands of the followers). The theory says that there is an external context that includes a social, economic, cultural, technological, ecological and political environment within which the constituents and the performance system reside. Within the performance system, there is an internal social, economic, cultural, technological, ecological and political environment within which goals are achieved.

According to Lynham and Chermack (2006), RLP seeks to address not "How can leaders be more effective in increasing the bottom dollar?", but "How can leaders increase their bottom dollar responsibly, with due regard to other stakeholders' needs?" Based on the interactions of the individuals who form that constituency, the constituency (followers) defines what is moral. In the RLP approach, "responsibleness" is about professional action. It is based on careful, reflective thought about responses; whether they are professionally right according to the context. Reflection is key, and considered thought before action will lead to professionally right action to suit a particular context. The three key criteria that determine what is professionally right are effectiveness, ethics and endurance. We know the dangers of solely being an effective leader (e.g. Hitler); a leader can be effective, yet also be unethical.

Thus through the RLP framework, the opportunities for responsible leaders to be social innovators can be seen from several points. The first is that RLP considers followers to be not only those within the organizations but also those stakeholders who are affected by or can influence the organization. Those stakeholders in the broader society are thus involved in the RLP process. Second, the context through which RLP takes place identifies almost the same contextual dimensions at which social innovation is aimed: social, economic, cultural, technological and environmental. Third, RLP is a value-embedded, social-change-driven approach that is more likely to lead to socially innovative initiatives. For example, Lynham and Chermack (2006) propose that RLP in action is more about leadership as a driver of a process rather than an outcome of performance. Within the RLP context, leadership needs to be understood as a "system-in-focus" in service to the broader performance system in the contextual environment; in other words, the broader society. Fourth, as noted earlier, reflection is a key aspect in both RLP and social innovation.

Social Innovation Through Relationships

RLR can be enacted as part of a social-innovation project, particularly as social relationships are an essential part of social innovation. As noted above, at the heart of Maak and Pless's (2006) RLR theory is the idea of the responsible leader. Responsible leadership involves building and sustaining good relationships with all stakeholders relevant to the organization's purpose. These stakeholders include not only those within the organization but those outside as well. In RLR theory, a responsible leader's key task is to be a weaver of relationships (Maak and Pless 2006).

In this process, the leader is expected to engage others as equals, introducing a variety of stakeholders. All the leader's attributes are used to bring in viewpoints from diverse stakeholders. The outcome from the integration of different viewpoints and demands of stakeholders could lead to socially innovative outcomes.

RLR has several ways in which to promote social innovation. First is that RLR is concerned with integrating differing stakeholders from within and outside the organization. Second, RLR is essentially concerned with building and maintaining the organization's social capital: the stock of active connections and human networks such as trust, mutual recognition, shared values, beliefs and understandings (Adler and Kwon 2002). The active social connections act to bind together people, and create mutual obligations and active communication networks. This introduces enormous tensions in stakeholder management. A responsible leader's duty is to make sure that these tensions are balanced as much as possible. The RLR-based leader aims to be humane and moral; demonstrating authenticity and integrity when caring for others. This leader displays relational intelligence: the ability to coordinate and cultivate relationships among stakeholder groups, applying both emotional and ethical intelligence to cope with issues when resolving ethical dilemmas. It is moral character and relational intelligence that distinguishes the good leader from the great (Maak and Pless 2006, p. 105).

These requirements of a responsible leader within an RLR framework offers a significant opportunity to enact social innovation (Fig. 7.1). On the other hand, it is also easy to see why RLR could be potentially used to champion social innovation. Socially innovative initiatives can result in building social capital. As Franz et al. (2012) put it, social innovation is a challenge for social sciences because social innovations become innovations by using the social aspect as an end as well as a mean. They note:

> …it is an a priori definition making the distinction easier between what might be socially innovative and what is not. It helps to solve the fundamental problem of any innovation (to become or not to be), i.e. the problem that we do not know whether it will be an innovation after all, since it is the success or failure of its diffusion, the eventual degree of generalisation which decides what can or cannot be considered an innovation. (p. 3).

In summary, the "social" aspect of social innovation demands that business leaders who are keen to initiate socially innovative ideas need to deal with the challenging social aspects of the innovation. This involves intense negotiations between stakeholders who may have opposing needs and wants. Relational intelligence offered in the RLR framework is a powerful tool for responsible leaders to achieve these social elements of innovation successfully and equitably.

Forms of Social Innovation

Moulaert et al. (2005) propose a three-tiered hierarchy of forms of social innovation; they are not mutually exclusive, but operate in integration with each other. The first form of social innovation is initiatives that are centered on alleviating or satisfying a human need (Fig. 7.1). These needs are of a certain character: they are unsatisfied because they are "not yet" or "no longer" required. A good example is microfinance schemes helping the disadvantaged in societies to develop a livelihood and maintain a steady form of income.

The second form of social innovation (labelled "micro" in Fig. 7.1) relates to opportunities in social relationships. According to Moulaert et al. (2005), these relationships are more about governance-related matters. These relate to satisfying human needs and increasing the level of participation, most notably, the marginalised in society. Compared to the first form, these initiatives are likely to be targeting macro- and group-level issues. Examples would be an innovative way to address youth homelessness in a particular community or encouraging children aged five to 12 years to keep fit through a low-cost multi-sport health and fitness program.

The third form of social innovation (titled "macro" in Fig. 7.1) relates to broader opportunities, especially in the socio-political arena, and to provide "access to resources needed to enhance rights to satisfaction of human needs and participation (empowerment dimension)" (Moulaert et al. 2005, p. 1976). This most complex of the forms of social innovation are those that explore ways to increase the socio-political capability and providing access to develop resources to safeguard rights that concern fulfilling human needs. These initiatives are likely to be at the national or even international level.

Elements of Social Innovation[2]

Using Dawson and Daniel's social innovation model (2010), we can identify attributes related to people, problem, process and goal in social innovation (Fig. 7.1).

The cases of Brandix and Unilever (Sri Lanka) (see Fernando 2007, 2010) can be used to explain the elements of social innovation. The single largest apparel exporter in Sri Lanka is Brandix (Brandix 2014). It employs 47,000 people across 42 manufacturing plants in Sri Lanka, India and Bangladesh. It runs a unique innovation program called "Disrupt Unlimited", where people are invited to submit an innovative idea that could change the current way of conducting business in the apparel industry. Once a year, Brandix hosts an event where major venture capitalists are presented with the ideas for potential funding and commercialization. Its social innovation programs have brought various accolades to the company, particularly regarding its sustainability initiatives. For example, it has been awarded the ISO 500001: 2011 certification for energy-management systems, the first apparel company in the world to receive this certification, and the Leadership in Energy and Environmental Design gold rating by the US Green Building Council.

Unilever (Sri Lanka) is a subsidiary of Unilever PLC. Operating in over 100 countries and employing 174,000, Unilever PLC engages daily with 2 billion consumers around the world (Unilever 2014). For matching long-term capitalism with responsible action, the company was awarded Corporate Economic Forum's C.K. Prahalad Award in 2012. In 2007, Patrick Cescau, its Group Chief Executive, was awarded Columbia Business School's Botwinick Prize in Business Ethics.

---

[2] This section includes an updated version of ideas first presented in Fernando (2007, 2010).

In the same year, Unilever PLC was ranked first in the Dow Jones Sustainability Index (see Fernando 2007; 2010). The Sri Lankan subsidiary, employing over 1100, is among the oldest and largest multinational companies in the country.

Brandix and Sri Lanka along with several other major companies pioneered the tsunami relief effort in Sri Lanka. Their initiatives in the immediate aftermath of the tsunami had a major impact on the Sri Lankan government and the United Nations relief programmes. The two companies' social-innovation initiatives during the tsunami relief efforts affected the four elements of social innovation: people, challenge, process and outcome.

People

Responsible leadership can be demonstrated by developing a social initiative where suffering is alleviated by meeting unmet needs of a community of people (Fig. 7.1). In a socially innovative initiative, the responsible leader needs to note that the people involved could be formal, informal or spontaneous groups that are drawn to the innovation due to a shared interest and common agenda.

According to Peterson and Seligman (2004), responsibility is not about preserving self interest, but being concerned of the common good. It is more about accepting the full range of consequences of an occurrence rather than recognising that one acted unethically. Brewer and Gardner (1996) and Dawes et al. (1990) note that employees who take responsibility has been found to generally empathize and develop a sense of identity with others. While aligned with the firm's profit making objectives, the social innovation must be useful for the community of people. Dawson and Daniel (2010) comment:

> Organizational innovation is necessarily a confluence of factors across various domains, such as, external environment and the operating context and culture, which are further moderated by numerous contingencies relative to the social concerns and interests of organizational participants. Taken as such, social innovation is more than product and process innovation, it is a concept which must recognize an essential commitment of the people for whom the change seeks to contribute. While business innovation remains rooted in the world of commerce and competition, social innovation has as a starting point the notion of social well-being and public good and seeks to benefit people in organizations, communities and society through direct and collateral outcomes of achieving greater social good (p. 19).

Thus the community of people to whom the social innovation is linked is a key force in the initiative.

Problem

The problem, or challenge, element of social innovation (Fig. 7.1) is looked at in a positive way—"What is the challenge?"—as opposed to a pessimistic view of "What needs to be fixed?" It should excite not only the leader but the employees and other stakeholders of the company. New strategies and approaches could be required to assist with the clarification, negotiation and prioritisation of initiatives when the challenge is ambiguous. Both RLP- and RLR-based leaders would be very context-driven, and would meet these challenges using the information available in the social, economic, cultural, technological and environmental contexts.

There can be several attributes of a challenge: internal or external, radical or apparently intractable, incidental or dynamic (shifting) (Dawson and Daniel 2010). For example, the Asian tsunami was a catalyst for many Sri Lankan organizations to engage in social-responsibility initiates. In Fernando (2007), I set out to explain how the original initiatives that started as an emergency response to a terrible natural disaster are now thriving social innovations. The case of Brandix is an example. After the tsunami, water wells along the coastal belt of Sri Lanka were contaminated with sea water and there was an urgent need to clean these wells. Brandix with its expertise and industry links on water purification, developed a comprehensive CSR initiative to provide clean water to affected areas (see Fernando 2007). Brandix constructed and maintained desalination plants with a two-fold process: first, processing contaminated well-water into clean drinkable water, and second, distributing of the drinkable water (Brandix 2006). The company's long-term CSR program involves the building of new desalination plants every year. I found that Brandix also cleaned around 4000 wells in Sri Lanka (Fernando 2007, 2010).

Most interviewees found decision making in the tsunami relief projects particularly hard. The Brandix leader said, "these [tsunami-related CSR decisions] were similar to the decisions I had to make under terrorist threats on my life to close down the factories and delay shipments. Then I had to make the call, and I did. At the time, we had never experienced anything like that before." (Fernando 2007, p. 5). In the context, there was a great urgency "to do something". He said:

> I had to make hard decisions. There was panic and I was concerned about wasting resources. I had to order everyone to work and meet the shipping deadlines because in the apparel industry, missing deadlines is committing suicide. A small group of employees were reluctant because they thought it was a hard, cold commercial decision. But for me, grief without a plan is more grief. While the factories were running, I decided that some employees should form into teams and we should go to those areas that no one had been to. So we sent several teams in a convoy carrying tents and basic emergency items to neglected areas especially in the East. (Fernando 2007, p. 5)

These first steps in a response initiative to a terrible natural disaster laid the foundations for the company's long-term social innovation. Nearly 35 months after the 2004 Asian Boxing Day tsunami, I reported the findings from interviewing the executives of Brandix on the evolution of the company's initial social-engagement initiatives (Fernando 2010). At 11 months, I found that Brandix focused mainly on providing water and tents. After 35 months, it had cleaned 4000 water wells, exceeding its original target by 700. Now, the company is building water wells around the country, mainly in low-income and rural areas where water is scarce. An initiative that started as an emergency response to a natural disaster to alleviate the suffering of affected communities has now become the main social-engagement initiative of this global apparel manufacturer.

In the case of Unilever (see Fernando 2007), after the tsunami, the directors had to make a challenging decision to restart operations. Because of the company's distribution network—one of the strongest, if not the strongest, in Sri Lanka—Unilever employees arrived first to the Eastern towns. Whether or not to publicise the relief work was a troubling decision to make. Unilever (Sri Lanka) interviewees said that they wanted to do the "right thing" by engaging in the relief efforts according to their conscience.

> Initially, they decided that Unilever should not use the tsunami CSR initiatives for enhancing its corporate image. However, according to the senior management team, in the absence of any publicity for their CSR initiatives, their stakeholders, both national and international, had wanted to know Unilever's contribution to the tsunami-relief effort. There had been increasing pressure from these stakeholders because some had channelled their resources through the company to direct them to affected areas. For example, ex-employees who were living abroad had sent funds to Unilever to be used in the relief effort. Hence, Unilever became concerned and decided to engage in "stakeholder awareness". According to the management team, "the Board decided to engage in focused awareness of our efforts, as opposed to a shotgun approach". They felt that this was appropriate because it was "more of a responsibility to account to our stakeholders than a strategy to exploit the tsunami for cheap commercial gain". One senior director said: As much as we didn't want to wave a flag, we needed to do the right thing by our conscience as well as seen doing the right thing because our stakeholders were expecting us to be seen. Stakeholders had to see the right thing been done–corporate image was important. (Fernando 2007, p. 5)

Unilever had to develop an awareness building campaign on the human tragedy because the company did not want to be seen as not contributing to the relief efforts. Therefore, the senior team decided to accept the publicity generated by their initiatives because the Sri Lankan government also needed to know how the multinationals in the country were contributing to the relief efforts. The two cases of Brandix and Unilever thus highlight some of the problems associated with socially responsible action.

Process

Getting the stakeholders on board to implement social innovation would involve the process dimension (Fig. 7.1). In this stage, the various stakeholder arguments against the initiative need to be negotiated and understood. The social-innovation process of an organization can depend on drivers and internal tools that act as regulators, reducing and amplifying the effects of the initiative.

Adapting from Fernando (2010, p. 8), the drivers of a firm allow a firm to place more priority on its chosen social initiatives. In both companies, stakeholders' demanded more publicity for the company relief efforts. Brandix managed these demands by developing the social initiatives into its overall strategy making process. Thus, the company integrated its CSR activities into its company strategy making. In the case of Unilever (Sri Lanka), the drivers for the initiatives were based on its mantra: *our brands, our people and our community*. Unilever claimed they "played to their strengths" (Fernando 2007, p. 5). That is, proven organizational resources, processes and techniques shaped the tsunami relief response.

Fig. 7.2 Socially responsible leadership and outcomes

Quadrant diagram:
- Vertical axis: Responsibility to Stakeholders (up) / Responsibility to Stockholders (down)
- Horizontal axis: Profits emphasize (left) / Social good emphasize (right)
- Quadrants: Ethical (upper left), Virtuous (upper right), Professional (lower left), Instrumental (lower right)

Goal

Finally, the goal element of social innovation stipulates that the solution should aim towards the increased well-being of the beneficiaries (Fig. 7.1). The four socially innovative responsible leadership outcomes identified in the model are virtuous, ethical, professional and instrumental.

Figure 7.2 further elaborates on these four outcomes. The horizontal axis shows the tension leaders have between emphasizing making profits on the one hand and doing social good on the other. The vertical axis shows the extent of leader responsibility towards the stakeholders versus stockholders. Responsible leaders' social initiatives that embody a high level of concern and responsibility to stakeholders while maintaining a profit focus can be expected to deliver more *ethical* outcomes. These outcomes are ethical as far as meeting the responsibility of making profits by discharging leaders' duties towards all stakeholders. Those initiatives that embody responsibility only to the stockholders and maintain a profit focus are likely to generate more *professional* outcomes. As opposed to these two outcome types, social-good-focused initiatives tend to execute more of a social-purpose, business-related mission. Those initiatives with high social good but tending to safeguard only stockholder interests could be identified as *instrumentalist* because it is very likely that initiatives that are focused on stockholders only, but with high social good, might have been developed to serve a profit-maximizing agenda that would enhance the company's reputation. In contrast, initiatives developed to have a high social good as well as meeting the needs of all stakeholders can be labelled as *virtuous*. These initiatives go beyond the ethical to a higher level of positive deviance (Cameron 2011), to have social good while safeguarding all stakeholder interests. This is not to say that the profit motive is abandoned—on the contrary, it is very much part of the initiative—but all stakeholder interests are still considered and, ideally, addressed.

Virtue is not a common concept in the business literature. In an examination of word usage in the *Wall Street Journal*, Cameron (2011) cites Walsh (1999), who found that from 1984 through 2000, publication of the terms "win", "advantage" and "beat" had risen more than by fourfold over that 17-year period. On the other hand, "virtue", "caring" and "compassion" appeared rarely in reference to business (p. 25). Bright (2006) claims that one key attribute of a firm's virtuous behavior is the unconditionality of social benefits: the "intention to create goods of first intent and to prudently use goods of second intent to instrumentally bring benefit to society" (p. 753). This is a critical condition in the context of our thesis and the main challenge of examining the authenticity of company expectations on social innovation activities seems to be on the intention to produce goods of first intent (considered a virtuous pursuit) or second intent (considered an instrumental pursuit) (Bright 2006, p. 752). In Fernando (2007), I observe how Unilever (Sri Lanka)'s initial response to the tsunami tragedy was concerning the production of goods of first intent. However, due to various competing stakeholder needs (Godfrey 2005, 2006), the company was forced to accept publicity particularly with the handover of LKR25 million it received from Unilever PLC to the Sri Lankan government. This action of accepting publicity associated with relief efforts can be identified as a good of second intent (Fig. 7.2).

In Fernando (2007, 2010), I note that those findings do not suggest that the two organizations' expectations were based solely on following second order goods. Both organisations' expectations at any stage of the relief operations did not show a need to solely generate goods of second intent (i.e., profits and reputation). I was confident that at least in the immediate aftermath of the tragedy, faced with the colossal human suffering and property damage, the need to spontaneously act without rational and strategic intent reduced the probability of solely producing goods of second intent.

A company's social innovation actions can be deemed to be less authentic if the goal is to only pursue goods of second intent such as increasing public image. Even if one assumes that organizations engaging in social innovation initiatives have only pure moral intentions, it would be hard to deny that the subsequent positive impact on reputation would increase profits. Culture, too, plays a role (Weaver 2001); for example, Sri Lanka's predominantly religious culture highly values charity and philanthropy. At a global level, there is hardly any doubt that Brandix's tsunami initiatives had a positive impact, particularly as the largest apparel exporter of Sri Lanka. Similarly, as a globally visible operation, one could argue that Unilever PLC could leverage goodwill among its stakeholders at a global level by pioneering the tsunami relief efforts in Sri Lanka. Therefore, both organizations show the dilemma that organizations associated with socially innovative action could fall into. That is, even if these organizations had the intention to produce first order goods, the by-products these actions generate could lead to second order goods such as increased reputation and profits. These outcomes could attract unfair criticism that organizations in the first instance engaged in socially innovative action to only produce goods of second order.

Virtuousness Through Socially Innovative Responsible Leadership

Here we explore the relationship between socially innovative responsible leadership and organizational virtuousness. As noted earlier, virtue ethics is increasingly gaining popularity among organizational behaviour scholars and more recently among leadership scholars. We noted earlier that the approaches used to integrate virtue ethics into organizational settings rely on Aristotelian or neo-Aristotelian virtue ethics (e.g. Tsoukas and Cummings 1997; McCloskey 2006; Sison 2011; Sison and Fontrodona 2012) positive organizational scholars (e.g. Cameron et al. 2004; Rego et al. 2011) and others (e.g. Melé 2009; Slote 1996, 2001; Swanton 2003; Bright et al. 2014) have proposed different approaches. Moore (2012), Fernando and Moore (2014), Beadle and Moore (2011), Crockett (2005), Van de Ven (2011) and Von Krogh et al. (2012) make Alasdair MacIntyre's interpretation of virtue ethics central to their discussions.

According to MacIntyre (2007), virtues are "dispositions not only to act in particular ways but also to feel in particular ways. To act virtuously…is to act from inclination formed by the cultivation of the virtues" (p. 149). The practice of virtues is at the heart of MacIntyre's argument. According to Fernando and Moore (2014), MacIntyre interprets virtues as being enacted "inside practices". These generate "internal goods" the pursuit of which lead to perfection of the products and excellence of the individual (MacIntyre 1994). Internal goods are valued for their own sake; not because of some other desired good (Moore 2012). The determination of the excellence of internal goods is made by the practitioners themselves (MacIntyre 2007, p. 188–9). However, scholars have noted that external stakeholders such as customers are also critical to develop relevant standards of excellence (see Beadle 2013, p. 685; Keat 2000, pp. 128–9; Moore 2012).

"External goods" are pursued for the sake of some further good; not for their own sake (Moore 2012). They are usually pursued for the access they give to internal goods which can be generated from the same or other practices (Fernando and Moore 2014; Moore 2013). To survive and continue the practices, they reside in institutions. Asian century business organizations are mostly interested in external goods such as reputation, profits and power; that is, generally, in success factors (Moore 2012).

Thus a responsible leaders' challenge would be to develop practice–institution combinations that aim to balance the "tension between the generation and prioritization of internal and external goods" (Moore 2012, p. 365). This is a complex task for the leader. The goodness of purpose of the organization is one key element that could guide the leader to meet this challenging task. From a leaders' perspective, the link to society in MacIntyrian virtue ethics is represented in the notion of a person's ultimate purpose in life. Through this purpose, the individual is expected to attain a state of well-being and maintain good relationships in the community. The pursuing of internal goods therefore has a good effect on the individual (i.e. individual good) as well as on the community (i.e. common good). This common good is the "goods of those types of communities in and through which the goods of individual lives are characteristically achieved" (MacIntyre 1994, p. 288). This link to the social level is amply explained by Moore (2012, p. 366) citing McCann and Brownsberger (1990, pp. 227–8):

> The normative character of MacIntyre's definition of a social practice...is secured within a larger account of the moral life as a whole. There must be some *telos* to human life, a vision anticipating the moral unity of life, given in the form of a narrative history that has meaning within a particular community's traditions; otherwise the various internal goods generated by the range of social practices will remain disordered and potentially subversive of one another. Without a community's shared sense of *telos*, there will be no way of signifying 'the overriding good' by which various internal goods may be ranked and evaluated.

This link to the common social good potentially allows responsible leaders to use social innovation as a way to enact virtue ethics.

The relationship between the goodness of purpose and success–excellence can be depicted as in Fig. 7.3. Following Moore (2012) and Fernando and Moore's (2014) line of inquiry, organizations can operate within any section of the two dimensions. Particular types of organizations, however, are likely to operate within certain areas. For example, consider the case of a concentration camp. It can strive to achieve excellence in how the camp is operated (bottom right). However due to the nature of the institution, a concentration camp is more likely to aim for success (bottom left). On the other hand, a charitable organization aiming towards achieving a good purpose would be on the top right rather than a more balanced position (see Fernando and Moore 2014; Moore 2012). It is important to note that a virtuous organization would not be placed on the top right corner (Moore 2012), but placed on the lower excellence side of the success-excellence scale (reflecting the good purpose, see Fig. 7.3). A non-virtuous organization or a vicious organization would have a bad purpose and, though aiming to follow success, might appear closer to the bottom of the boundary (Moore 2012).

From a MacIntyrian perspective, the responsible leader will have to recognise that organizations are moral projects (Moore 2012). He describes the undeniable

Fig. 7.3 Success-excellence relationship with goodness of purpose (With kind permission from Springer Science+Business Media: Journal of Business Ethics, Fernando, M., & Moore, G., 2014. MacIntyrean virtue ethics in business: a cross-cultural comparison. Online first, 1–18. Adapted from Crockett and Anderson, 2008, see Moore 2012)

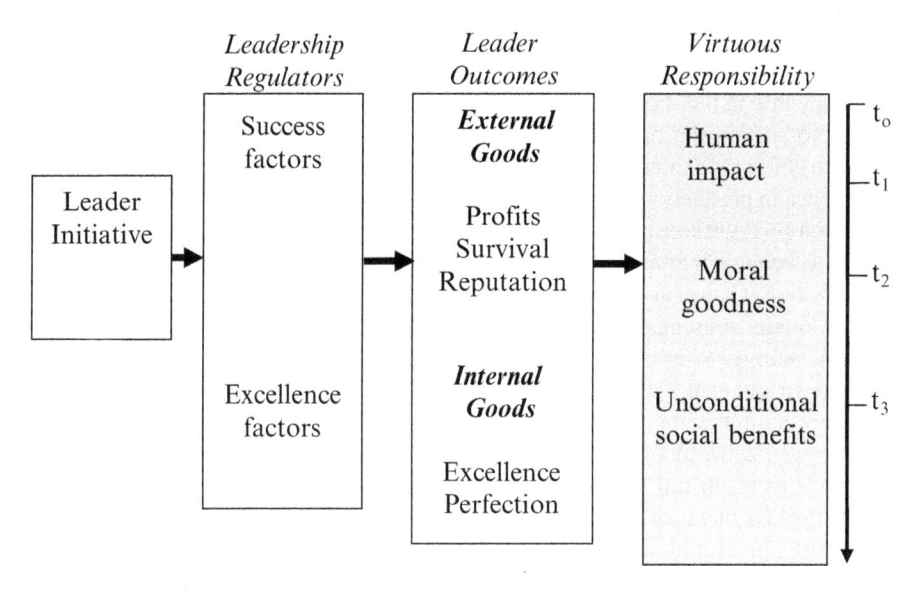

```
Leadership        Leader          Virtuous
Regulators        Outcomes        Responsibility

┌─────────────┐   ┌──────────┐    ┌──────────────┐
│  Success    │   │ External │    │              │   ⎡ t₀
│  factors    │   │  Goods   │    │   Human      │
│             │   │          │    │   impact     │   ⎯ t₁
Leader  →     │ → │  Profits │ →  │              │
Initiative    │   │  Survival│    │   Moral      │   ⎯ t₂
│             │   │ Reputation│   │   goodness   │
│             │   │          │    │              │
│  Excellence │   │ Internal │    │ Unconditional│   ⎯ t₃
│  factors    │   │  Goods   │    │ social       │
│             │   │          │    │ benefits     │
│             │   │ Excellence│   │              │
│             │   │ Perfection│   │              │
└─────────────┘   └──────────┘    └──────────────┘
```

Fig. 7.4 Virtuous responsible leadership

tension between practice and the institution, which extends to a tension between excellence (production and prioritization of internal goods) and success (production and prioritization of external goods). Unless leaders responsible actions sustain the core practices on which the organization is formed, the organization itself (the practice-institution combination) will not survive (Moore 2012).

The virtuousness of leaders' initiatives can be examined based on the balance between success and excellence. Virtuous organizations need to strike this balance, with the emphasis just on the side of excellence (Moore 2012). We can develop Fig. 7.4 to extend the case for a virtuous approach to responsible leadership. In Fig. 7.4, leadership regulators can either enhance or suppress the virtuousness of the leader initiatives. Success factors as a regulator of leaders' actions refer to those processes that drive leaders' pursuit of external goods such as profits, survival or reputation. Empirical studies by Fernando and Moore (2014) and Moore (2012) have found that the pursuit of external goods is typically driven through financial activity, customers, suppliers, employees and brand management. RLP-based leader actions with the focus more on performance are likely to target success factors than excellence factors. Excellence factors, on the other hand, act as regulators when leaders use organizational processes to generate internal goods by seeking both excellence of the outcomes through products or service and the fulfillment of the constituents. RLR-based leader actions with more emphasis on relationships are likely to target excellence factors more than success factors.

However, leaders' actions can consist of a mix of success (RLP) and excellence (RLR) factors, with different emphasis placed on internal and external goods. Properly balanced initiatives aligned with firms' core business activities can generate both external and internal goods. The timeline indicates that while RLP-based success factors and external goods are relatively more short-term oriented, RLR-based excellence factors and internal goods are relatively more long-term oriented. That is, while in the short term (t_0-t_1), the leaders' focus will be more on generating profits to sustain the organizations' objectives, in the long term (t_2-t_3), the focus shifts to generating internal goods (i.e. through relationship building into delivering excellence in products and service, and perfection of the individuals). The impact of organizational virtuousness through leadership is conducive to a situation where the desire to achieve human excellence is embedded in the culture and context of the organization (Cameron et al. 2004).

The model presented in Fig. 7.4 helps to further examine the virtuousness of leaders' actions to examine how Bright et al.'s (2006) attributes of virtuousness overlap. Bright et al. (2006) propose that virtue represents the excellence of character. They claim that this trait can reside in people and entities such as organizations. At the organizational level, the notion of virtuousness requires leaders to foster their followers to reach full potential and highest aspirations. More importantly, in the context of the thesis of this book, the three attributes set a standard for leaders to engage in social initiatives and align these with organizational strategy (Godfrey and Hatch 2007).

The human impact outcome of a leader's actions is its effect on improving the living conditions, resilience and general wellbeing of constituents (Bright et al. 2006). Based on the MacIntyrian view of individual good and common good, actions that maximize both are likely to generate positive human impact for all constituents. In this process, no constituent should have more access to a resource and benefit than others. To be considered virtuous, a leader's actions should also pass the moral goodness test, which is based on people and organizations' character traits. Leaders championing this particular attribute would believe in the action because it is the correct action to safeguard the best interests of the internal and external goods of the organization. Leaders championing this particular attribute would initiate action because it is the "right thing to do" (Bright 2006), in terms of protecting the interests of internal and external goods of the organization. According to Arjoon (2000), the concept of "the good" relates to what takes place within the confines of communities. He asserts that when community members contribute to the whole with the best of their capacity, recognizing the legitimate needs of other members, those actions generate common good. In producing this common good, leaders should aim to achieve human excellence in initiatives that exceeds instrumental reciprocity (i.e., an intent to generate a specific response in or from others, see Peterson and Seligman 2004). Intent is a key dimension in determining the extent of moral goodness but is notoriously difficult to determine. Leaders' responsible decision making should be based on whether an action is the correct thing to do even when the outcomes clearly indicate lack of definable benefits. For example, when leader behavior is designed with an instrumental purpose, such action cannot be defined as contributing to moral goodness (Weiser and Zadek 2000). As noted earlier, desirable character traits in leaders is integral to assessing the moral goodness of their initiatives. However, only those outcomes where leaders act to the best of their abilities and recognizing the rights of others add value to the common good would demonstrate moral goodness.

Finally, any leader action to generate organizational virtuousness should satisfy the unconditional social benefit criterion. This criterion stems from Aristotelian ethics (eudemonia), that wellbeing is an integral part of virtuous action, not an outcome of virtuous action (Park and Peterson 2003). As noted earlier, Bright et al. (2006) describe unconditional social benefit as an intention. The intention in the first place is to generate goods of first intent (internal goods). They are chief or first order goods, which deserve interest in them, as in the case of common good initiatives and concern for others (Bright 2006). However, interest in second order goods is amoral because these are pursued for attaining something secondary, such as profit, reputation and power (Bright 2006). The generation of second order goods (external goods) is required to be used wisely to bring common good to society. According to Bright, "social and economic interests are complementary. The pursuit of economic interests for the promotion of social interests is virtuous and genuine, whereas the sole pursuit of economic interests risks ingratiation" (p. 752). Thus if a leader accepts a green house gas emissions target only for the sake of obtaining increased business, any outcomes generated from such an action are classed as goods of second intent, and without virtue (i.e., an action taken with the intention of solely producing profits without concern for the common good and legitimate rights of others). However, if goods of second intent (e.g., increase in sales) are produced as a by-product without intention while aiming to achieve first order goods (e.g., accepting green house gas emission targets), it can be classified as virtuous (Bright et al. 2006).

In summary, in this chapter we considered an integrated perspective of responsible leadership. This chapter has examined the value of socially innovative responsible leadership, extending the RLP and RLR approaches and focusing on how responsible leadership can develop socially innovative initiatives (Fig. 7.1) that are virtuous (Fig. 7.4). In the Asian century, with the focus shifting gradually from performance to relationship building, RLR-based responsible leadership shows promise in encouraging socially innovative responsible leadership, which—in theory, at least—promises virtuous outcomes. With high social impact and due concern for all stakeholders, firms have the opportunity to choose the right balance between success and excellence factors. This opportunity to balance short-term and long-term needs and goals provides a road map to shape appropriate drivers and regulators to secure the best socially innovative responsible leadership outcomes.

Conclusion

The premise of the book is based on the shift in economic and political power from the Western bloc of nations to Asia, particularly China and India. To successfully thrive in the new economic order, the role of corporations and corporate leaders will also need to change. Responsible leadership has been presented in Western research as a leadership approach that is more humane and value-laden. Previous chapters have examined two key theories of responsible leadership: RLP and RLR. While these theories explain some mechanisms of *what* responsible leadership is, more recent contributions have extended these theories and proposed novel ways for *how* responsible leadership can be enacted. These two distinct theories demand different attributes from leaders. In this chapter, the key contribution to the existing literature, based on changes in the economic and political order, has been an examination of socially innovative responsible leadership. Furthermore, the chapter has examined how RLP and RLR could be integrated and extended to include virtue in socially innovative responsible leadership. The discussion in this chapter thus further extends the current Western-based literature on responsible leadership from a mostly prescriptive approach to a pragmatic approach relevant to the Asian century.

References

Adler, P. S., & Kwon, S.-W. (2002). Social capital: Prospects for a new concept. *Academy of Management Review, 27*(1), 17–40.
Alter, K. (2004). *Social enterprise typology*. www.4lenses.org/setypology. Accessed 25 Apr 2015.
Arjoon, S. (2000). Virtue theory as a dynamic theory of business. *Journal of Business Ethics, 28*(2), 159–178.
Auriac, J. (2010). Corporate social innovation. *OECD Observer, 279*, 32.
Austin, J. E., Leonard, H., Reficco, E., & Wei-Skillern, J. (2004). *Corporate social entrepreneurship: A new vision of CSR* (Harvard Business School Working Paper No. 05–021). Boston: Harvard Business School.
Australian Government White Paper. (2012). *Australia in the Asian century*. Canberra: Australian Government.
Baregheh, A., Rowley, J., & Sambrook, S. (2009). Towards a multidisciplinary definition of innovation. *Management Decision, 47*(8), 1323–1339.
Beadle, R. (2013). Managerial work in a practice-embodying institution: The role of calling, the virtue of constancy. *Journal of Business Ethics, 113*(4), 679–690.
Beadle, R., & Moore, G. (2011). MacIntyre: Neo-Aristotelianism and organization theory. *Research in the Sociology of Organizations, 32*, 85–121.
Beeson, M. (2014). *Regionalism and globalization in East Asia: Politics, security and economic development*. New York: Palgrave Macmillan.
Bloomberg. (2013). *China eclipses U.S. as biggest trading nation*. http://www.bloomberg.com/news/2013-02-09/china-passes-u-s-to-become-the-world-s-biggest-trading-nation.html. Accessed 25 Apr 2015.
Boschee, J. (2001). Eight basic principles for nonprofit entrepreneurs. *Nonprofit World, 19*(4), 15–18.
Brandix. (2006). Water is life: Care for our own. *REACH*, pp. 7–8.
Brandix. (2014). *Enter the world of Brandix*. http://www.brandix.com/brandix/index.php
Brewer, M. B., & Gardner, W. (1996). Who is this" we"? Levels of collective identity and self representations. *Journal of Personality and Social Psychology, 71*(1), 83.
Bright, D. (2006). Virtuousness is necessary for genuineness in corporate philanthropy. *Academy of Management Review, 31*(3), 752–754.
Bright, D., Cameron, K., & Caza, A. (2006). The amplifying and buffering effects of virtuousness in downsized organizations. *Journal of Business Ethics, 64*(3), 249–269.
Bright, D., Winn, B., & Kanov, J. (2014). Reconsidering virtue: Differences of perspective in virtue ethics and the positive social sciences. *Journal of Business Ethics, 119*(4), 445–460.

Bull, M., Crompton, H., & Jayawarna, D. (2008). Coming from the heart (the road is long). *Social Enterprise Journal, 4*(2), 108–125.
Bull, M., Ridley-Duff, R., Foster, D., & Seanor, P. (2010). Conceptualising ethical capital in social enterprise. *Social Enterprise Journal, 6*(3), 250–264.
Cameron, K. (2011). Responsible leadership as virtuous leadership. *Journal of Business Ethics, 98*(1), 25–35.
Cameron, K., Bright, D., & Caza, A. (2004). Exploring the relationships between organizational virtuousness and performance. *American Behavioral Scientist, 47*(6), 766–790.
Caulier-Grice, J., Davies, A., Patrick, R., & Norman, W. (2012). Social innovation overview: A deliverable of the project: "The theoretical, empirical and policy foundations for building social innovation in Europe" (TEPSIE), European Commission – 7th framework programme. European Commission, DG Research, Brussels.
Chapple, W., & Moon, J. (2005). Corporate social responsibility (CSR) in Asia: A seven-country study of CSR web site reporting. *Business & Society, 44*(4), 415–441.
Choi, N., & Majumdar, S. (2015). Social innovation: Towards a conceptualisation. In S. Majumdar et al. (Eds.), *Technology and innovation for social change* (pp. 7–34). New Delhi: Springer.
CNBC. (2015). *US dethroned as world's billionaire capital.* Available at www.cnbc.com/2015/10/15/us-dethroned-as-worlds-billionaire-capital.html. Accessed 31 Oct 2015.
Crockett, C. (2005). The cultural paradigm of virtue. *Journal of Business Ethics, 62*(2), 191–208.
Crockett, C., & Anderson, A. (2008). *A grounded theory of virtue: From purpose to praxis* (Working paper).
Dawes, R., van de Kragt, A., & Orbell, J. (1990). Cooperation for the benefit of us-not me, or my conscience. In *Beyond self-interest* (pp. 97–110). Chicago: University of Chicago Press.
Dawson, P., & Daniel, L. (2010). Understanding social innovation: A provisional framework. *International Journal of Technology Management, 51*(1), 9–21.
Dees, J. (1998). Enterprising nonprofits. *Harvard Business Review, 76*, 54–69.
Dees, J. (2001). *The meaning of "social entrepreneurship".* Paper presented at the Centre for Advancement of Social Entrepreneurship (CASE), Fuqua School of Business, Duke Univesity, Durham, NC.
Dees, J., Emerson, J., & Economy, P. (2002). *Strategic tools for social entrepreneurs: Enhancing the performance of your enterprising nonprofit* (Vol. 207). New York: Wiley.
Ekbal, N. (2009). *The great Muslims of undivided India.* Delhi: Kalpaz.
Fernando, M. (2007). Corporate social responsibility in the wake of the Asian tsunami: A comparative case study of two Sri Lankan companies. *European Management Journal, 25*(1), 1–10.
Fernando, M. (2009). *Going beyond climate ethics: Virtuousness in climate change initiatives.* http://www.nccr-climate.unibe.ch/conferences/climate_policies/working_papers/Fernando.pdf. Accessed 12 Apr 2014.
Fernando, M. (2010). Corporate social responsibility in the wake of the Asian tsunami: Effect of time on the genuineness of CSR initiatives. *European Management Journal, 28*(1), 68–79.
Fernando, M. (2011). A social innovation based transformative learning approach to teaching business ethics. *Journal of Business Ethics Education, 8*, 119–138.
Fernando, M., & Moore, G. (2014). MacIntyrean virtue ethics in business: A cross-cultural comparison. *Journal of Business Ethics,* Online first, 1–18.
Franz, H.-W., Hochgerner, J., & Howaldt, J. (Eds.). (2012). *Challenge social innovation: Potentials for business, social entrepreneurship, welfare and civil society.* Berlin: Springer.
Gallo, F. T. (2011). *Business leadership in China: How to blend best Western practices with Chinese wisdom.* Hoboken: Wiley.
Godfrey, P. C. (2005). The relationship between corporate philanthropy and shareholder wealth: A risk management perspective. *Academy of Management Review, 30*(4), 777–798.
Godfrey, P. C. (2006). A reply to bright: Virtuousness and the virtues of the market. *Academy of Management Review, 31*(3), 754–756.
Godfrey, P. C., & Hatch, N. W. (2007). Researching corporate social responsibility: An agenda for the 21st century. *Journal of Business Ethics, 70*(1), 87–98.

Grameen Bank. (2015). *Founder.* Available at http://www.grameen-info.org/grameen-founder-muhammad-yunus/. Accessed 25 Oct 2015.
Gupta, V., & Hanges, P. J. (2004). Regional and climate clustering of societal cultures. In R. J. House, P. J. Hanges, M. Javidan, P. W. Dorfman, & V. Gupta (Eds.), *Culture, leadership, and organizations: The GLOBE study of 62 societies* (pp. 178–218). Thousand Oaks: Sage.
Gupta, V., Levenburg, N., Moore, L., Motwani, J., & Schwarz, T. (2009). Anglo vs. Asian family business: A cultural comparison and analysis. *Journal of Asia Business Studies, 3*(2), 46–55.
Haley, G. T., & Tan, C.-T. (1996). The black hole of South-East Asia: Strategic decision making in an informational void. *Management Decision, 34*(9), 37–48.
Haley, G. T., & Tan, C.-T. (1999). East vs. West: Strategic marketing management meets the Asian networks. *Journal of Business & Industrial Marketing, 14*(2), 91–104.
Heiskala, R. (2007). Social innovations: Structural and power perspectives. In T. J. Hamalainen & R. Heiskala (Eds.), *Social innovations, institutional change and economic performance* (pp. 52–79). Cheltenham: Edward Elgar.
Hochgerner, J. (2009). Innovation processes in the dynamics of social change. In J. Loudin & K. Schuch (Eds.), *Innovation cultures. Challenge and learning strategy* (pp. 17–45). Prague: Filosofia.
Hockerts, K. (2010). Social entrepreneurship between market and mission. *International Review of Entrepreneurship, 8*(2), 177–198.
Hofstede, G. (1993). Cultural constraints in management theories. *The Academy of Management Executive, 7*(1), 81–94.
Hofstede, G. (1998). A case for comparing apples with oranges: International differences in values. *International Journal of Comparative Sociology, 39*(1), 16.
Hofstede, G. (2003). Cultural constraints in management theories. *Readings and Cases in International Management: A Cross-Cultural Perspective, 1*, 17.
Hofstede, G. (2010). The GLOBE debate: Back to relevance. *Journal of International Business Studies, 41*(8), 1339–1346.
Hofstede, G. (2011). Dimensionalizing cultures: The Hofstede model in context. *Online Readings in Psychology and Culture, 2*(1), 8.
Hotta, K. (2009). Effect of changing governance system: Result of Western style management adoption to Japanese culture of ambiguity. *Journal of Systemics, Cybernetics and Informatics, 7*(1), 66–71.
Howaldt, J., & Schwarz, M. (2010). Social innovation: Concepts, research fields and international trends. In K. Henning, & F. Hees (Eds.), *Studies for innovation in a modern working environment-international monitoring* (Vol. 5). Aachen: IMA/ZLW.
Jamali, D. (2007). The case for strategic corporate social responsibility in developing countries. *Business and Society Review, 112*(1), 1–27.
Keat, R. (2000). *Cultural goods and the limits of the market.* London: MacMillan Press.
Kesselring, A., & Leitner, M. (2008). Soziale Innovation in Unternehmen. In *Studie erstellt im Auftrag der Unruhe Privatstiftung.* Wien: Zentrum für Soziale Innovation.
Knowledge@Wharton. (2009). *Muhammed Yunus: Lifting people worldwide out of poverty.* Available at http://knowledge.wharton.upenn.edu/article/muhammad-yunus-lifting-people-worldwide-out-of-poverty/. Accessed 29 Oct 2015.
Lee, S.-H., & Oh, K. K. (2007). Corruption in Asia: Pervasiveness and arbitrariness. *Asia Pacific Journal of Management, 24*(1), 97–114.
Lynham, S. A., & Chermack, T. J. (2006). Responsible leadership for performance: A theoretical model and hypotheses. *Journal of Leadership & Organizational Studies, 12*(4), 73.
Maak, T., & Pless, N. M. (2006). Responsible leadership in a stakeholder society–A relational perspective. *Journal of Business Ethics, 66*(1), 99–115.
MacIntyre, A. (1994). A partial response to my critics. In J. Horton & S. Mendus (Eds.), *After MacIntyre: Critical perspectives on the work of Alasdair MacIntyre* (pp. 283–305). Notre Dame: University of Notre Dame Press.
MacIntyre, A. (1998). Practical rationalities as forms of social structure. In K. Knight (Ed.), *The MacInytre reader* (pp. 120–135). Cambridge: Polity Press.
MacIntyre, A. (2007). *After virtue* (3rd ed.). London: Duckworth.

Mair, J., & Marti, I. (2009). Entrepreneurship in and around institutional voids: A case study from bangladesh. *Journal of Business Venturing, 24*(5), 419–435.

Martin, R. L., & Osberg, S. (2007). Social entrepreneurship: The case for definition. *Stanford Social Innovation Review, 5*(2), 28–39.

McCann, D. P., & Brownsberger, M. L. (1990). Management as a social practice: Rethinking business ethics after MacIntyre. In D. M. Yeager (Ed.), *The Annual of the Society of Christian Ethics 1990* (pp. 223–245). Washington, DC: Georgetown University Press.

McCloskey, D. (2006). Hobbes, Nussbaum, and all seven of the virtues. *Development and Change, 37*(6), 1309–1312.

Melé, D. (2009). Integrating personalism into virtue-based business ethics: The personalist and the common good principles. *Journal of Business Ethics, 88*(1), 227–244.

Meredith, R. (2009). *From China: The world's new car capital.* http://www.jcbgchina.cn/html/html/chinabiz/20090423/50.htm. Accessed 25 Apr 2015.

Moore, G. (2012). Virtue in business: Alliance boots and an empirical exploration of MacIntyre's conceptual framework. *Organization Studies, 33*(3), 363–387.

Moore, G. (2013). Re-imagining the morality of management: A modern virtue ethics approach. In H. Harris, G. Wijesinghe, & S. McKenzie (Eds.), *The heart of the good institution* (pp. 7–34). Dordrecht: Springer.

Mort, G. S., Weerawardena, J., & Carnegie, K. (2002). Social entrepreneurship: Towards conceptualization and measurement. *American Marketing Association. Conference Proceedings, 13*, 5.

Moulaert, F., Martinelli, F., Swyngedouw, E., & Gonzalez, S. (2005). Towards alternative model(s) of local innovation. *Urban Studies, 42*(11), 1969–1990.

Mulgan, G., Ali, R., Halkett, R., & Sanders, B. (2007). *In and out of sync: The challenge of growing social innovations.* London: NESTA.

Mumford, M. D. (2002). Social innovation: Ten cases from Benjamin franklin. *Creativity Research Journal, 14*(2), 253–266.

Park, N., & Peterson, C. (2003). Virtues and organizations. In *Positive organizational scholarship: Foundations of a new discipline* (pp. 33–47). San Francisco: Berrett-Koehler.

Perrini, F., & Vurro, C. (2006). Social entrepreneurship: Innovation and social change across theory and practice. *Social Entrepreneurship, 23*(1), 57–85.

Peterson, C., & Seligman, M. E. (2004). *Character strengths and virtues: A classification and handbook.* Washington, DC: American Psychological Association.

Pless, N. M. (2007). Understanding responsible leadership: Role identity and motivational drivers. *Journal of Business Ethics, 74*(4), 437–456.

Pol, E., & Ville, S. (2009). Social innovation: Buzz word or enduring term? *The Journal of Socio-Economics, 38*(6), 878–885.

Porter, M. E., & Kramer, M. R. (2006). The link between competitive advantage and corporate social responsibility. *Harvard Business Review, 84*(12), 78–92.

Pot, F., & Vaas, F. (2008). Social innovation, the new challenge for Europe. *International Journal of Productivity and Performance Management, 57*(6), 468–473.

Population Reference Bureau. (2014). *World population data sheet 2014.* Available at http://www.prb.org/Publications/Datasheets/2014/2014-world-population-data-sheet/data-sheet.aspx, Accessed 12 Dec 2014.

Redding, S. (1990). *The spirit of Chinese capitalism.* New York: Walter de Gruyter.

Rego, A., Ribeiro, N., Cunha, M. P., & Jesuino, J. C. (2011). How happiness mediates the organizational virtuousness and affective commitment relationship. *Journal of Business Research, 64*(5), 524–532.

Rodrigues, J., & Baker, G. A. (2012). Grameen Danone foods limited (GDF). *International Food and Agribusiness Management Review, 15*(1), 127–158.

Sackmann, S. A. (2006). Leading responsibly across cultures. In T. Maak & N. Pless (Eds.), *Responsible leadership* (pp. 122–137). Oxon: Routledge.

Sayers, L. (2014). *Why all-sector innovation is the key to unlocking potential.* http://www.themandarin.com.au/11769-luke-sayers-sector-innovation-key-realising-australias-full-potential/?pgnc=12014. Accessed 25 Apr 2015.

Sison, A. J. G. (2011). Aristotelian citizenship and corporate citizenship: Who is a citizen of the corporate polis? *Journal of Business Ethics, 100*(1), 3–9.
Sison, A. J. G., & Fontrodona, J. (2012). The common good of the firm in the Aristotelian-Thomistic tradition. *Business Ethics Quarterly, 22*(2), 211–246.
Slote, M. (1996). *From morality to virtue*. Oxford: Oxford University Press.
Slote, M. (2001). *Morals from motives*. Oxford: Oxford University Press.
Sondergaard, M. (1994). Research note: Hofstede's consequences: A study of reviews, citations and replications. *Organization Studies, 15*(3), 447–456.
Swanton, C. (2003). *Virtue ethics, a pluralistic view*. Oxford: Oxford University Press.
Taatila, V. P., Suomala, J., Siltala, R., & Keskinen, S. (2006). Framework to study the social innovation networks. *European Journal of Innovation Management, 9*(3), 312–326.
Teiwes, F. C., & Sun, W. (2007). *The end of the Maoist era: Chinese politics during the twilight of the cultural revolution, 1972–1976*. Armonk: M.E. Sharpe.
Thompson, J. L. (2002). The world of the social entrepreneur. *International Journal of Public Sector Management, 15*(5), 412–431.
Tixier, M. (1994). Management and communication styles in Europe: Can they be compared and matched. *Employee Relations, 16*(1), 8–26.
Tsoukas, H., & Cummings, S. (1997). Marginalization and recovery: The emergence of Aristotelian themes in organization studies. *Organization Studies, 18*(4), 655–683.
Turnbull, S. (2011). Worldly leadership: Challenging the hegemony of Western business education. *Journal of Global Responsibility, 2*(2), 170–187.
Unilever. (2014). *Introduction to Unilever*. http://www.unilever.com.au/aboutus/introductiontounilever/
Van De Ven, B. (2011). Banking after the crisis: Towards an understanding of ranking as a professional practice. *Ethical Perspectives-Katholieke Universiteit Leuven, 18*(4), 541–568.
Von Krogh, G., Haefliger, S., Spaeth, S., & Wallin, M. W. (2012). Carrots and rainbows: Motivation and social practice in open source software development. *MIS Quarterly, 36*(2), 649–676.
Wagner-Tsukamoto, S. (2005). An economic approach to business ethics: Moral agency of the firm and the enabling and constraining effects of economic institutions and interactions in a market economy. *Journal of Business Ethics, 60*(1), 75–89.
Walsh, J. P. (1999). Business must talk about its social role. In T. Dickson (Ed.), *Mastering strategy*. London: Financial Times/Prentice Hall.
Warner, M. (2014). *Understanding management in China: Past, present and future*. Abingdon: Routledge.
Wang, B. X., & Chee, H. (2011). *Chinese leadership*. New York: Palgrave Macmillan.
Watson, P. (2000). Managing people- the key activity for site managers. *Construction Manager, 5*(10), Chartered Institute of Building, 48–49.
Weaver, G. R. (2001). Ethics programs in global businesses: Culture's role in managing ethics. *Journal of Business Ethics, 30*(1), 3–15.
Weiser, J., & Zadek, S. (2000). *Conversations with disbelievers: Persuading companies to address social challenges*. New York: The Ford Foundation.
Whelan, G. (2007). Corporate social responsibility in Asia: A Confucian context. In *The debate over corporate social responsibility* (pp. 105–118). Oxford: Oxford University Press.
Witzel, M., & Warner, M. (2013). *The oxford handbook of management theorists*. Oxford: Oxford University Press.
Yunus, M. (2007). *Creating a world without poverty: Social business and the future of capitalism*. New York: Public Affairs.

Chapter 8
The Future for Responsible Leadership

Introduction

The responsible leadership field is still in its formative years: current responsible leadership research focuses more on clarifying the attributes of the concept and process than on the outcome variables, such as its link to productivity and organizational performance. But if the claims regarding responsible leadership are valid, the benefits to be derived at the individual, organizational and societal levels in the Asian century are too vast to gloss over. Thus this concluding chapter will address the need to develop appropriate research designs to capture and apply the concept of responsible leadership. It will emphasize the need for scholars to contribute theoretically and empirically to the development of responsible leadership discourse as well as approaches to teaching responsible leadership in business schools, so that leaders have the necessary skills and tools to enact responsible leadership in the Asian century.

Potential of Responsible Leadership

Researchers frequently assert that responsible leadership provides greater inclusiveness at work, superior ethical practices and greater effectiveness and profitability (e.g. Maak 2007; Maak and Pless 2006). As the responsible leadership field is relatively new, much of the work in this area has been based on conceptualisations. Very little work has been done on testing responsible leadership theories empirically. That is, the current research seems to have made significant strides towards clarifying the attributes of the concept and process, rather than exploring the outcome variables, such as its link to productivity, organizational performance and social wellbeing. Responsible leadership could benefit from developing new links and ways of managing and leading people in organizations; for example, the link between responsible leadership and "presenteeism"—workers' loss of productivity, even when they are at work, due to a health condition or personal context such as a sick relative at home (Iverson et al. 2010). Studies in the Netherlands (Alavinia et al. 2009), Denmark (Hansen and Andersen 2008), Canada (Caverley et al. 2007) and the United States (Goetzel et al. 2004) suggest that presenteeism because of health conditions is a growing problem. Other studies have shown a relationship between a number of personal variables (e.g. health conditions and health risk factors) and organizational variables (e.g. managerial leadership style, available resources and restructuring) linked to the generation of presenteeism (Iverson et al. 2010).

Responsible leadership, with its broader concern for stakeholders, could conceivably reduce the productivity loss from presenteeism. Using RLP and RLR approaches to socially innovative responsible leadership, leaders have the opportunity to balance the urge to make profits in a virtuous manner. Thus responsible leadership could be used as an independent variable to assess changes in presenteeism. In this process, mediating or moderating effects of variables such as intention to quit, employee engagement, individual spiritual well-being, job satisfaction, job commitment and organizational citizenship behavior could describe the influence and impact these variables have in the relationship between responsible leadership and presenteeism.

Scholars wishing to pursue this line of inquiry need to now develop appropriate research designs to comprehend and apply the concept of responsible leadership in business organizations.

These research designs can be developed in several ways. First, empirical studies on responsible leadership need to use more extensively established constructs and variables from other related fields. For example, there is potential for responsible leadership scholars to continue developing the field empirically by more fully integrating established constructs and variables from psychology (see special issue of the *Journal of Management Development* on the influence of psychology on responsible leadership, Volume 31, Issue 5, 2012), religious studies (Pruzan and Miller 2006) and philosophy domains to extend the research base and infuse further methodological rigor and academic credibility.

Second, rather than using quantitative methods alone, empirical studies could be developed based on qualitative methods to gain depth of insight. In addition, the field could also benefit from adopting mixed-method approaches (Greene et al. 1989). According to Sydenstricker-Neto (1997), mixed-method approaches generate novel ways for conceiving and implementing evaluation. Caracelli and Greene (1997) propose that the use of these alternative methods shows a clear and authentic attempt to be reflexive; to be accountable and be critical of the practice of evaluation.

Finally, similar to the developmental cycle of most management concepts, responsible leadership contributions are limited at the moment mostly to the North American and European settings. Future research could focus more on cross-cultural and comparative studies. For example, new research on responsible leadership among US and Chinese business leaders would broaden the relevance of responsible leadership to a global scale, and provide an extraordinary opportunity to examine the interplay of Asian wisdom traditions with established Western leadership approaches. As with several recent new management concepts, scholars might find that the growth in the interest in responsible leadership could have been due to Western desires to adopt Eastern views of life and wisdom traditions. For example, studies could examine how responsible leadership practices are enacted in Chinese, Japanese, Indian, African and other business settings. Of particular interest would be how the responsible leadership field evolves to fulfill its potential to make the degree of responsibility experienced by leaders, followers and other stakeholders in the leadership process across the globe the focal point in explaining the effectiveness of leadership in a wide range of institutional and cultural contexts. Although a large amount of research on cross-cultural aspects has compared and contrasted national cultural differences, very few contributions have examined the managerial implications of the cultural variations of organizational members living in the same locality but of different ethnic origins (Hofstede and Bond 1988). A single style of responsible leadership behavior might not be relevant and effective concerning such groups of followers.

Responsible Leadership: Another Management Fad?[1]

Various approaches to management have come and gone with great frequency (Fernando 2001; Staw and Epstein 2000). Is responsible leadership another management fad? The literature on management fads shows that leaders are keen to integrate those management concepts that are new and let go of those that have little currency. Staw and Epstein (2000), both of the University of California at Berkeley, attempted to examine whether popular management approaches such as total quality management, management by walking around and zero-based budgeting helped to increase profitability in organizations. In US based industrialized organizations, they found no relationship between the adoption of popular management approaches and profitability. However, these scholars were able to find some surprising outcomes as to why these management approaches are popular. They found higher worker satisfaction, lower turnover and better ethical work relationships. When popular management approaches were adopted by the sample organizations, their study also showed an association with increase in leaders' (e.g., CEO's) short-term pay independent of organizational performance. These researchers then examined whether CEOs were rewarded for integrating popular management approaches without a demonstrated link to improving the bottom line. Public perception of the use and implementation of the popular management approaches could have influenced corporate boards to increase CEO pay. Staw and Epstein (2000) claim that the adoption of popular management approaches by leaders may show to the board of

---

[1] This section includes an updated version of ideas first presented in Fernando (2001).

directors that the leader may be proactive, is visionary and therefore, deserves a higher pay.

Staw and Epstein's study, published in the prestigious *Administrative Science Quarterly*, suggests that not organizational performance, but organizational reputations can be improved through integrating popular management approaches. What signs indicate that responsible leadership is another management fad? What suggests otherwise? A strong indicator that responsible leadership is not a fad is the clear integration of the notion at a fundamental level to almost all leadership approaches and styles. Earlier we noted that responsible leadership helps to connect leaders with stakeholders in a manner that promotes their levels of motivation and commitment to achieve meaningful social change that can create sustainable value (Pless 2007). Hence, a responsible leader is primarily required to follow organizational goals effectively and responsibly, both inside and outside the organization (Pless 2007). At a fundamental level, this notion of responsibility, although implicit in leadership theory and practice, was lost with the rising expectation of profit maximization. The advent of responsible leadership has made explicit what was always implicit. With a wider approach of a leader-stakeholder relationship view point, it tackles the assumptions of most of traditional leadership theory (which is overly focused on the leader-follower interactions, internal to the organization). In this sense, I believe that responsible leadership is far from being another management fad. However, Staw and Epstein (2000) claim that the cause for the shorter life cycles of most popular management approaches may be due to the rapidly changing social patterns than the actual inefficiencies of management approaches. In contrast, responsible leadership might in time lose its gloss and popularity in the academic and popular press, but in practice, the notion of responsibility will be central to the effective and humane functioning of organizations and communities. Staw and Epstein (2000) recommend a healthy skepticism toward unproven management techniques; thus, responsible leadership scholars have the task of carrying out rigorous research into the concept of responsible leadership to realize its potential.

Developing Responsible Leaders

The purpose of writing this book would not be fulfilled without highlighting the importance of the role of teaching and learning in the area of responsible leadership. The recent corporate scandals, such as at Volkswagen and Barclays, JPMorgan Chase, Goldman Sachs and other banks, suggest not simply morality problems, but something more serious: business schools have been charged with incubating criminals (Zingales 2012). The erosion of ethical standards across the business world is compounded by economists considering their subject divorced from morality.

In a presentation at the National Centres for Competence Research in Bern, Switzerland (2009), I made the case for integrating virtue ethics into climate-change modeling. At question time, I was told by an economist that it would not make sense, nor would it be possible, to integrate the subjective nature of ethics into economic modeling. Zingales (2012) suggests, economists unintentionally teach business students about greed. Zingales is worth quoting at length:

> My colleague, Dr Gary Becker, pioneered the economic study of crime. Employing a basic utilitarian approach, he compared the benefits of a crime with the expected cost of punishment. While insightful, Dr Becker's model, which had no intention of telling people how they should behave, had some unintended consequences. A former student of Dr Becker's told me that he found many of his classmates to be remarkably amoral, a fact he took as a sign that they interpreted Dr Becker's descriptive model of crime as prescriptive. They perceived any failure to commit a high-benefit crime with a low expected cost as a failure to act rationally, almost a proof of stupidity. The student's experience is consistent with the experimental findings I mentioned above. In other words, if teachers pretend to be agnostic, they subtly encourage amoral behaviour without taking any responsibility. True, economists are not moral philosophers and we have no particular competence to determine what is ethical and what is not. We are, though, able to identify behaviour that makes people better off. When economist Milton Friedman said the one and only responsibility of business is to increase its profits, he added: "So long as it stays within the rules of the game, which is to say, engages in open and free competition without deception or fraud." That is a very big caveat —and one that is not stressed nearly enough in our business schools (Zingales 2012).

I assert that the best way to teach ethics is not as standalone classes but as a topic that is integrated into all core courses. These classes have the potential to recognise the reputational and other costs of not following ethical standards in industry. Moreover, it highlights to students the broader social issues of promoting self-interest (Zingales 2012).

Business schools across the world are now embracing the systematic development of responsible leadership to deliver subjects in the undergraduate and postgraduate programs. The UN-led Principles of Responsible Management Education initiative (PRME) has been a major driver for the growing interest on the topic of responsible leadership. This 2007 initiative is recognised by over 500 leading business schools and academic institutions in over 80 nations. Some of these include more than one-third of the *Financial Times*' top 100 business schools (see http://www.unprme.org/participants/index.php for a list of signatories to the PRME initiative). PRME is a network for academic institutions to promote corporate and social sustainability. It primarily offers a framework for the integration of universal values into curricula and research. Looking towards the future, with the continuing number of reported corporate scandals and the growing intensity of social and business issues linked to climate change, intellectual property rights and other human rights, the interest in the field is poised to grow.

Given the rising expectations that business schools will integrate business ethics into their curricula, in 2010 I was entrusted by my faculty with the task of developing a new final-year undergraduate subject on responsible leadership. In my university, the initiative was part of working towards Association to Advance Collegiate Schools of Business (AACSB) accreditation. The subject was based on a new pedagogical approach to teaching responsible leadership, which I termed Social Innovation-Based Transformative Learning (SIBTL).

In Fernando (2011), I explain how the SIBTL approach was applied first to teaching business ethics and governance, a subject that undergraduate students took in the final year of their Bachelor of Commerce. Building on this experience, I developed a new Responsible Leadership subject using the SIBTL approach. I use Fernando (2011) here to explain how the SIBTL approach is implemented in the new subject.

There are several motivating factors for using the SIBTL approach to teach responsible leadership. After conducting a literature review on the business ethics teaching literature, Rossouw (2002) identifies "three basic positions that with regard to the purpose of teaching business ethics can be distinguished" (p. 412). The first position focuses on cognitive competencies where students are able to make sound ethical decisions in business. These competencies include moral awareness, moral understanding and moral reasoning. The second position involves behavioral competence; using moral imagination to develop ethically sound innovations to business problems. These approaches develop moral courage to "improve the morality of business behavior" (Rossouw 2002, p. 414). The third position involves those that focus on developing managerial competencies. Rossouw (2002) identifies these as "the ability to discern the systemic implications of organizations for moral behavior" (p. 415). He laments that most business ethics teaching approaches are based on either the cognitive or behavior oriented approaches and calls for teaching based on integrated approaches where all three competencies are targeted. He claims that otherwise there will "always remain a distance between the conclusion of a logical argument about business ethics and the resolution to act upon that conclusion" (2002, p. 423); resulting in students having the knowledge of what to do in a challenging ethical situation but failing to act responsibly.

As opposed to the learning by children, adult learning occurs when adults are exposed to a real life context (Knowles 1980, 1990; Delahaye 2005; Wenger 1998). Based on the Andragogy school of learning, engaging in social interaction also enacts the principles of action learning and experiential learning (Fernando and McLean 2010; Dewey 1938). A teaching approach in responsible leadership that requires students to socially interact with others in a business setting would develop not only cognitive competencies but more so their behavioral and managerial skills. Thus a responsible leadership teaching approach that integrates all three competencies would inspire students to interact with others and through that experience become aware of their assumptions and other worldviews. Based on Habermas's (1971)) instrumental, communicative and emancipatory knowledge, the transformative-learning theory (Mezirow 1990, 1991, 1997, 2000) suggests an ideal foundation to developing an integrated teaching and learning approach.

Transformative Teaching and Learning Through Social Innovation

Although transformative learning has been effective in teaching students in fields such as sociology (Langan et al. 2009), arts (Butterwick and Lawrence 2009) and medicine (MacLeod and Egan 2009), its use in responsible leadership teaching is relatively novel. Transformative learning works under the assumption that those who reflect today as part of the thinking process will be reflective practitioners of the future (Duarte 2010). Challenging student assumptions is critical for the success of transformative learning (Cranton 2002). By requiring students to critique their assumptions of daily practices where long-term interests are compromised for short-term convenience, Brookfield (1995) claims that a strong commitment can be generated in students to engage in ethical action under challenging situations. Using social innovation as a context, this commitment can be oriented towards generating positive social change (Brookfield 2000).

Challenging students' assumptions to encourage reflection and critique of their assumptions should take place in a conducive environment, "combined with safety, support, and a sense of learner empowerment" (Cranton 2002, p. 66). Unlearning needs to take place in students before new interpretations of a situation and required actions can take place (Starbuck 1996). In classroom settings, the biggest obstacle for teachers in challenging student assumptions leading to unlearning is developing the all-important context for students to reflect and critique. An assessment to develop a socially innovative response for a social problem provides a suitable context for students to reflect and critique. The idea is to develop a strong enough context that trigger critical thinking and critical reflection in students.

Cranton (2002, p. 66) identifies seven stages for transformative learning:

1. An activating event that typically exposes a discrepancy between what a person has always assumed to be true and what has just been experienced, heard or read.
2. Articulating assumptions; that is, recognizing underlying assumptions that have been uncritically assimilated and are largely unconscious.
3. Critical self-reflection; that is, questioning and examining assumptions in terms of where they came from, the consequences of holding them and why they are important.
4. Being open to alternative viewpoints.
5. Engaging in discourse, where evidence is weighed, arguments assessed, alternative perspectives explored and knowledge constructed by consensus.
6. Revising assumptions and perspectives to make them more open and better justified.
7. Acting on revisions, behaving, talking and thinking in a way that is congruent with transformed assumptions or perspectives.

In the responsible leadership subject I developed and teach, a project based on social innovation is used to enact transformative learning. Following Cranton's (2002) process for transformative learning, the social innovation project is developed as the activating event where students through critical thinking and critical reflection identify a gap in their assumptions and the experience of engaging in the project. It leads students to "recognizing underlying assumptions that have been uncritically assimilated and are largely unconscious" (Cranton 2002, p. 66). By "behaving, talking and thinking in a way that is congruent with transformed assumptions or perspectives" (Cranton 2002, p. 66), and the experience of communicating the gap in their assumptions and learning new meanings of the situation are likely to lead students to a reformulated or novel interpretation of the event.

The Subject

MGMT351: Responsible Leadership was launched in 2011 as a core subject in the management major in the Faculty of Business, University of Wollongong. Expanding on the introductory view of leadership offered in MGMT110: Introduction to Management and MGMT201: Organisational Behaviour, this subject examines the topic of responsible leadership in depth and from a variety of perspectives. Currently, the course is taught on a collection of readings and case studies and is yet to use a core text. I teach about 250 students annually at our campuses in Wollongong, Singapore and Malaysia.

The students examine different approaches to leadership, including ethical leadership, and address current issues relating to leadership such as sustainability and human rights through leaders' influence on shareholders, employees, communities and society. Students engage in experiential learning activities, case studies and analysis, scenario-based problem-solving activities, highly interactive lectures and extensive classroom discussions. By engaging in these activities, students are expected to develop responsible leadership skills in order, and ideally to apply them effectively in their personal and professional lives. The learning outcomes in this subject are:

1. Demonstrate a deep understanding of the various leadership theories.
2. Identify and explain the ethical dimensions of leadership.
3. Explain the influence business leaders have on the well-being of various stakeholders.
4. Identify and critically evaluate the key challenges of responsible leadership.
5. Identify and apply appropriate responsible leadership styles to assess, evaluate and deal with contemporary business challenges.
6. Demonstrate an understanding of the use of specified information communication technology tools.

These learning outcomes were developed after extensive discussion and development within the Faculty and university education and other relevant committees. The demand for resources and the link to faculty and discipline qualities in achieving the learning outcomes are explained in the following Table 8.1.

Phrases such as "critical thinking", "critical evaluation" and "critically analyze" in the learning outcomes and subject description demonstrate the intention to use transformative learning in the subject. The learning outcomes also indicate support for using an integrated approach to developing the cognitive, behavioral and managerial competencies of the student. Consider for example learning outcome number four: identifying and critically evaluating the key challenges of responsible leadership. The face-to-face classroom sessions during the 13-week period consist of 2 h lectures and a 1 h tutorial per week. Classroom sessions are designed to engage students in a manner to promote critical reflection. To inspire such reflection, I take students through an emotional journey. For example, we would discuss the tensions involved in abortion and euthanasia debates. In the front-half of the subject, various modes of teaching such as case studies, films, storytelling and role plays are used to

Table 8.1 Link to teaching strategies and faculty and discipline qualities

Teaching strategies & resources	Faculty & discipline qualities
The following teaching strategies, learning resources and subject design features may be used to enable achievement of the identified learning outcomes:	*The identified combination of learning outcomes, teaching strategies and resources relate to achievement of the following Faculty and Discipline Qualities*:
This highly interactive subject uses experiential learning activities, group case studies and analysis, scenario-based problem-solving activities, interactive lectures and extensive classroom discussions. Tutorial classes promote student discussion and problem solving, and provide support for student assessment tasks Through these activities, the students will explore responsible leadership skills from both a theoretical and practical perspective in order to apply them effectively in their personal and professional lives	1. Informed: Students will be introduced to appropriate research-based, conceptual and applied knowledge of responsible leadership, and develop skills for independent thinking and life-long learning
	2. Innovative and Flexible: By developing their understanding of responsible leadership, students will be innovative in their thinking and work practices, able to apply creativity and logical analysis to current leadership issues
	3. Socially Responsible: By developing an understanding of how to engage in responsible leadership, students will appreciate the ethical dimensions of leadership and make informed choices for the benefit of stakeholders
	4. Connected: In recognizing the importance of responsible leadership to the general well-being of stakeholders in business, students will appreciate the links between ideas and practice in responsible leadership
	5. Communicators: by engaging in assessable individual and group work, students will demonstrate interpersonal, written and verbal communication skills and develop an understanding of intercultural communication practices

From the MGMT351 Subject Development Proposal, UOW

expose and engage students in developing critical reflection and critical thinking. Thereafter, as the major assessment, students work in groups to generate a socially innovative response to a unique social problem in the community.

Assessments

Students are required to undertake three items of assessment: a film-based critique of responsible leadership (worth 30 % of total marks), a socially innovative responsible leadership group project (also worth 30 %) and the final exam (worth 40 %). The assessments are designed to help students identify and develop responsible leadership skills. As a team of consultants, student groups of three or four members work together to (a) research and explore a business organization and (b) propose a social-innovation-based approach to enact responsible leadership in the selected organization. Students apply social innovation to a real business organization and one of its leaders to develop a powerful and convincing argument for their selected organization to adopt a social-innovation initiative demonstrating responsible leadership. The report must contain the following sections:

1. A brief description of each group member's contributions to the report.
2. A brief introduction outlining the key facts of the selected business organization and its leader.
3. A description of the social innovation.
4. A proposed implementation of the social innovation consisting of a definition of the innovation, an explanation of how the organization can enact its key elements through responsible leadership and a description of measurable qualitative and quantitative targets.
5. Recommendations to the organization's top management.

This assessment can consist of either field or desk work. The social innovation must be linked to at least one of the concepts/theories discussed in the course, and students must both define social innovation and explain how to enact the key elements of the definition through the proposed initiative. The marking criteria for the project report are awarded as follows:

(a) Addressing assigned tasks (15 %).
(b) Adequacy of analysis (20 %).
(c) Clarity and conciseness of arguments (10 %).
(d) Use of social innovation to propose initiatives demonstrating responsible leadership behavior (25 %).
(e) Comprehensiveness of the initiative (20 %).
(f) Referencing, spelling, punctuation and report structure (10 %).

Content of Social-Innovation Projects

One example of the responsible leadership social innovation project focused on a local branch of a national chain of liquor stores in Australia (identified as ABC here). The objective of the project was to examine the branch's leader, and propose a socially innovative approach to enact responsible leadership within the business. The social issue in focus was environmental sustainability; specifically, the issue of increased consumer waste. The group focused on the store manager as the leader in focus. He or she has the responsibility for advocating "lightweight" wine bottles to suppliers and the community, so that a reduction in glass waste can occur. The project group went on to analyse the effect people have on social innovations, as well as examining the challenge, process and goal, as per Dawson and Daniel's (2010) model. The group then examined sustainability measures so that the organization could monitor the targeted results of the social innovation. These included financial measures, such as calculating and scrutinising net profits, as well as reexamining the value of the social capital produced, and exploring the relationship with suppliers as a social measure. These measures were used to make a business case that the social innovation proposed would be beneficial in achieving social well-being. The group report (slightly altered here to preserve anonymity) noted:

> Our research has found that glass bottles are by far the most popular choice of material used within the beverage industry as a means of packaging, especially the wine industry, with 95 % of wine distributed in glass. A primary reason for this choice in material is due to its symbolic meaning, as a higher quality glass infers a superior product. However, when heavy glass bottles are not recycled properly by consumers and are tossed into regular landfill, it becomes extremely detrimental to the environment as glass in regular landfill will never decompose.
>
> In an attempt to confront this evolving issue, we have formulated a social innovative solution based upon the notion of "lightweight" glass wine bottles, which actively involves ABC. This packaging technological advancement involves manufacturing a lighter-weight wine bottle by reducing the wall thickness, without negatively affecting the integrity of the bottle. The manufacturing process of lightweight glass is a relatively new development and a growing trend within the United Kingdom. This manufacturing process is most definitely a viable action that can be applied here in Australia within the wine industry, capitalising on costs savings and environmental benefits.
>
> We have suggested that ABC's Store Manager undertake the responsibility of an advocate in getting suppliers to use lightweight glass wine bottles. In order to accomplish this, we suggest that the Store Manager offer a reduced stocking/shelving fee to any supplier who uses the environmentally friendly bottles, which can also act as an incentive for suppliers to adopt this innovative packaging. This is only part of the social innovation program we have in mind for ABC, as this approach is rather a proactive tactic in solving the issue of increased packaging waste from the beverage industry, which we believe is important for the sustainability in solving this environmental problem. We understand that this course of action may take longer to implement on behalf of the suppliers, as extensive research and design is needed before implementing this into their production. That is why we also have ABC employing a loyalty program that encourages their customers in not only purchasing the wine brands that do utilise a lightweight glass bottle; but also, and most importantly, returning the empty lightweight bottles back to the store so that ABC can recycle the glass in the most environmentally efficient manner.
>
> However, during our investigation we asked local members of the community whether they would be willing to return the empty wine bottle back to ABC, and unfortunately most responded that it would serve as rather an inconvenience in storing empty wine bottles at their place until they visited the store again…. With this information, our social innovation will entail customers receiving loyalty points every time they purchase a lightweight wine bottle, and for every 14 bottles purchased, they will receive a complementary bottle. In addition to this, if the customer returns nine empty lightweight bottles, they will receive a complementary bottle. The latter application aims at increasing customer's commitment in fulfilling the goal of environmental sustainability.

The social-innovation-based transformative learning approach used in the teaching and learning of MGMT351: Responsible Leadership at University of Wollongong goes beyond the limited skill, behavioral or cognitive-based singular approaches to a broader and more integrative approach. It promotes student engagement in real-life organizational ethical and social issues. Despite its challenges, this approach helps teachers develop the students' all-important moral character. This inclusive approach has more potential to trigger critical reflection by challenging students' assumptions, beliefs and attitudes.

Conclusion

This chapter addressed those issues concerning the future of responsible leadership. It looked at the need to develop appropriate research designs to capture and apply the concept of responsible leadership in the Asian century. It emphasized the need for scholars to contribute both theoretically and empirically to the development of responsible leadership discourse. An often ignored area in the development of new topics such as responsible leadership is teaching and learning approaches. Especially as the economic and political landscape shifts from a more Western to an Asian base, these teaching and learning approaches will play a vital role in the development of responsible leaders.

References

Alavinia, S. M., Molenaar, D., & Burdorf, A. (2009). Productivity loss in the workforce: Associations with health, work demands, and individual characteristics. *American Journal of Industrial Medicine, 52*(1), 49–56.
Brookfield, S. (1995). *Becoming a critically reflective teacher*. San Francisco: Jossey-Bass.
Brookfield, S. D. (2000). Transformative learning as ideology critique. In J. Mezirow (Ed.), *Learning as transformation: Critical perspectives on a theory in progress*. San Francisco: Jossey-Bass.
Butterwick, S., & Lawrence, R. L. (2009). Creating alternative realities: Arts-based approaches to transformative learning. In J. Mezirow & E. W. Taylor (Eds.), *Transformative learning in practice: Insights from community, workplace, and higher education*. San Francisco: Jossey-Bass.
Caracelli, V. J., & Greene, J. C. (1997). Crafting mixed-method evaluation designs. *New Directions for Evaluation, 74*, 19–32.
Caverley, N., Cunningham, J. B., & MacGregor, J. N. (2007). Sickness presenteeism, sickness absenteeism, and health following restructuring in a public service organization. *Journal of Management Studies, 44*(2), 304–319.
Cranton, P. (2002). Teaching for transformation. *New directions for adult and continuing education, 93*, 63–72.
Dawson, P., & Daniel, L. (2010). Understanding social innovation: A provisional framework. *International Journal of Technology Management, 51*(1), 9–21.
Delahaye, B. L. (2005). *Human resource development: Adult learning and knowledge management*. Milton: Wiley.
Dewey, J. (1938). *Logic: The theory of inquiry*. New York: Henry Holt.
Duarte, F. (2010). Addressing student synicism through transformative learning. *Journal of University Teaching and Learning Practice, 7*(1), 4.
Fernando, M. (2001). Are popular management techniques a waste of time? *The Academy of Management Executive, 15*(3), 138–141.
Fernando, M. (2011). A social innovation based transformative learning approach to teaching business ethics. *Journal of Business Ethics Education, 8*, 119–138.

Fernando, M., & McLean, P. D. (2010). Embedding notions of community in the teaching-research nexus: A case study. In M. Devlin, J. B. Nagy, & A. M. Lichtenberg (Eds.), *Research and development in higher education: Reshaping higher education* (Higher Education Research and Development Society of Australasia (HERDSA) annual international conference, pp. 289–299). Milperra: Higher Education Research and Development Society of Australasia.

Goetzel, R. Z., Long, S. R., Ozminkowski, R. J., Hawkins, K., Wang, S., & Lynch, W. (2006). Health, absence, disability, and presenteeism cost estimates of certain physical and mental health conditions affecting U.S. employers. *Journal of Occupational and Environmental Medicine, 46*, 398–412.

Greene, J. C., Caracelli, V. J., & Graham, W. F. (1989). Toward a conceptual framework for mixed-method evaluation designs. *Educational Evaluation and Policy Analysis, 11*(3), 255–274.

Habermas, J. (1971). *Knowledge and human interests*. Boston: Beacon Press.

Hansen, C. D., & Andersen, J. H. (2008). Going ill to work: What personal circumstances, attitudes and work-related factors are associated with sickness presenteeism? *Social Science & Medicine, 67*(6), 956–964.

Hofstede, G., & Bond, M. H. (1988). The Confucius connection: From cultural roots to economic growth. *Organizational Dynamics, 16*(4), 5–21.

Iverson, D., Lewis, K. L., Caputi, P., & Knospe, S. (2010). The cumulative impact and associated costs of multiple health conditions on employee productivity. *Journal of Occupational and Environmental Medicine, 52*(12), 1206–1211.

Knowles, M. S. (1980). *The modern practice of adult education: From pedagogy*. Cambridge: Englewood Cliffs.

Knowles, M. S. (1990). *The adult learner: A neglected species* (4th ed.). Houston: Gulf Publishing.

Langan, D., Sheese, R., & Davidson, D. (2009). Constructive teaching and learning: Collaboration in a sociology classroom. In J. Mezirow & E. W. Taylor (Eds.), *Transformative learning in practice: Insights from community, workplace, and higher education*. San Francisco: Josey-Bass.

Maak, T. (2007). Responsible leadership, stakeholder engagement, and the emergence of social capital. *Journal of Business Ethics, 74*(4), 329–343.

Maak, T., & Pless, N. M. (2006). Responsible leadership in a stakeholder society–A relational perspective. *Journal of Business Ethics, 66*(1), 99–115.

MacLeod, R., & Egan, A. (2009). Transformation in palliative care. In J. Mezirow & E. W. Taylor (Eds.), *Transformative learning in practice: Insights from community, workplace and higher education* (pp. 111–121). San Francisco: Jossey-Bass.

Mezirow, J. (1990). *Fostering critical reflection in adulthood: A guide to transformative and emancipatory learning*. San Francisco: Jossey-Bass.

Mezirow, J. (1991). *Transformative dimensions of adult learning*. San Francisco: Jossey-Bass.

Mezirow, J. (1997). Transformative learning: Theory to practice. In P. Cranton (Ed.), *Transformative learning in action: Insights from practice – New directions for adult and continuing education* (No. 74, pp. 5–12). San Francisco: Jossey-Bass.

Mezirow, J. (2000). Learning to think like an adult: Core concepts of transformation theory. In J. Mezirow (Ed.), *Learning as transformation. Critical perspectives on a theory in progress*. San Francisco: Jossey-Bass.

Pless, N. M. (2007). Understanding responsible leadership: Role identity and motivational drivers. *Journal of Business Ethics, 74*(4), 437–456.

Pruzan, P., & Miller, W. C. (2006). Spirituality as the basis of responsible leaders and responsible companies. In T. Maak & N. M. Pless (Eds.), *Responsible leadership* (pp. 68–92). London: Routledge.

Rossouw, G. (2002). Three approaches to teaching business ethics. *Teaching Business Ethics, 6*(4), 411–433.

Starbuck, W. H. (1996). Learning by knowledge-intensive firms. In M. D. Cohen & L. S. Sproull (Eds.), *Organizational learning* (pp. 484–515). Thousand Oaks: Sage.

Staw, B. M., & Epstein, L. D. (2000). What bandwagons bring: Effects of popular management techniques on corporate performance, reputation, and CEO pay. *Administrative Science Quarterly, 45*(3), 523–556.

Sydenstricker-Neto, J. (1997). *Research design and mixed-method approach: A hands-on experience.* http://www.socialresearchmethods.net/tutorial/Sydenstricker/bolsa.html. Accessed 20 Aug 2010.

Wenger, E. (1998). *Communities of practice: Learning, meaning, and identity.* New York: Cambridge University Press.

Zingales, L. (2012). *Do business schools incubate criminals?* http://www.bloomberg.com/news/articles/2012-07-16/do-business-schools-incubate-criminals-. Accessed 26 Apr 2015.

Chapter 9
Appendix: Sample Asian Century Leader Interviews

Introduction

The following Asian business leader interviews are provided as examples to illustrate the thesis developed in the book. Interviewed business leaders were encouraged to talk about their leadership experience in terms of leading a business organization in Asia, particularly in China. I identified leaders who would be able to present a cross-cultural experience of their leadership approach. Most interviews took around 60 min. Interview questions included understanding of leadership, expectations of an Asian century responsible leader, impact of the Asian century on responsible leadership, and the role of Confucian and guanxi practices on responsible leadership.

Jia Li, Co-Founder, Baixing.com, China

Career

In the third year of my university study, I started my own website. And in the next year, I used the website to earn about 50,000 US dollars. This meant big money for me as a student. And after that I sold the website and I invested all my money that I earned from the website into business. I am a Certified Trainer for Microsoft in China. I was the speaker for nearly all official Microsoft events in East China. After I graduated from university, I faced the difficult problem of deciding whether I should start a company by myself, or join Microsoft. I decided to start a company by myself and one of my friends. The company was called Topwin Digital Technology Company. But immediately after I started the company for about 6 months, I found a problem with myself. Before I was a trainer and a web master, and I was able to attend to all the business functions by myself. I was just an individual contributor, and I could only attend to something by myself. But after I launched Topwin, with my friend, we had to hire several people but found that I had absolutely no idea of managing people. So here I was. I had some money and several talented people, but I didn't have the faintest idea of how to manage people and also, how to use money effectively. So I became frustrated and at the time I thought it was too early for me to start a real company. I ran the company for 6 months. We already broke even. At the time of my leaving the company, we had five employees. Even with five people I found very hard to manage them. I knew that I need to fix this weakness of myself, so that is when I decided to join Microsoft.

Moneywise, it was a really stupid deal because, at Microsoft, I earned only about 20 % of my income from when I ran my own company. But my intention was to learn at Microsoft how to manage people. And I must say the job at Microsoft was very interesting. It was to start a new, nation-wide partner network for Microsoft. Before I joined Microsoft there was no onsite customer service for enterprise users in China. So we were building the whole network covering all cities around China, for all Microsoft enterprise customers. We built it from scratch. We started recruiting partners, we trained partners and we certified them. Within 3 years we built the first Microsoft nationwide customer service partner network in China, which had 28 partners.

And by the end of the third year, this network won the award from Microsoft Headquarters with the top customer satisfaction rating globally. We had a 99 % customer satisfaction rating. At the time, I was the Channel manager. Then I became the Business Development Manager and I was responsible for developing more business for our partners within Microsoft. So my task essentially was to ask everyone within Microsoft for more business to our partners. After 3 years in total at Microsoft, I quit Microsoft and joined eBay.

The reason to join eBay was driven by several factors. My former boss at Microsoft was also at eBay, and he was the CEO of the eBay new venture in China. He had a headcount to hire one employee, so he asked me whether I would like to join him. I said not really, because what I was doing with Microsoft was very successful. I was also going to be promoted. But I said I am happy to listen to what he was going to do and what type of business proposition he had in mind. The business was focused on making it an online classified website. He gave me an example 'A' license in China means like the highest level of driver license in China. There were many drivers with 'A' license that could not find a job. While at the same time, there were lots of people looking for 'A' license drivers and this website was a place to connect 'A' license drivers with jobs. I loved the idea because it was 'meaningful', so I quit Microsoft immediately and joined this small team. I held the posts of Marketing Manager, Committee Manager and Marketing Director at eBay over a 3 year period. And after about 2 years, this website became the top online website in China. Also we received the award from eBay global as the fastest growing team in the eBay classified group globally. But my third year at eBay was the worst time for eBay in China. eBay failed in China, totally except our new venture.

eBay.com.cn competed with Taobao which is an online website, similar to eBay. eBay spent about 400 million U.S dollars in China to compete with Taobao. But it failed. Taobao is the subsidy of Alibaba. And after that eBay global decided to quit China and eBay sell ebay.com.cn to Taobao.com and eBay closed PayPal in China. At the time we were the only business unit remaining in China, and they also want to do something with us, because they want to stop spending money in China. At the time, we were worried, so we went to the U.S. to talk to the CEO of eBay, John Donahoe. We made a business proposal about China to John and he said "Don't ask me anything about China, you are absolutely right, much more right than me, I have no idea about China, just do it!"

So we thought, this is a good opportunity for us. Because, on one side, eBay wants to stop spending money in China, and on the other side, our team had a very good reputation with the global eBay team and with the CEO. So we made a proposal to eBay, saying, "how about we spin off from eBay and you keep some rights in the future like to buy back the company it means you can stop investing money into the business immediately, but you keep your opportunity in future". eBay agreed, so we spin off from eBay, running as a real start-up. At that time we had three founders. One was my former boss at Microsoft. We knew each other for about 13 years. And the other co-founder I knew him for about 15 years.

We kept growing like an independent start-up, we went to venture capitalists to have access to investment funds. After 5 years, in 2011, we became the number one online website in China. However, at the time I felt like change. My personality is such that I like new things, new challenges constantly. I had already stayed in the company for about 6 years, so I want to do something new. I decided to study in U.S to fix my biggest weakness, bad English and narrow vision. Then I spent a year to prepare an application, eventually I got admitted by Stanford University. Just before I went to U.S, my partner called me saying "the company is in trouble, we need you to come back to fix the problem". So I gave up the offer, went back to my start-up. But I still wanted to study in U.S, so I was looking for another part-time program. Finally, I got admitted by Columbia University.

I went back to the company for about 10 months, 'fixed everything'. And right now the company goes back to the right check. And in the past 6 months I tried to balance among company work, my study in the U.S. and my family in Australia. I found it is impossible. Even though I had worked 14 h per day, I still couldn't make everything right. I knew I have to scarify one part for the other two. So I quit the company to devote all of my time on my study and family.

The Greatest Leadership Challenge

The greatest leadership challenge I have is with managing people. For example, I had to shut down the Beijing office because of business downturn. But I didn't know how to explain to the employees who have worked so hard. For many, it was their first job. And my personal preference was that I like to work with friends, that's my personal preference. But the reality is Beijing office contributed little to the overall business, but costs were significant. I had tried to find a way to keep the Beijing office operating for 1 year. At the end of that year, I couldn't find a way to keep it going.

My co-founder said that he would talk to the employees. But I said no, that's my decision, that's my team, I have to face them during this tough time. I think this is the most difficult time of my entire career. There is a conflict of my interest into people you have worked with and trained and the goal of sustaining and growing the business. I was struggling for a while.

Responsible Leadership

In terms of the differences between responsible leadership and general leadership, the case of laying off my people at the Beijing office is a good example. Normally in China, by law we have to give affected employees 1 month's pay in addition to a month's pay for each year of service, so it is called $N+1$. For example, an employee who worked for 5 years would receive a termination package worth 6 month's pay. But I went beyond this. I paid $2N+1$ as a severance package, and found a job for everyone. I think this I had to do as a responsible leader. So I think responsible leaders should think of the benefit of the company over personal preference, this is first. The second is to take care of your employee, not only what is required by law, also by yourself as a person. In return, a leader can expect to gain the respect and trust from employees.

So how would responsible leaders achieve high profits responsibly? In the Beijing case, I convinced myself this way. I mentally made sense of the shutting down of office in this way. Every employee in the Beijing office holds stocks of my company. So if the company becomes successful in future, everyone becomes successful, moneywise. If the company fails, staying in a failed company is meaningless for anyone. So that's how I convinced myself: make the company a success, then the company's success will compensate everyone who is even leaving the company. That was my way of making sense about this decision.

Leading in Asia

Since the Internet industry is the most special industry in China, internet entrepreneurs are not typical entrepreneurs in China. In most of the traditional industries in China, the management has to build a very strong relationship with local governments. For example, as a real estate developer company, the CEO has to have a very strong personal relationship with many high rank officials. Otherwise, for instance, your business has no chance to get land for the business.

Jia Li, Co-Founder, Baixing.com, China

Recent Changes in Chinese Business Culture

Ten years ago, if you ask a CEO in any company, "what makes you successful?", the answer normally will be "relationships". But right now they will tell you about 60 % is about relationships, 40 % is about management. Ten years ago, most companies are family businesses. Nearly all of the top executives were relatives. The issue with the leadership of family business were trust. How could I trust professional managers, who are not my family members, to manage my money? With more family business leaders going to business schools in U.S or Europe, they know how to manage their businesses without hiring relatives. As a result, nowadays, most successful family businesses hire professional managers to manage their companies.

I don't think that Confucian's teachings and practices influenced me. Conversely, in the internet industry, normally, we have to think in the reverse, sometimes, in a fashion of almost anti-Confucian manner. Because tech start-ups gain its momentum by destroying traditional rules and establishing new ones. But this will be different for most of the traditional industries. I heard about some programs in the U.S., they teach about the philosophy from Confucianism. There is an old Chinese saying for business people, harmony is the source of money. Most traditional Chinese business people believe in this.

The most important lesson that I have learned is being patient, thinking about issues carefully. In my start-up, at the very beginning, I wanted to make everything happen as quickly as possible. Before long, I realised in the long run, I didn't get good pay-off with this was of working. In some projects, when I spend ten days to think about an issue before jumping in and doing something, it got good results in the end. In summary, doing the right thing instead of doing the thing right is my new motto.

Comparing Western and Eastern business cultures, I think the biggest gap is in terms of the nature of the business contract. Western business people respect formal contracts more than their Chinese counterparts. My business partner and myself, we are best friends, we have known each other for more than 10 years, so we trust each other. In China, you can only trust someone who had known each other for a very long time. Especially when co-founding a business, one always look for friends. Comparably, in the U.S, doing business is much easier because most people will comply with the terms of the contract signed between the two parties. When I first worked with Americans, I found they spend a lot of time on negotiating contracts. However, after the contract is signed, they will just do whatever was agreed in the contract. In China, you would provoke people if you negotiate for a while on contractual terms. They normally relate this action with not trusting them. Thus, contracts are always signed quickly, roughly. You have to spend a lot of time communicating during the work in progress. Furthermore, when the company becomes bigger, say has 100 employees, it is very hard to manage by talking through every day on every detail. That's why a lot of companies, which have great business opportunities can't grow beyond 50 employees.

Summary

Summarising the above, it is much harder to be a leader in China. You have to handle all kinds of relationships. You have to train your employees to be professional. It is hard in China to recruit professional managers. On the flip side, the good thing is, once you have built several great relationships, doing business becomes easier.

Bernie Landy, President, BlueScope China

Career

I'm a career professional in the steel industry. I've worked in the steel or metal associated industries since 1978 and spent most of my career in sales or marketing, mostly in Australia but since the late 1980s, I became deeply involved in the international; side of the steel business.

I travelled a lot to Asia countries in the late 1980s and in 1990, I was appointed to the position of Managing Director of the trading business in Singapore to manage the South East Asian trade for BHP Steel. Then in 1992, I went to Hong Kong and took care of the North Asian business. So I got a lot of experience in those years, in Asia particularly. Those days, I was also involved in the exporting business to the Middle East and the USA.

From 1992 onwards, I returned to Australia and worked in the Australian domestic market in senior sales and marketing positions, but much of that time I still had a deep involvement in the export business. So export was my responsibility in two or three jobs that I had. So I could sum up that stage of my career by saying that I was successful in sales and marketing, also successful in developing and growing customer relationships in a variety of different regions, and I guess that's what made me qualified to come to China.

When I came over to China, my task was to grow the business. I'm in a full profit and loss role now looking after 3 quite large business units, each with their own manufacturing operations over a diverse geographic footprint (eight different locations in China, approx 2000 employees), so my job has evolved and got bigger, but there is still a very strong sales and business development focus in this market, which has been growing up until now.

I grew up in country Victoria in Australia. My parents were working class. We had a very extroverted family. I was an average student at school, but did my best. Probably as I grew in to a younger adult, I always had a lot of determination. I finished up being captains of football teams and basketball teams and I think I started to learn some leadership skills in that era. Playing a lot of sport, I was always around a lot of people, it teaches you to be sociable, teaches you leadership responsibilities. Even though I was only working part time jobs, I was given responsibility in those jobs so all that helped to prepare me for my career. I also was holding down part time holiday jobs in very much adult environments, from the age of 16 onwards. So I was earning my money from the age of 16, probably I had a fair bit of drive and determination to do that because our family didn't have much money so I learned to be somewhat self-sufficient.

Leadership

The first thing about leadership is that you need to earn the confidence and trust of the people with whom you interact. I would certainly start with colleagues and employees; bosses of course; definitely customers; the people in the other functions of your business that need to cooperate with you for you to achieve what you need to in your job. I think also, leadership is being a role model for the people in your organization. Leadership is about courage; not letting politics be a distraction in a business, being open and honest about what you are trying to achieve, communicate effectively and broadly. And I think being very transparent is an important quality of a leader.

I think establishing that trust with your colleagues, employees, customers, suppliers, all of the people that are essential to the success of your business, very early on to establish that trust, that the working relationship with those who influence the success of the business is the top priority. I think very quickly understanding the key drivers of the business, particularly financial drivers. Well firstly even before all of that I'd say that coupled with forming excellent relationships is making sure that your organization is a safe organization for your employees to work in. No one should come to work and go home injured. So that's definitely foremost.

So then I was beginning to talk about the financial numbers, so that's obviously very important, understanding the key impacts such as the margins that you earn for your products that you sell, the cost structure of your business, the overhead structure, the main business performance indicators that you need to have to watch; or your dashboard. You need to know the key ratios of your business, you have to have a very good understanding of and know what levers to pull to make sure that you get whatever outcomes are expected of you from bosses and your shareholders.

In terms of leadership challenges, I think there are always difficulties with the different types of personalities, the different interests that are involved in a business. You know sometimes, misalignment of performance expectations can cause problems. For example, a manufacturing guy might have 'lowest cost' and 'highest output' as his or her key performance indicator, but the guy who runs the sales department might be wanting to make products that might not necessarily have the highest throughput but could have the highest profit margin, it might even cost a bit more to make.

So that's a key challenge I think that organizations have to get across. I'll sum it all up by saying- its 'alignment' amongst the various functions that are in the business to make sure that they are all pursuing one set of goals and they all understand the direction in which the organization is heading- I think the challenge is that people understand their role and their responsibility in delivering against an aligned set of objectives that the company has.

Advice for Leading Successfully

Probably the first advice I would give is to think back over one's career so far and think about the best leaders that he or she has ever worked for. And I'd ask them to tell me what were the key characteristics of those excellent leaders that they've seen, either inside or outside the organization. I'd ask them to what extent have they applied what they've seen through their experience about how good leaders lead and what were their characteristics? I'd ask them to think about how they might apply those characterises to their own approach. I'd actually point out some very good leaders in their own organization, I would say to the young leader "please watch those people and try and understand the characteristics that they exhibit as a leader, and try and apply those characteristics to your own leadership style." So that's one point, I'd really appeal to their experience about what they've seen in the past. I'd have a discussion 'with them about what is their set of values that they bring into the organization' and 'what do they think is important'.

So' I'd be saying to them, "what's your set of values?" I'd ask them first before I broadly talked about our own set of values and I'd be looking for a match of those values. If there were strengths and weaknesses that came out of that in terms of the value set, I'd be coaching that leader, I'd try and coach them on what the really important values are that our organization holds close to the heart.

If the leader was working for me, I'd also be very clear up front on what I expect in terms of output and performance, and I'd give them two or three things to focus on in the short term, not a lot of things. I'd probably say "these 10 things are important but what you really have to get right in the first 90 days or 180 days of your job are these three things. And if you progress well with those I'll start to emphasize the other things as you go ahead." I'd also ask one other thing, I would also ask them to come back after 90 days after they have started their job and give me their first impressions of what they've seen, and give me some early indications about what opportunities they are seeing and what needs to be changed.

Leading in China

There are some 'cultural differences'. I think people here in China do approach their daily work and the way they make decisions in a different way. So if I summarise the Western way of management is, "give me lots of data, give me lots of facts, I want the black and white story, I want all the information in front of me to make a decision, I expect everyone to be on board, I expect you to be very clear in your communications and to tell me what's going on in the business, tell me what the opportunities are for improvement, be very open, very frank". In Asia, and China it is different; well let me talk about China first. Probably it is a little bit more of a challenge to get people to respond to you that way. They expect the boss to make the decisions a lot of the time, they look to the boss for leadership, they look to the boss to be right, and they look to the boss to take care of them. And probably they accept the consequences of poor performance a bit differently from what we would in a Western context. Because there's this tendency about 'saving ones face' particularly in China.

Being from a Western background I actually want people's input, I'm using the same model I just described, I say "please tell me, I'm thinking out loud here, tell me if my ideas are stupid or otherwise" and they won't tell you, they're reluctant to tell you in a group if your idea is a poor one. The ones that really do know you and whom you've established a relationship will come up to you outside the meeting and say "boss well you asked for this feedback, I didn't want to give it to you in the meeting but here it is, that was a stupid idea". So it's a lot more difficult to draw people out, particularly in a group situation, in a team situation. So you have to think about how you actually extract people's opinions and their recommendations to get the best out of what they have to offer. In my experience, after a time, and if the team has been together for a reasonable period of time, you can get them to act the way you want them to, but it's not a natural tendency.

Moving to a different characteristic, I find also that developing a sense of urgency is a challenge. People in China because, I don't know why, but they seem to think there is plenty of time to do things. You have to be really clear and unambiguous about deadlines and about what you are expecting to get back, be very concise. It's more difficult to leave it totally up to someone's initiative to come back with what you want so you've got to be pretty descriptive in giving direction.

I think that one positive thing is that it is a bit easier to get alignment here in China; because as I said, they look to the boss. So as long as you are very clear with what you want and you explain the context and they believe in what you are saying is right and they agree with the direction, they can come on board pretty quickly. On that point, I think there is little difference between Western society and China, people like to get clear directions, they like to know that the path that they are heading on feels and sounds a bit like the right path to be on; it gives them confidence and they will do what's necessary to deliver against that direction.

Well it's probably delivering on all those characteristics that I've described as what makes a leader. It's certainly giving your people the direction and confidence in you as you as a leader, making sure that the direction is clear, making sure that people not only know what the direction is but they know what their role is in helping the organization deliver against the objectives and strategy that it has; and also giving honest clear open feedback to the people about their performance.

Responsible Leaders

What I would expect of responsible leaders is very clear. I talked a little bit about the values, personal values but the organization – definitely needs to have a clearly defined set of values. It needs to define the boundaries about how it is going to operate. We used the example of the environment; so the board of directors, the chief executive has to give the organization a sense of direction about what their expectations are on the environment, what their expectations are on safety, what their expectations are on taking care of their employees, how they're going to treat their customers, how they're going to treat their suppliers, so I'm talking about all the stakeholders here; that's probably step one.

Responsible Leadership and Profits

Often you see new chief executives that have come into a company, and have to start with, not necessarily a clean sheet of paper. They often want to define a set of values as a first step or "totem" for their leadership. Such a set of values gives direction to the whole organization; and actually that causes you to make decisions in a particular way. So for example we could save a lot of cost if we did not have the same attitude to occupational health and safety that we have. But because we want to be a safety leader, you know when we even design a plant we will make sure that we have the appropriate amount of guarding, and top quality lighting, and give our people the best safety equipment, we'll give them training, we'll do everything possible to prevent them from harm; that adds to cost and we know that a lot of our competitors do not do that, so they have a cost advantage. Despite that, we go ahead and make the necessary investment in safety, and for the environment for that matter. It actually causes you to think about doing other things in your business better than your competitors so that it neutralises the cost of putting a certain value in practice. We have to do things in our organization that are within the boundaries (values) we've set for ourselves. We can't go outside of a boundary and miss some critical safety, or other steps because we want to save some costs or produce faster; we won't avoid working safely or protecting the environment to save costs or whatever.

So that's really up to leadership and the board of directors of the company to set the standard and give the direction to people so that it's very clear- and again it gets back to the alignment I talked about, people have to be aligned to that way of doing business and decisions have to be made consistent with the direction that the leadership of the company has set.

Impact of Leading in Asia on Responsible Leadership

It's very clear that some things get done differently in Asia compared to other parts of the world. There are different regulations; different ways that employers tend to treat their people, different approaches to environmental management. A lot of those, a lot of those constraints are probably more relaxed than Western society in some ways. Now I think this is changing, particularly in China where the general population is very concerned about things like water safety, quality of the air that they breath, occupational health and safety, payment and conditions all that sort of stuff. To be very crude, there was probably a time where companies could exploit these differences and enjoy the cost advantage and enjoy the lesser constraints on operating in a certain country relevant to their home country, but again I think this gets back to the set of values that you operate by.

I guess you've got to look at it from the point of view of; how your directors and shareholders view that and how does it compare to your set of values if you are actually going to take advantage of the differences going in to a new investment venue. eg if you drop your environmental standards and you don't make the investment in safety, and you're not going to worry too much about how you pay people. Responsible leadership is really about sticking to the set of values that your company has and possibly not taking advantage or exploit the differences that exist in other economies. Even if you can, within the norms or regulations of a new investment venue, you should not compromise your value set. There are some things that will challenge you, some things that you may not be able to control, but keep to values wherever you can influence or control.

Some foreign companies coming into China have possibly not managed closely to their values and some employees have engaged in business conduct that they would not otherwise use in other countries where they do business; and finally that has come back to bite them. Whether that has been deliberate or not it's hard to say, but certainly I think that as far as responsible leadership is concerned; the company's value systems have been loose if it has enabled leaders to adopt those practices.

It's the responsibilities of leadership, and again this is right from the top of the company, to be very clear about what it expects from its leaders in terms of how it conducts itself in the various communities in which it operates. It's almost like if you're not going to do a certain thing in Australia, then you're certainly not going to be allowed to do a different thing in China.

And leadership needs to be supported with the right governance processes to ensure that those things that you can control business practices to the best of your ability. It is very interesting sitting in China now just how much attitudes have changed even in the space of 1 year, since the new Chinese government leadership has come in and it has actually Set some clear expectations of what appropriate business conduct looks like. There are now changes evident in areas such as the standard of entertainment, the standard of gifts people give to one another, in a business context; a lot of that has taken a much, much more conservative turn in the last 12 months or so. There have also been several high profile anti-corruption actions against government officials and also some foreign companies.

Guan xi, or the forming of mutually rewarding relationships in business is a deeply entrenched characteristic of the business culture in China. For example, the people you went to university with are still the guys you're doing business with 25 or 30 years later, that is very real and there is nothing wrong with that. Having strong networks and long standing relationships and longevity of business are all very strong in the Chinese value system, so that can be very hard to compete with if you're relatively new to the country and you're at an early stages of forming your relationships. So that I think is a challenge. Whether the business conduct is acceptable or not that's another matter, I believe that's going to change very rapidly in China. Corruption is certainly something, as well as the things I've mentioned before, that the community over here value very highly as well as clean air, clean water, good food, safety, a safe environment. They don't want to see their leaders enriching themselves through corrupt business practices. So over time the community pressure will start to have a greater impact over here I think.

Future of Leadership

In terms of the future of leadership, I'd like to see the best characteristics of the cultures and businesses that are operating in the global business community all come together and we see the best characteristics of each being exhibited in a typical leader. So the typical 'global' leader will understand different countries and cultures, different economies, different commercial practices etc., and will be able to adapt to such differences. Adaptability, tolerance, flexibility while remaining true to values will be the desired characteristics of a leader.

So leaders will have to understand those differences, understand the impact it will have on their business and have a much more flexible and culturally sensitive approach to leading. It's not just black and white, it's not just KPIs or the numbers, it's the subtleties in doing business in different environments and economies and learning to get alignment across the different challenges that presents.

Simon Linge, President, NS BlueScope Indonesia

Career

My background is in establishing businesses that are successful for the long term. Within that is a program leadership model that is effective particularly in an Asian context, but in any site. I think that is probably why I've been offered and asked to come into this role. I've been in this role for about 6 months. But my history with BlueScope is, I'm now in my 26th year with this organization. Originally, my career was in a group within the BHP called BHP transport and logistics. So, my background is very much more in transport logistics and supply chain. I started my career in human resources and principally that career started in industrial relations and negotiating with people like the maritime unions. I moved in to operations, which ran from the port of Port Kembla in Australia for BHP for a few years. Then, subsequently I went into management/sales/marketing for a few years. Then, when BlueScope became a separate entity from BHP, a lot of my work was with the steel works so they asked me to be part of that future rather than go with BHP Billiton as the merging occurred, which suited me and my family at the time. I did some commercial roles and shipping logistics. Then I was asked to lead the Malaysian steel business in mid 2005 to the end of 2007. That was a turn around for that business. From there I was asked to go to China for 3 years with one of our businesses there. That was successful. Then I went to a New Zealand pacific island business for 2 ¾ years and was leading that business. It was not a turnaround business, which was more about changing the culture and bringing the business into the twenty-first century. I then went off to the US leading an investment proposal for BlueScope and a joint venture business in the US. Then I was asked to come to Indonesia to try and lead a turnaround in our Indonesian business that has been in a steady decline for probably 4–5 years. That's my personal journey that brought me to Indonesia.

In terms of background, yeah I came from a very humble background. My father and mother were both accountants and financial people. I was born in the United Kingdom. I came from a working class background so I was always instilled with a strong work ethic and an ethic about what was right or wrong. So I had a very strong value set. My wife would say that my value set is sometimes too strong. If something tramples on my value set, I have a difficult time with it. I didn't have a background particularly in business. I did have a background in taking on leadership roles in school and a lot of that was given to me because of managing to a set of values so I had respect from my colleagues in school. I was never the popular kid in school and I was never in the geeky group. I was kind of in the neutral zone where I could work with anybody in the school environment. I played a lot of sports, particularly rugby. And that led me to believing in operating in a team and the power of being successful when you work in a team. Those would probably be the key influences.

Leadership

For me, leadership is giving your people a sense of direction and a sense of possibility against whatever the realities are of the day. So it's also giving them a sense of positiveness even when times are tough. It's also making sure that there are a set of values or ethics or guiding principles about how a business should operate and where it should stand in terms of internal stakeholders. So employees understand how they will be recognized and rewarded and dealt with, but also external stakeholders in the sense that you and your organization are trustworthy and credible and that they know where you stand, and the consistency of your values and behaviors.

Challenges of Leadership

It's lonely at times, so there's not always the opportunity to have confidence. It's recognizing that you don't have all the answers. Particularly in the Asian context, there's an expectation that the leader has the answer. So it's balancing that and making sure you can actually draw out of people their very best of who that person is without them feeling like you're just giving them the answer. I think that's one of the challenges of leading in Asia. I think one of the challenges is not only reminding yourself that you don't have all the answers, but that every minute of everyday people are observing what you do more so than what you say and will be making judgments on you every minute of the day.

Responsible Leaders

I would expect clarity about right and wrong, a clarity that ultimately you're responsible for your shareholder and performance of the business, clearly, but you also have a responsibility to act ethically. You also have a responsibility to recognize that you have the livelihood of X number of people, whether it's a small number or large number, within your workforce. You are trying to guide them towards success. Particularly in an Asian context, where there's a great deal of aspiration in the region, individual aspiration as well as collective aspiration. So you have a responsibility to guide them, as individuals and collectively as a team, to a better place than from when you arrived.

Responsible Leadership and Profits

I think obviously this catches to some degree, not solely, but to some degree of the issue of corruption. Not completely, I think the question is broader than that. I think as a responsible leader, part of looking at your business, leading your business and the people within it and the stakeholders around you is to look at the long term and balancing short term needs and long term requirements. A responsible leader would say, if anything that could give you a short-term benefit but does so at the expense of your long-term aspirations and credibility, they wouldn't take that short-term opportunity. And that gets back to what your values are and what you stand for and in an organization like BlueScope. We have the good fortune of both of our shareholder being very clear about where they stand on the issues of ethics, not only corruption, but also in clarity in how to treat safety and the environment. It would be easy to take shortcuts and to deviate from our standards for short-term benefit, but that will ultimately give you longer-term pain. In Asian and developing countries, regulations are opaque. I think sometimes that is done deliberately to potentially give advantage to certain companies that might air on the lower side of standards.

But I think typically in developing countries, it's actually because they are not quite sure the way to frame the regulations. Rather than phrase it in a way that copies a particular country or particular standard, it becomes loose or is framed loosely. As a result, that could lead you to "we can do this legally" but if you are very clear about your standards that you operate to globally, you can say you aren't prepared to take such actions regardless of what the regulations say. A good example would be environmental standards around one of our facilities here in Indonesia are the level of emissions. The Indonesian standard is to allow higher emission levels than we normally operate within our facilities globally. We operate our facilities at the standard we employ across our global footprint. We think if we do not do this then we are not acting ethically and in 10 year's time we will have a problem as we will be judged by what we have or have not done. The things you can do for balancing short term profit, we can strip out some incremental costs and improve our profits, but doing so we would be giving ourselves a challenge for the long term and not acting as responsible as we need to.

Impact of Leading in the Asian Century on Responsible Leadership

Recognizing that it is very tempting in terms of accelerating your business performance. It's very tempting to deliver an answer. You have had experiences in different countries or from a developed country and to try to overlay that answer in a directive way, but I don't believe that builds a sustainable business in Asia. As an expat, there is an automatic credibility that you are given when entering an organization in another country. The company you work for has entrusted, so you immediately therefore, there is an assumption that you must be one of the better performers because you were given the opportunity to move away from your home country and to work in a different country that clearly those people must be very good. In the Asian culture, there is an element of submissiveness, at least an unofficial level of submissiveness; you find other ways of being dealt with. At least at face value people will agree with what you asked them to do. You really just need to make sure you are being inclusive, that you find a way of bringing people into the answers. In all the Asian countries I've worked in, that has been the case. I was reminded of this of when I arrived in Indonesia after time in NZ and the USA. In one of my early management team meetings here, the team said "tell us what to do and they will follow". I guess my answer immediately was "that's not the way it's going to work here, we are going to work out what to do as a team." I've got some good experiences from other countries and other businesses, but that doesn't mean it's right in an Indonesian setting. One of the other attributes of that is that I will not live in Indonesia for the rest of my life; I will not be part of BlueScope for the rest of my life. So it is important that the local team be equipped and able to take the business forward for the next 10 years, not me. That's one of the challenges, is getting it to be sustainable and to be carried forward by people within the country you're operating in.

Challenges and Opportunities in Different Markets and Cultures

Every market is different. So if I take the first part, markets, yeah I think there are differences in markets, but there are also a lot of similarities. Because of both BlueScope's longevity in the region and also the positioning of BlueScope, both are products of people's professionalism and responsible leadership there are a lot of similarities. There are very different challenges by markets from a cultural point of view, and I can come back to that in terms of differences. Malaysia is a mature market and it's history has helped shape some of that. So it's British colonial history has helped shape the way, at least the baseline of activity in a way that is quite British or even Australian in context because I guess Australia has also had a British colonial past and so some of the frameworks are similar. And equally some of the standards are very similar for both Singapore and Malaysia. So often, for instance, for building codes they will reference Australian standards. China is a very different beat. I certainly went to China thinking that it would be a homogeneous market, and clearly that is not the case. It's very regional with different dynamics. Weather, climate and topography in places can be a significant issue as well and there are substantive differences, north, south, east, west, across the markets. And again it's history lends itself to authoritarian rule again partly being the geography being so large and diverse. Indonesia is a mix of the two. It has a different colonial past with the Dutch being here and the Japanese for a short amount of time. Because the Dutch used Indonesia as a trading vehicle, they didn't leave any significant legacies in terms of institutions, so that's been an interesting differential. And again, backed by authoritarian rule, you could say Malaysia has been one party in power for 60 years, but there's at least a political process, whereas in Indonesia, up until the swearing in of the new President there hasn't really been a big successful democratic transfer of presidential power in 60 years. Corruption is an issue in all 3 countries, but in Indonesia its probably more public and more expected than it is in Malaysia or China.

From a cultural point of view, there are different cultures in Malaysia. You have a greater mix of cultures. You have the Malay population, which constitute about 55–60 % of the population, Chinese, which is 30 % percent, and Indian, which is 10 %. In terms of ethnic backgrounds, you tend to find workforce groups surrounds certain activities, so the Malay population within our business works as engineers or operators, a little bit of HR and administrative activities. The Chinese would typically be the engineers and the accountants and the sales people because most of the customers are of Chinese ethnic backgrounds. The Indian population fit in around trades people, so electricians, mechanics, mechanical people and transportation and logistics. There's also what I would describe as a bigger gene pool of excellent people. So there's high competition for them, but it's easier to get really core people because a lot of the Chinese have been taught overseas now and you get that in Malaysia as well. Indonesia interestingly, a lot of Indonesians who are educated outside Indonesia don't come back to Indonesia until much later so you don't have that external influence yet. We are just starting to see it now; the 40 and 50 somethings who have worked and lived overseas have come back. So that gives me strong hope for the country over the next 40 years, that those people will help naturally pull up the capabilities levels of the country.

Future of Leadership

Hopefully, within the Asian context it will be more broad-based than figurehead leadership. I still think globally there is a strong and probably growing focus on presidential leadership, where the focal point of leadership rests with an individual. The failure or success of a country or a business rests with an individual. Successful leadership is when you got a team of people who are successfully leading the business.

I think there's an expression, which is 'what is old is new again.' I'm sure if I spoke to my grandparents, they would look horrified at some of these concepts because isn't that what you're supposed to do? It's doing the right thing. And not quite a utopian view of the world, but kind of being ethically stable and I guess a lighthouse or foundation stone that provides the anchor point for how people operate. You're seeing it already in organizations, they are clearly being held to account for, as seen in the banking industry. But there are construction companies in Australia today that are being held to account for behaviors in terms of projects in the Middle East and Asia. There are German companies that have been successful in the short term in China that have been held to account. In Asian countries it is politically/publicly easy to hold foreign companies up as the pariah. And as long as foreign countries recognize that then they will look to do the right thing. And say to themselves "If I can't be successful in the short term because of that, then I need to make the decision to either not be in that market or alternatively I need to sustain myself in that market and play along with the game. And as part of that, I will demonstrate to stakeholders, including government about what I'm doing and ask the question of Government to move others to that standard."

Ultimately, Asian governments will start to crack down on corruption, particularly as the country becomes more developed and greater separation of certain powers starts to occur. And the other part of that is they will not be able to attract foreign direct investments if they cannot deal with the issues of corruptions. If companies like BlueScope are going to be held to account for their behavior of making sure they operate responsibly, be it safety, environment, dealing with employees, dealing with customers and/or issues of corruptions, and others are not held to account then eventually, if we are not being successful, we will exit and say one of the reasons we are exiting is because we don't feel we can be successful because others are not being held to account on responsible leadership. The more foreign companies do that then the more the Asian governments will have to crack down. You can see it in China now. The new leadership in China is saying that this is an issue. Not just an economic issue but also a political issue. Corruption isn't just people taking money, but also turning a blind eye to certain activities or not meeting regulations, etc. But I think you see it in Korea with similar announcements about larger organizations being pursued for not following appropriate behavior. It's going to be an ongoing push from countries on business to start holding them accountable, and the GFC has been part of that. Business has been tainted by the actions of some businesses pre GFC. The pressure will continue to be on us to show we are a responsible member/part of society.

Atul Gogna, Vice President, Strategic Marketing, NS Bluescope Coated Products, Singapore

Responsible Leadership in Asia

In Asia, the environment is far more complex than in the West because there are a lot of unsaid social norms and expectations, often unique to local culture, which a good manager has to keep in mind.

Besides requirements of the Western model of responsible leadership, the Asian context requires additional sensitivity and capabilities to manage these unspoken norms. For instance, if an employee has violated some procedure and is removed within agreed contractual agreement and local law, it still may not be perceived as fair by the workforce and may lead to resistance.

Another aspect of the Asian context is higher demands on a leader to uphold ethical business conduct in spite of potentially negative consequences to the business. Legal and economic systems are still evolving in many developing Asian countries, particularly in South East Asia. Sometimes local competitors employ business practices that would not be possible in a developed Western jurisdiction. A responsible leader therefore has to be even more careful about how they're going about their business. He/She would have to balance a lot of objectives and provide extensive education to make sure that their team members not only understand the Asian rules, but also start to understand the Western expectations of responsible leadership.

Challenges Facing Leadership in Asia

The biggest challenge is understanding people's emotional make up and unspoken social norms. In many Asian cultures, people often don't voice their opinions or differences openly. Sometimes it is out of respect for the other person's culture and sometimes out of fear of consequences. In general Singapore context is very similar to any Western developed country. What makes it slightly challenging is that you encounter two kinds of groups here in work situations. One comprises the local Singaporeans, who have a unique culture of their own and the other, expatriates from many countries, who bring with them their own myriad values. But the Singaporeans all speak English, are well-educated and well-travelled internationally. And most expatriates make an effort to adapt. So it is not too difficult for each group to communicate and understand each other. Also the rule of law is very strong in Singapore so you don't encounter challenging situations from a business practices perspective.

Future of Leadership in Asia

I don't think it will be very far from where it is currently, although the challenges mentioned above will definitely reduce. Each Asian country has a very strong culture of its own and people are very fond of their culture. There is a certain degree of resurgent pride in Asian culture. There was a time when Asians were quite in awe of the West, but now are more mature in balancing international norms with their own Asian culture. Hence some of the peculiar social norms and challenges of leadership are likely to remain.

However due to higher education and international travel, there is likely to be greater understanding and tolerance amongst people. Simultaneously the governments and public systems are likely to become a little more transparent. So the challenge of responsible leadership in Asian context should be easier in the future.